ENCYCLOPEDIA
OF
WOMEN'S WIT,
ANECDOTES
AND STORIES

Also by the Author

The New Talkamatics: Easy Way to Verbal Power and Persuasion
10 Days to Miracle Speech Power

ENCYCLOPEDIA

OF

WOMEN'S WIT,

ANECDOTES

AND STORIES

Cathy Handley

Prentice-Hall, Inc.   Englewood Cliffs, New Jersey

Prentice-Hall International, Inc., *London*
Prentice-Hall of Australia, Pty. Ltd., *Sydney*
Prentice-Hall of Canada, Ltd., *Toronto*
Prentice-Hall of India Private Ltd., *New Delhi*
Prentice-Hall of Japan, Inc., *Tokyo*
Prentice-Hall of Southeast Asia Pte. Ltd., *Singapore*
Whitehall Books, Ltd., Wellington, *New Zealand*

Library of Congress Cataloging in Publication Data
Main entry under title:

Encyclopedia of women's wit, anecdotes, and stories.

  Includes index.
  1. Women–Anecdotes, facetiae, satire, etc.
I. Handley, Cathy, 1931-
HQ1233.E5   305.4   81-21073
                          AACR2
ISBN 0-13-276584-5

    Printed in the United States of America

This book is dedicated
to the memory of my mother,
Aline Norvell Thompson

The editor is grateful to the publications and individuals who contributed to this encyclopedia. Permissions and Acknowledgments are listed on pages 333 - 347.

What This Book Can Do for You

At long last—a long-overdue reference book of wit and wisdom by and about women.

In the past, in collections of quotations and sagacity, few remarks were credited to women.

Since the beginning of the women's movement, raconteurs, librarians, writers, speakers, business and professional people, educators and club members have often searched for a "good story" or an "apt comment" by or about women. Often, however, the search has been difficult—or fruitless.

WHAT THIS BOOK CONTAINS

To meet this need, this book contains over 2,000 items of wit, anecdotes and stories by and about some famous—as well as less famous—women.

In all, there are over 800 different categories of quips and quotes. The book's categories include age, birth control, careers, communism, face lifts, marriage, money, shopping, sex and other timely topics.

Under these various contemporary categories are all of the *individual* items, ranging from sad to wry to hilarious. You'll find Jill Ruckelshaus saying, "We (women) have been raised in a society where we have met the government, and it is not us."; Ginger Rogers reflecting, "Activity is life itself."; and Eva Gabor, true to the Gabor heritage, remarking, "Men are the same wherever you go—attractive."

WHY THIS BOOK IS ESPECIALLY VALUABLE

In this volume, you find women of earlier days making surprisingly pertinent comments on vital issues of today. But what is *especially* valuable is that the book is juicy with feminine insight and amusing tidbits of today's *new woman*. I believe no other book offers so many fascinating comments and anecdotes by and about contemporary women—often on subjects ladies in previous times did not speak out on.

THE BOOK IS EQUALLY VALUABLE TO MALE SPEAKERS

Because so many men today find themselves speaking and writing about today's woman, men speakers and writers will find this book as valuable to them as it is to women readers.

Male communicators who need current material on the fair sex will find this book a treasure trove. They can easily find thought-provoking and applause-earning comments to adorn their writing and speeches, and doubtless will receive comments on their ability to select good material about today's headline-making sex.

TWO HELPFUL GUIDES

The book's arrangement uses a simple A-B-C format. Especially helpful are the comprehensive, easy-to-use table of contents and index. The table of contents has references ranging from "advice" to "knowledge" to "women's lib."

The index is a quoter's index, which gives the name of the person making the remarks. If you wish a quotation from a scientist, you can quickly scan the quoter's index for such names as Marie Curie and Rosalyn Yalow.

Although this book—like today's typewriter, tape recorder and copying machine—is an indispensable tool for people who must communicate effectively with one another, it has one other great value: its stories and sayings shower the reader with insights, smiles and laughter. Best of all, it enables you to pass on these feminine truths and mirth to others ... to enlighten and brighten their days with women's wonderful wit and wisdom.

Cathy Handley

CONTENTS

LIST OF SUBJECTS

11

ABSENCE

In the old days, ptomaine poisoning was a coverall.... If you missed a show and you were young, it meant you were having an abortion. If you were old, it meant you were having a face lift.

— Ruth Gordon

(As the war drew to a close, General Eisenhower flew home briefly for a triumphal parade but had to return immediately to Europe.) Afterwards, Harry Butcher wrote a best seller called "My Years With Eisenhower." Mamie, still alone, teasingly threatened to write one titled: "My Years Without Eisenhower."

— Ruth Montgomery

ACHIEVEMENT

The devotion of thought to an honest achievement makes the achievement possible.

— Mary Baker Eddy

It's like a friend of mine used to say, "Don't worry about me. I've done everything I started out to do, and a whole lot more that I didn't plan on."

— Minnie Pearl

ACCOMPLISHMENT

I think you ought to make up your mind just what you want to do, then go ahead and do it. That's the only way to get what you want.

— Hetty Green

You know when it comes to spending your life, there have to be some things neglected. If you try to do too much, you can never get anywhere....

— Hetty Green

If one can take a truly impersonal viewpoint, then it does not matter who writes the novels or paints the pictures or discovers the new planet. If it is women's function to hold the world together while these things are being accomplished, let her take pride in that. Or let her try to hold things more together.

— Phyllis McGinley

In a speech delivered at Mississippi University for Women: "Women, here and now in this present time, dare, dare to dream, exercise your imagination, conceive new patterns. Think sequentially, analyze critically and brood creatively about your purpose and your man's purpose. Are they really different? Are not both of you to become a spouse—a parent—and a worker? This nation needs all the talent its people, men and women, possess to help solve the magnitude of problems facing it today."

— Marjorie Bell Chambers

ACCOUNTS PAYABLE

A wife explaining her "accounts payable" system to a friend: "Well, actually, I pay my American Express Card with my Master Charge and my Master Charge with my Bank All-Purpose card ... and my All-Purpose card with my Visa Card....and so it balances out..."

ACTING

Actress Ellen Burstyn said that she always "considered acting a healing art."

You learn timing, you learn to react, and you learn to work and work until you get it right.

— Jane Wyman

(About Joan Crawford) She is like a slot machine—you put in a nickel and out comes a perfect performance.

— Jean Negulesco

I'm in bed with Burt (Reynolds) during most of the play. Oh, I know it's dirty work, but someone has to do it.

— Carol Burnett

Acting's not something you learn; you either have it or you don't. Oh, you can learn to move, to breathe, but the other is ingrained.

— Dame Judith Anderson

If I know my mother is out front, I might just as well not perform. She totally destroys the illusion for me, everything I do becomes absurd.

— Glenda Jackson

Bette Davis said she prepared for a role by remembering the advice of Claude Rains: "I learn the lines and pray to God..."

Susan Hayward, explaining her preference for playing stage roles in big theaters: "If I flop, I'm going to flop in a big way."

Good acting is opening the doors to that part of the role you see in yourself, and partnering that with your imagination and invention.

— Meryl Streep

It's fine to start out as a curvy biz-whiz ... but it takes all the talent you've got in your guts to play unimportant roles.

— Joan Blondell

Writing is the most important thing. Even a bad director can't mess up a good script. Writers are my god. I'm no genius. If they don't give me a good script on paper, I can't pull it off.

— Barbara Stanwyck

ACTING—ROLE

Because she played so many exotic and "barefoot" parts in her film career, Rita Moreno once said, "I have the most scarred-up feet in town."

(About appearing in a revival of "Cat On A Hot Tin Roof") I think I'll do it while I can still get myself in the slip.

— Elizabeth Ashley

For a woman it is not easy. They used to look at you in the movies as a mother, as a prostitute or as a sex symbol. It is not easy to find good parts.

— Claudia Cardinale

Zsa Zsa Gabor telling Joe Hyams about her decision to allow her head to be shaved for a movie role: "I am a famous actress. I will do anything for my art and to improve the picture. In any case, they are giving me a $100,000 bonus."

About ten years ago Claudette Colbert came up to me at an Elsa Maxwell party and said, "Bette, you have the most enviable career in this town. You began playing older women before you had to, and now no one will know when you must make the switch." Now I know she was right.

– Bette Davis

A producer, Samuel Goldwyn, took Barbara Stanwyck to task on a point of acting technique, but this was nearly 15 years ago, when she starred in his sentimental classic, Stella Dallas. While admitting that one of her crying scenes had moved him to tears, he thought it might be still more effective if she played it without tears herself, but fighting to hold them back. They reshot the scene that way and Goldwyn wept more than ever. "It was," he told friends later, "one of the happiest moments of my life."

– Frank S. Nugent

I've never acted a scene in my life—I live them all. In the test film of a television program I am planning, I play an international girl reporter. During almost the entire episode, I think my life is endangered. I'll never forget the faces of my fellow actors when, after rehearsal, I said to the cameraman: "Okay, turn 'em over!"—and then ran in the opposite direction. They couldn't understand my quick exit. It seemed to contradict the instruction to start the cameras. But I had to run into the scene; I had to run far enough to come in panting, hot with perspiration and panic.

This kind of "acting" is letting your body say it for you. For example, for one sequence of the picture 'Sudden Fear' I went through nine days of hysteria, and I mean hysteria. What was wanted was unrestrained emotion. I was truly in terror just as truly as I have laughed, been in love, been a lady, been a shrew ... I can only live an acting scene.

– Joan Crawford

ACTION

Rule of action: *Never* hesitate, or stop, or draw back in the middle of an action, whatever may happen. But *never* commence an action without

having given a long and sustained scrutiny to all its possible con-
sequences (all the possibilities..) in every sphere in which the mind is
not compromised, *give oneself the benefit of anonymity* ("follow the rules
and customs").

— Simone Weil

ACTIVITY

Activity is life itself.

— Ginger Rogers

Painting's not important. The important thing is keeping busy.

— Grandma Moses

Gloria Swanson believes in activity: going into pictures at 14, onto the
stage at 43 and into fashion at 52. At 80, she painted a picture for a
first-day cover to go with a stamp commemorating the U.N. Decade for
Women and at 81, published her memoirs.

ACTRESS

The prettier she (an actress) gets, the worse she acts.

— Gene Shalit

(On being rehired as an actress) It's just like social life ... you ain't
going to be asked to somebody's house again if you stink up their party.

— Miriam Hopkins

Being an actress is a humiliating business, and, as you get older, it
becomes more humiliating because you've got less to sell.

— Katharine Hepburn

I was on the brink of beginning to understand my career as an actress
when I gave it up.
   I regret I didn't stick to it for another five years because I believe I
might have made a real name as Grace Kelly.

— Princess Grace of Monaco

(After using a Southern accent in a couple of her movies) I sometimes
have trouble reverting to my normal speaking voice. I was talking to a
friend the other night, and instead of saying, "Goodbye," I said, "Y'all
come back and see us real soon now, y'hear?"

— Sally Field

ADOPTION

Adopting kids is terrific, but I have enough ego so that I want to pass on something of myself.

– Kate Jackson

ADVENTURE

This is my year of daring. I'm trying everything from Chekhov to pratfalls.

– June Havoc

Old age in itself doesn't frighten me.... What upsets me is the idea that a woman who is no longer young must renounce the illusion that every time she goes out in public she may have the pleasant surprise of a sentimental adventure.

– Francoise Sagan

Fate has mapped out an adventurous career for me, and I manage somehow to live up to its requirements, but at heart I am not much different from the stay-at-home girl who started hoursekeeping fourteen years ago in a flat in Independence, Kansas.

– Osa Johnson

ADVICE

So the children are now experiencing—and handling beautifully—the small shock I remember experiencing when, as a young girl, I called on my mother for advice and, for the first time, she answered: "Kathryn, *I don't know.*" They are, you see, coming to realize that I don't have all the answers, that there are some answers *they* must now give *me*.

– Kathryn Crosby

One time top gossip columnist Elsa Maxwell was asked if she'd had any problems because of her appearance—heavy, with features reminiscent of a bulldog—entering her world of celebrities and "High Society." She explained there'd been no problems but that she'd had a happy life by following her father's advice, "Treat the light things in life very seriously, and the serious things very lightly."

AFFAIR

Columnist Abigail Van Buren once advised a reader it wasn't an "affair" unless it was the whole enchilada.

AGE

Age is the enemy and it brings no gifts.

— Simone Signoret

In this business, age has terrible economic residuals.

— Barbara Feldon

No woman should ever be quite accurate about her age. It looks so calculating.

— Oscar Wilde

Careful grooming may take 20 years off a woman's age, but you can't fool a long flight of stairs.

— Marlene Dietrich

I haven't got this "romantic" feeling about age. I think we rot away, and I think it's a damn shame.

— Katharine Hepburn

A woman advice columnist says that just because you can't rock all night doesn't mean you can't waltz for an hour.

When asked her age by a newspaper interviewer, jet setter and designer Maxime de la Falaise McKendry said, "We mustn't get too technical, must we, darling?"

A newspaper reporter tactfully tried to ask Angie Dickinson's age by saying, "I'm afraid I forgot how old you are." "So have I," she shot back.

AGE—ENTHUSIASM

Anyone growing older without enthusiasm has got to manufacture it, pretend it. Do it until it becomes like self-hypnosis. Manufacture enthusiasm as you go and grow.

— Maggie Kuhn

AGE—GROWING OLD

Every time I think that I'm getting old, and gradually going to the grave, something else happens.

— Miz Lillian Carter

AGE—IMPROVING WITH

My daughters Zsa Zsa, Eva and Magda and I are like good wine—we improve with age.

— Jolie Gabor

My life? It gets better all the time. What would be the point of getting older if you didn't get better—in every way?

— Marlo Thomas

AGE—OLD

It's not how old you are, but how you are old.

— Marie Dressler

(Speaking to TV's "Rhoda," as Rhoda's mother) I'm a very young "old woman," but you're a very old "girl."

— Nancy Walker

A cosmetician says it's old age when people start telling you you're looking good, but no one says you're good-looking.

(On the "Flo" TV show) Mama, paying the bill for Flo's neon sign, says, "I had some (money) put away for my old age and who knows when that will be?"

I'm not afraid of old age—it's nothing to fear. I will be a very wise and serious old lady. As I get older, I get quieter, because now I know myself better.

— Sophia Loren

(American women have been) liberated from the old-age syndrome. There are no "older women" in America today. Women are all young in mind, young in spirit; they can wear any kind of clothes.

— Halston

There are six myths about old age: 1. That it's a disease, a disaster. 2. That we are mindless. 3. That we are sexless. 4. That we are useless. 5. That we are powerless. 6. That we are all alike.

— Maggie Kuhn

My most successful achievement after reaching age 65 was becoming 66. And after that, it was getting to be 67, 68, and right up to where I am now, 82. My after-65 career has been as happy, as resultful, and as satisfying as my pre-65 period.

— Ruth Gordon

AGE—WHEN ASKED YOURS

Writer Bill Fay reported that Aunt Fanny (a part created by Fran Allison on The Breakfast Club) once told the show's listeners that she was about 25 years old, then added, " 'Course it's the second time around."

I'm somewhere between being 60 and being called.

— Woman Chef

Wanda the waitress, when asked her age, always answers, "plenty-nine."

When a computer operator was asked her age, she said, "I'm 15-celsius."

Youthful Figure: the answer you get when you ask a woman her age.

— Modern Maturity

AGGRESSION

It is said that men are innately more aggressive than women. Conditioning, not sex hormones, makes them that way. Anyone seeing women at a bargain-basement sale see aggression that would make Attila the Hun turn pale.

— Dr. Estelle Ramey

AGING

When I have time I will think about growing old.

— Sheilah Graham

An elderly woman, when asked how one reaches the age of 94, replied: "The best way you know how."

Time goes by and every day you do get a little older. In my case it's been an improvement.

— Madeline Kahn

There's a lot of information directed at and about youth, career making and being young mothers, but we must teach young women to see ahead 20 years. None of us can ward off the penalties of age, but we can learn to think ahead. We're so youth-oriented, we don't want to think about being 60 or 70.

— Lillian Hellman

AID

Helen H. Hull, often called the "First Lady of Music" for her help to musicians, said, "...it is a great pity that the government does not financially aid our artists ... Remember, I said aid, not subsidize."

ALBUM

(About her album's sale) It's doin' real well. Could do better if more people bought it.

— *Dolly Parton*

Erma Bombeck once referred to a "make-believe" comedy album titled "The Family That Plays Together Gets on Each Other's Nerves."

ALIVE

Actually everything is of interest. Indeed I would say that one is only really alive when one is open to all impressions and is prepared to laugh too.

— *Soraya*

ALONE

My best company I find in myself ...

— *Greta Garbo*

What a lovely surprise to finally discover how unlonely being alone can be.

— *Ellen Burstyn*

A woman can't be alone; she needs a man. A man and a woman support and strengthen each other. She just can't do it alone.

— *Marilyn Monroe*

> Whose sleeves do you enfold
> While leaving me to lie here
> Night after night
> Alone on my wildest robe?

— *Lady Sagami*

Few things daunted sparkling Bea Lillie in her performing career. But one thing did. Lillie's dressing room, even between acts, looked like a salon. Her one real fear, she admitted, was being alone.

AMBASSADOR

If an ambassador leaves his post with fallen arches, a weakened liver, bursitis in his right arm, a healthy skepticism about the futility of making the world over and a firm resolve not to take another big job for a reasonable length of time, he has done the best he could.

— *Clare Boothe Luce*

AMBITION

I wanted to grow up to be Billy the Kid.

— Elizabeth Ashley

I always wanted to grow up to be a Va-Va-Voom Lady.

— Lola Falana

Suzanne Somers knew very early what she wanted to be when she grew up: "Important."

— Barbara Grizzuti Harrison

(On her life's ambitions) I wanna go to Milwaukee in the worst way ... and be someone tall.

— Bette Midler

... my ambition is to be the oldest woman in the world, and every day brings me nearer my goal.

— Jean Marsh

When you set your heart on something, and when it's all you want to do in the world, you have to pay for it and I did. I took life on the chin.

— Katherine Anne Porter

Men who care a lot about their work are respected. Women who care a lot about their work are objects of suspicion and are sometimes called schemers ... ambitious. And the word ambitious now takes on negative connotations because it is used about a woman.

— Mary Tyler Moore

(Writing in *Seventeen* magazine) If you tell me that there are obstacles in the way of your ambition that make it impossible to pursue, then I know it's not a real ambition. There are always obstacles. The "perversity of events," as someone once called it, is always ready to lick us. Events are never right for achieving what we most want to achieve. If this were not so, there would be no real fun in being 17—or even in being alive.

— Helen Gahagan Douglas

I had just returned from a meeting of the National Organization for Women (NOW) when my five-year-old daughter greeted me with the news that she wanted to be a nurse when she grew up. "'A nurse!' I said. 'Listen, Lisa, just because you're female doesn't mean you have to settle for being a nurse. You can be a surgeon, a lawyer, a banker, President of the United States—you can be anything!' She looked a little dubious. 'Anything? Anything at all?' She thought about it, and then her face lighted with ambition. 'All right,' she said. 'I'll be a horse.'"

— Meg F. Quijano

AMBITION—BLIGHTED

(On an interview with Arnold Bennett) She (writer Dorothy Dix) found Bennett extremely formal—either very shy or very withdrawn. She got nowhere until she pointed her pencil at him: "Mr. Bennett, I've always been sorry for you because of your—your blighted ambition."

"What?" She had startled him. "How's my life blighted?"

"You've always wanted to run a hotel."

Bennett's eyebrows shot up. "Why ... as a matter of fact, Miss Dix, I have. But how the devil did you find that out?"

"You told me so, in your books." Her smile widened. "Every time one of your characters comes a cropper, he keeps a hotel. It happens over and over."

Arnold Bennett shook his head in astonishment. "By George, I never quite realized it. You're right." The ice suddenly thawed, "and we had a lovely time," Dorothy said. Also, she got a striking interview.

— Hartnett Tikane with Ella Bentley Arthur

AMERICA

America is my country, Paris my home town.

— Gertrude Stein

I have a deep feeling for America. I'm definitely a product of this continent... *We're* the privileged ones.

— Diane Keaton

America is for me—Americans love to encourage young talent... In England, you practically have to be white-haired to get a good role. America uses the wisdom of the older people, but it's a young country and uses the energy and ideas of youth.

— Dana Wynter

I left America with a feeling of peace and contentment, the feeling that comes with a sense of accomplishment, of a mission fulfilled. I left with a deep sentiment of gratitude toward the great American public—most especially the women—who supported my work, who gave me a chance to bring hope to thousands of children threatened by the great crippler, infantile paralysis.

— Sister Kenny

I come to America to rest. It is always thrilling to return to America. I never escape—I don't want ever to escape—the spark of emotion one can feel only by coming back to one's native land. That sounds like poetry.

It is.

The American spirit always survives, no matter what its environment. It is something geography can never change.

— Nancy Astor, M.P.

AMERICAN DREAM

(When speaking at the Democratic National Convention) I feel that, notwithstanding the past, my presence here is one additional bit of evidence that the American Dream need not forever be deferred.

— Barbara Jordan

ANALYSIS

In analysis you learn all about how you behave, the things that won't work for you, the things you don't do right—and that's your research. Then you leave the doctor's office and go back into your life where everything's happening and you're in the middle of it, and that's your field work. That's where you try to learn to change some of the patterns you've got caught up in.

— Linda Lavin

ANGEL

In grade school, Patricia Harris tried out to be an angel and the teacher told her angels were white.

ANIMAL

I think animals are wonderful—all animals ... They have no chips on their shoulders—they're never mad at you, and they never misunderstand you.

— Jean Arthur

ANIMAL—CAT

You can't look at a sleeping cat and be tense.

— Jane Pauley

Two little girls looking at a grey-striped mother cat in a box, surrounded by her new-born kittens. One little girl said to the other, "We didn't even know Tiger was engaged!"

Four-year-old Diana came back excited from viewing the neighbor's new kitten. "They have two boy kittens and three girl kitties," she said. "How do you know?" her aunt asked. "Mother picked them up," said Diana, "and looked. I think it's printed underneath."

ANIMAL—COW

Riddle: When do cows wear bells? Answer: When their horns don't work.

> *— Agriculture Dept's Children's Book*

ANIMAL—DOG

Dogs are here on earth to teach us. They have taught me how to be serenely patient, and they have taught me about love—fundamental love.

> *— Doris Day*

(When asked her dog's age) "Eighteen months," Doris Day replied. "They're all eighteen months."
   I hesitated. "You mean like women are always twenty-nine?"
   "Exactly."

> *— Molly Haskell*

ANIMAL—HUNTING

To kill something for fun or luxury is to me the most insane and inhumane act of man.

> *— Loretta Swit*

ANSWER

There are days when I feel I could have given a softer answer. I'm kinda tough.

> *— Ann Landers*

ANTISLAVERY

The first black woman to speak out publicly against slavery was Sojourner Truth. She was born a slave and called "Isabella." Though she could not write or read, when she became free, she traveled to many states and spelled out her anti-slavery message.

APARTMENT

A woman who rents apartments to career women advertises: "Too much month left after the money?"

APPEARANCE

(Regarding her flamboyant appearance) I'm very real where it counts—inside.
                                            — Dolly Parton

I don't look this way out of ignorance. It's my gimmick.
                                            — Dolly Parton

There's always one girl at every party who makes the others wish they'd gone to the movies.
                                            — Phyllis Diller

Men aren't going to bother learning about your 24-karat heart unless it's wrapped in an attractive package.
                                            — Adrien Arpel

(Describing newscaster Jane Pauley) She has that regal austerity—half chic, half matronly, a little provincial—of a woman older than her years because of her position.
                                            — Aimee Lee Ball

APPEARANCE—CLOTHES

I don't wear brassieres. They restrict my breathing.
                                            — Mamie Van Doren

I don't like bikinis because I can't wear them myself—just jealousy.
                                            — Beatrice Lillie

You know, don't you, that the bikini is only the most important invention since the atom bomb?
                                            — Diana Vreeland

According to one woman, every time her marriage broke up, her wardrobe improved.

A wit once said that the high heel may well be the most potent aphrodisiac in the entire field of clothing.

One girl-watcher's comment: "High heels create a wanton swing of the hips and more hustle to the bustle."

If women follow that very short skirt fad, they're fools. But then, we are fools.

— Ava Gardner

I don't like anything (in clothes) that's exaggerated. I've often said a fashionable woman should be attractive ... not an attraction.

— Pearl Nipon

Inscription on the T-shirt of a young lady in a creative-writing class: "Good readers make good novel lovers."

Maybe the naked truth is glorious, but I like a bit of chiffon here and there.

— Elsie Janis

Gingham is all right tactically but pale pink chiffon should be within arm's reach, when arms are reaching.

— Elsie Janis

I think the human body is a glorious thing. But I really think it's more exciting for a woman to be dressed. It's sexier.

— Dyan Cannon

Before this time (her movies, *Diamond Lil* and *She Done Him Wrong*) clothes were made for the flat chest and small shoulders. I brought out the bust. I've started other trends besides sex, you know.

— Mae West

A woman's skirt should be like a diplomatic conference—long enough to be decent and short enough to hold people's interest.

— Andre Francóis Poncet

Movie actress Jacqueline Bisset says she loves good fabrics and, like the French, wears her clothes "till they die."

One secret of a woman's clothes is that sweaters and pants should fit well enough to show you're a woman but loose enough to show you're a lady.

— Department Store Buyer

Reminiscing about Hollywood, designer Edith Head pointed out that in the 1930's and 40's a movie star wore dazzling diamonds and furs, "even if her character was on poverty row. That was the way to win a rich husband and live happily ever after—and it always worked."

One day Barbara Gibson, secretary to Rose Kennedy, was called in to see a new evening dress Mrs. K. had tried on. The secretary told Mrs. K.

she looked fabulous ... adding, "You look thirty-eight." With a teasing smile, Mrs. K. said, "You mean twenty-eight, don't you?"

APPEARANCE—CLOTHES SHOPPING

Comedienne, Totie Fields strolled in to a snobbish boutique and demanded "hot pants." When the saleslady said, with high hauteur, that they did not carry anything over a size 9, Totie gleefully slapped both her buttocks with both her hands and announced, "That's perfect; I'll take two pairs.!"

The average Frenchwoman, before ordering a dress, first tries to get an entrance to the famous leading creators of fashion—to be invited to their shows. Then she goes through the shops in order to get a special material, a special lace, a special flower, a special ribbon that she has seen, for the special price she wants to pay. Then her little *Copiste* (whose address she will sooner die than give to her best friend) copies the chosen model as exactly as possible. Sometimes she has been happy enough to get a copy of the original toile. These toiles of grande couturiers are the most precious things craved by the Frenchwoman. There is a real gangsterism in stealing them.

— Anita Joachim Daniel

APPEARANCE—EYES

(Talking with a reporter) Really, I ought to be at work right now, but when I looked at you I thought you might be worth a few minutes' talk, for you haven't got city eyes, you never can tell anything to anybody with that kind of eyes; not that I'd ever try to tell anyone what to do or how.

— Hetty Green

APPEARANCE—FACE

She looked as if she'd wrinkled her clothes and ironed her face.

If I had to get by on nothing but a pretty face, I'd drown myself.
— Anna Magnani

My own face, as a child, has some distant and filtered quality, as thought I wasn't sure whether I might not disappear at any moment.
— Judy Collins

A woman's face may be her fortune, but along about middle age, her fortune no longer gains interest.

— Mary McCoy

(Speaking about using a makeup foundation) Doris Day once said she's found that men think freckles are provocative if they can see only half of them.

They say people make their faces after a certain age, but it is also true that before a certain age people's faces help to make them.

— A character in Violet Clay *by Gail Godwin*

APPEARANCE—FACE—IMPERFECTIONS

Tennis player Chris Evert loves to joke. At a match in Phoenix, Chrissie's face was a bit broken out so she instructed the announcer to introduce her with, "She is the greatest woman player in the world. She has won Wimbledon and Forest Hills. And she is currently sporting a new zit on her chin...."

APPEARANCE—FACE LIFT

If you think you need a face lift—then you probably do need a face lift.

— Ann Landers

Eat, drink and be merry today, for tomorrow you may have to dye your hair and have your face hoisted.

— Elsie Janis

Ever so often someone asks me if I've had my face lifted and I say, "Would I look like this if I had?"

— Bette Davis

I realize I could do with some improvements, but I know I would miss even the bits I don't like if they were to disappear.

— Lauren Bacall

When Betty Ford came home from the hospital (after her face lift) she asked her husband, Gerry Ford, "Do you love me?" And he said, "Yes, but if my wife finds out she'll kill me."

— Bob Hope

(Commenting about a famous woman's face lift) When your house needs repair, you fix it, so why not repair your face? It's the opposite of being a slob.

— Princess Luciana Pignatelli Avedon

(Describing skinny Katharine Hepburn) Not much meat, but choice.
— Spencer Tracy

(When asked her measurements) Why do you need by the numbers what you can see with your eyes?
— Gina Lollobrigida

Hollywood gossip columnist: "A certain movie actress is teed off by the fact that sister Eva has never svelte better."

Barbara Walters asked, about Dolly Parton's overblown figure, "Is it all you?" Dolly cagily replied, "Well, let's just say if I hadn't had it on my own, I'm the kind of person who would have had it made!"

While Raquel Welch was starring at Caesar's Palace, an employee remarked: "We got a headliner who's built better than the hotel."
— Earl Wilson

I stood in front of the mirror the other morning and assessed myself (my figure). Imagine, if you will, the state of Texas. I look terrific in Amarillo, but by the time I hit Dallas and Fort Worth, I begin to blouse, and don't thin out again until Corpus Christi. (But after Houston, who hangs on to see Corpus Christi?)
— Erma Bombeck.

APPEARANCE—GROOMING

Chanel, sitting on the stairs as she always did at one of her openings, noticed a middle-aged American in the crowd with a long glamour girl hairdo and an ensemble that foreshadowed today's "layered" gypsy frowziness. She exclaimed, "Oh my God, that flying hair, those flying scarves! Does that poor thing really think that autumn can be concealed with spring foliage?" That led her to philosophize, and her remarks should be pasted on every dressing table mirror: "A young girl can get away with throwing on any old rag; an older woman has to have clothes of superior cut and fabric. What counts is neatness, neatness, neatness. Sloppiness adds years."
— Alice Leone Moats

APPEARANCE—HAIR

My hair is like I am ... It's moody.
— Louise Lasser

Phyllis Diller refers to her "mix-master-styled" hair.

(Upon learning Beverly Sills' red hair matched hers exactly) How in the world did you get my recipe?

— Lucille Ball

An actress commented that her hair was hooked on a London tricologist's shampoos and conditioners. "It (her hair) goes into withdrawal if I run out."

When Ethel Merman saw her gorgeous lamé and palette costumes for *Call Me Madame*, she exclaimed to designer Mainbocher, "My gawd, you've made a lady out of me." Mainbocher smiled and then asked what she expected to do with her hair (worn in a rather unique arrangement: high in front and in something of a pony tail in back). Merman said, "Honey, I'm going to wash it."

APPEARANCE—HAIR (BLONDE)

Blondes have more fun, but brunettes have more time.

— Margo Smith

Raymond Chandler remarked of his femme fatale in *The Long Goodbye:* "There are blondes, and then there are blondes."

It's hard work being a brunette. One of the nicest things about being a blonde is that people don't expect you to make conversation.

— Martine Carol

APPEARANCE—HAIRCUT

Mother to teenage daughter: "You'd better get a haircut—you're beginning to look like a boy."

— Sparks

(Fashion editor Eugenia Sheppard, on a new Italian haircut) "Hacked off at the nape of the neck and a little slept-in on top."

APPEARANCE—POSTURE

If you let your body slump, everything goes out of shape. You get rolls where you don't have rolls.

— Dinah Shore

My mother was always after me to stand up straight. She said it made your clothes look good and kept you healthy. "Don't sit like a safety pin," she'd say. In her day one wore big corsets with bones in them, but even when she didn't have one on, her mother told her to imagine there was a bone going from her wishbone to her bellybutton. It sounds uncomfortable, but it works. If that part of your body's in order, the rest falls into place.

– Dina Merrill

APRIL FOOL

Don't believe that "You're a knockout" expression in his eye. There are April fools of both sexes.

– Elsie Janis

APRON

TV star Donna Reed in an interview said that viewers used to call her the "apron lady" because she always wore one in the show. She explained she was always in the kitchen whipping up something or other "because that's what a woman's role was expected to be."

ARGUMENT

I've never won an argument with her (his wife Rosalynn), and the only times I thought I had, I found out the argument wasn't over yet.

– Jimmy Carter

ARISE

He who rises late must trot all day.

– Cross stitch motto by designer Brendan Gardner

Jimmy usually wakes before I do and brings me my orange juice and the paper about six-thirty. If I'm still asleep, he sometimes lets me linger a little longer, But this one morning he woke me and said, "I'm sorry, dear, but you'll have to get up. There's so much work on your desk that when I put your paper on it, it slid right off."

– Rosalynn Carter

A woman with empty arms is an empty woman.

— Debbie Reynolds

ART

Paint what's in your head.

— Georgia O'Keefe

It's not enough to be just good.

— Louise Nevelson

Supporter of the Arts, Joan Mondale (wife of Walter Mondale) is known as Joan of Art.

Alma Thomas once dismissed a local pastor with the words, "Art is my religion."

(Commenting on the prices paid for her snow scenes) People would be better off buying chickens.

— Grandma Moses

(On why she could paint winter scenes any month) If you know something well, you can always paint it.

— Grandma Moses

Gloria Vanderbilt (as quoted by Laura Bergquist) said of her painting: "I don't believe in studying. Either you've got it or you haven't."

Peggy Guggenheim, patroness of 20th century art, in sponsoring young artists, adopted the motto: "Buy a painting a day."

Any art is the result of a development rather than a spontaneous thing. A person works, and as they work they ripen, and their experiences are brought forth when needed.

— Fanny Brice

It's as if my mind creates shapes that I don't know about. I thought someone could tell me how to paint landscape, but I never found that person. I had to just settle down and try.

— Georgia O'Keefe

It is my belief that the serious artist insists upon the sanctity of the world; even the despairing artist insists upon the power of his art to somehow transform what is given. It may be that his role, his function, is to articulate the very worst, to force up into consciousness the most perverse and terrifying possibilities of the epoch, so that they can be dealt with and not simply feared; such artists are often denounced as vicious and disgusting when in fact they are—sometimes quite apart from their individual conceptions of themselves—in the service of their epoch, attempting to locate images adequate to the unshaped, unconscious horrors they sense.

– Joyce Carol Oates

ASPIRATION

Far away there in the sunshine are my highest aspirations. I may not reach them, but I can look up and see their beauty, believe in them and try to follow where they lead.

– Louisa May Alcott

ASSAULT

Henry entered no plea Thursday to charges of assault causing bodily harm and threatening his wife December 22 near Lake Luce. Appearing in court, he stated: "I can't understand why I was charged and arrested. After all, it was only my wife."

ASSETS

I told my girls to leave something on—keep a little chiffon on. A woman's greatest asset is a man's imagination.

– Ann Corio

ASTROLOGY

When one of (her daughter) Mary's sons was about six years old, he heard her say, "I'm Jewish," and he said, "You are? I thought you were Capricorn!"

– Dorothy Rodgers

ASTRONAUT

A woman comic asks: "If athletes get athlete's foot, do astronauts get missile-toe?"

Sally Ride, future astronaut, commented about NASA'S space shuttle training program: "...your basic once-in-a-lifetime opportunity ... You don't have to be very feminine, or very masculine, or a color, or a race. It's people in space."

ATTACK

Though she was married to a British trader named Thomas Bosworth, an American Indian woman, Creek Mary, loved freedom. During the Revolutionary War era, she got together a group of male warriors and stormed Savannah, attempting to drive out the British.

AUCTION

Whenever I hear of a celebrity auction, I send in a bid for Robert Redford

– Joan Rivers

When attending an auction, one elderly woman to another: "Jane, here's one place you can get something for nodding."

AUDIENCE

The audience scares me.

– Tamara Louwe

I love audiences more than anything in life. I'm a junkie for a crowd.
– Elizabeth Ashley

A benefit audience usually sits there resenting all the money they've spent.

– Jean Stapleton

Regarding audience members who cough through plays, Hermione Gingold told Walter Winchell: "All persons should be medically examined before being allowed to buy theater tickets."

The only reason I have a career at all is the audiences. The people in the business don't like me, directors, producers ... I think the only obligation I have in the theater is to the audience.

– Elizabeth Ashley

AUDITION

I'm a terrible "auditioner"! I'm a performer, not an auditioner!
– Beverly Sills

In hearing audition candidates or in accepting pupils of my own, I am always on the look-out, of course, for a great voice; but, if a pupil comes to me with real musical feeling, I will not refuse to teach her simply because she lacks greatness. The real musician can do more good in the world, perhaps, than merely the glamorous star! So, sing anyway! Sing and love it, and give all the pleasure to others that you can.

– Ernestine Schumann-Heink

AUTO

Belligerent-looking woman to male filling station attendant: "Fill *him* up!"

Bumper sticker on a woman's car: "I may be slow, but I'm ahead of you."

I don't know how a car knows when you're ready to sell it ... but it knows.

– Erma Bombeck

Richard Cameron gave his wife Kathy Cameron, Revlon's fragrance evaluator, the New Jersey auto license plate "Scent 1."

Celeste Holm, looking at a low-slung foreign car: "It's fine, but foreign cars always remind me of things you trip over on the top of the stairs."

A woman doctor who's driven the same make car for two decades, buys a new one every four years. "And every four years," she says, "I get the very latest 'disprovements.'"

AUTOGRAPH

Larry King got the thrill of his life recently when a little girl ran up and asked for his autograph.

"I said okay and asked her what she wanted me to write," King said. "She said, 'Just sign it Mr. Billie Jean King.'"

AVIATION

Pioneer aviatrix Louise Thaden, on being hired by Beech Aircraft as a factory representative: "I think I got that job by being a woman. They could show that even *I* couldn't bend one of their planes."

(About why she became a flyer) You'd have to search for the reason in my childhood. I was born in a hovel, but I was determined to soar up among the stars. What I love about flying is being up there all alone with nobody to help you but yourself.

– Jackie Cochrane

Jacqueline Aurial, who set a world speed record for women, in an article by Helen Markel Herman: "When I began to fly, I suddenly discovered that my life before had not been full and joyous, but empty and superficial ... I felt as though I had been caught in a vise, slowly suffocating ... Suddenly I wanted to know the truth, to find out what was important to me. And the truth is with me when I fly."

My flight has added nothing to aviation. After all, literally hundreds have crossed the Atlantic by air, if those who have gone in heavier-than-air and lighter-than-air craft are counted and those who have crossed the North and the South Atlantic. However, I hope that the flight has meant something to women in aviation. If it has, I shall feel it was justified; but I can't claim anything else.

— Amelia Earhart

Some features of the (solo trans-Atlantic) flight I fear have been exaggerated. It made a much better story to say I landed with but one gallon of gasoline left. As a matter of fact, I had more than a hundred. The exact quantity I remember because I had to pay a tax for every gallon imported into Ireland!

I did *not* land within six feet of a hedge of trees. I taxied to the upper end of a sloping pasture and turned my plane into the shelter of some trees, as a matter of course. It made a much better story the other way, I admit.

No flames were threatening to burn my plane in the air. I did have some trouble with my exhaust manifold, of which I shall tell you later. There was no extreme hazard from that cause, however.

I did not kill a cow in landing—unless one died of fright. Of course, I came down in a pasture and I had to circle many other pastures to find the best one. The horses, sheep, and cows in Londonderry were not used to airplanes, and so, as I flew low, they jumped up and down and displayed certain disquiet. I really was afraid that an Irishman would shoot me as I stepped out of the plane, thinking that I was just a 'smart alec' from some big town come down to scare the cattle.

— Amelia Earhart

AWARD

When Carol Channing won a Tony Award, she thanked her mother for "whatever you did."

When singer Marian Anderson received a Congressional Gold Medal, engraved on it was the inscription of her favorite spiritual: "He's Got The Whole World in His Hands."

Accepting an award from the Notre Dame Club of Chicago, Lucille Ball, bowled over by the University president, Rev. Theodore Hesburgh, said: "I know you've done all kinds of things for Notre Dame, but my God, I didn't realize you were that attractive."

When Candice Bergen, who did not complete her undergraduate work, received an award as Woman of the Year and a gold bean pot, bestowed by Harvard's Hasty Pudding Theatricals, she told her audience: "Today as I proudly cradle this pot, I can look back on several visits by the Dean of Women at Penn. who once asked me: 'Candice, what will you be without your B.A.?' I can now tell her she was right: nothing."

AWARD—OSCAR

When Barbra Streisand received the Oscar for *Funny Girl*, she said, "Hello, Gorgeous."

I received my prized Academy Award statuette at about the same time that I finally wheedled out of my husband, Harmon O. Nelson, Jr., the tenaciously guarded secret of his middle name. It was "Oscar." To tease him, I began to call my statuette "Oscar." Soon, "Oscar" was adopted by the industry—and that's how the Academy Award statuettes got their nickname.

– Bette Davis

BABY

My baby will have the career of a baby.

– Shirley Temple Black

Most women would rather cuddle a baby than a typewriter or a machine.

– Phyllis Schlafly

Seven-year-old Shirley spent her piggy-bank contents to buy a package of bubble gum for each member of the class. When the teacher asked the occasion, the little girl replied, "Last night I became a sister. Mom had a baby."

I'm beginning to feel it's time for me to have babies. I want babies, but I'm not quite ready to get married. I can't do one without the other. I've heard it's been done, but my mother wouldn't like that—and I must keep her respect.

– Diana Ross

BABY—ABORTION

Betty Ford rejoiced in an interview that abortion had finally "been taken out of the backwoods and put into the hospitals where it belongs."

When Midge Constanza was White House advisor: "(At the present time) You do have a right to an abortion, but you have to report the pregnancy within 48 hours, then be examined by two doctors, two Senators and the Speaker of the House."

Gloria Steinem once asked if I would add my name to a list of prominent women admitting an illegal abortion. Pleased to be considered prominent I felt I had let Gloria down by never having had an abortion. "In my case, Gloria, the supply has always been equal to the demand."

– Barbara Howar

BABY SITTER

I guess you could say that I baby-sat for a couple of generations of Americans with "I love Lucy," "The Lucy Show" and "Here's Lucy" ... That makes me very happy.

– Lucille Ball

Though they had four children and 15 grandchildren living within 30 miles, a retired couple was noted for taking trips and, when they were at home, working on many community activities. "Why are we always so busy?" said the grandmother. "Well, you sure can't baby-sit, if they can't catch you at home."

BACKGROUND

TV Host: "...and you really were in the background as woman and wife?" Anne Morrow Lindbergh: "Oh, yes— 'How do you do?' people would say, looking past me to Charles."

BALANCE

God balances everything out. My theory is that God gives you either straight white teeth with lots of cavities or crooked stained teeth with no cavities. In the same way, if someone were not as attractive, then she might be much more intelligent.

– Farrah Fawcett

When I go to work, I have to fix my hair, put on makeup, get dressed up, show up on time, sweat, work, and do as I'm told. So I am very, very careful never, ever to do any of those things any other place in my life— that's the only way I can keep my life balanced. If I adhere to any kind of social behavior, then I would be doing double time. What you see is what you get. I pretend for a living; I don't pretend for free. I don't owe the world any more pretense. I'm like the United Fund: I overgive that way every time I go to work.

– Elizabeth Ashley

BANK ACCOUNT

A Christian has a nonlimited bank account. He has all the gifts of God.
— *Woman Minister*

"Of course, we have money left in the bank," a woman said to her husband. "I still have four checks left."

The re-entry homemaker took a job in a small office and among her chores was handling the firm's receivables. After several days of depositing checks, she phoned the bank and asked for the firm's balance. The bank clerk inquired, "What is your balance as of this morning?" Replied the ex-homemaker, "I asked you first!"

BARGAIN

Really think hard before passing up what you know to be a great bargain. You will know it is a great bargain if it gives you a feeling roughly equivalent to the feeling you had when you met the man of your dreams.
— *Elin Schoen*

BATH TUB

All women look alike in the bath tub.
— *Edith Head*

BATHROOM

The bathroom has become the only sanctuary in the American home that insures diplomatic immunity from every chore possible.
— *Erma Bombeck*

BEARD

The big difference is that the people who wear goatees at the Waldorf had 'em before bop.
— *Sarah Vaughan*

BEAUTY

It is God who made woman beautiful; it is the Devil who makes her pretty.

— Chinese Proverb

Sarah Bernhardt proposed, to preserve their beauty, that blondes bathe in white wine and brunettes in claret.

There should be as little merit in loving a woman for her beauty, as a man for his property, both being equally subject to change.

— Alexander Pope

I leave the serious sun baking to the young, who will learn to regret it in a few years. Sun produces more lines than a broken heart.

— Dinah Shore

If I could have only one beauty aid, it would be a man. A woman cannot really look her best unless she is making an effort for a man, or, even more effective, men.

— Carroll Baker

If you read the papers, you will notice that no girl with short hair has made an advantageous marriage lately. So what's the sense of looking like a shaved bulldog?

— Elizabeth Arden

The mother, speaking of her new baby, said to a feminist friend, she'd prefer that the tyke grow up to be beautiful rather than brainy. The shocked feminist said, "Why beautiful ... *today?* There'll be so many more opportunities possible for a girl." "Yes," said the mother, "but there'll be a lot more men who can see than who can think."

I believe the key to good looks is self-esteem, and self-esteem means self-discipline—in all areas of one's life. But I still want to taste everything life has to offer—in moderation: good wine, a spoonful of chocolate mousse, some pasta if I avert my eyes from the garlic bread, a triple feature when I want to relax, a day of doing nothing ...

— Dinah Shore

God's woman has a fantastic source of beauty right at her elbow. She has a master cosmetologist beside her to erase the hard lines of anger. With a touch of His hand, He can soften her rigid skin into the beautiful flawless complexion of kindness. He rejuvenates her cheek bones by gently brushing them with the fresh glow of understanding. Her mouth glistens with the ointment of gentleness. He lets the inner fire of her soul add extra sparkle to her eyes, and they are bright with forgiveness. When he finishes with His work, He sends her out into the world He made, turns the floodlights up, and we all see she is a BEAUTY.

— Joyce Landorf

I have noticed that most of the beautiful women I have known in my life were nearsighted and had poor memories. Why, I used to fume, is this always, accursedly so? They never notice the sights you want them to see; they never remember the person, book, or event you want to discuss! Yet one might as well postulate a divine providence from this. Few things in our world are as sad as the fading of the looks of a beautiful woman; why, then, should she be able to catch every reflection of her diminishing allure in a passing shop window or a pursuing mirror? Why should she even remember how much better her hair, eyes, skin looked twenty years ago?

— John Simon

BEAUTY—CONTEST

Rina Messinger, Miss Universe, on beauty contests: "Why is it more proper to compete on intelligence than on beauty, when both are allotted by God?"

So you have to parade around for 20 minutes in a swimsuit. By doing that, you can win $10,000 to study whatever you want.

— Lee Meriwether

More than anything else, I wanted to be beautiful. That's why I was always decorating myself, to improve on nature. Once I saved the ripe red cherries from dinner and instead of eating them I braided them into my hair. My brother helped me. When we were through, he said I looked pretty. It was the first time anyone had said that to me, ever, and I threw my arms around his neck and kissed him. But my mother found us and said, Lilly, you must eat your dessert, not wear it.

— Lilly Daché

BEAUTY—INNER

But the kind of beauty I want most is that hard-to-get kind that comes from within—strength, courage, dignity.

— Ruby Dee

My feeling is that beauty is strictly internal. It comes from within, and concerns one's circulation, and I don't mean the newspaper kind.

– Gloria Swanson

"Beauty comes from within," was always being said to TV star Bonnie Franklin. "Any girl hearing that." says Franklin, "knows she's ugly."

BEAUTY—RECIPE

(When asked why she was so good-looking at age 60) I come from good stock—I inherited good bones ... Find some time to be quiet and have two good friends you can trust. Then you can be beautiful and stay beautiful.

– Lena Horne

BEAUTY—RITUALS

In London, most of my clients are of the aristocratic class; but this woman was of the middle class—"in trade" as they say over there; very rich, very charitable, very much beloved by her employees ...

She came to my establishment at regular intervals and stayed two weeks at a time, having every conceivable kind of treatment. And between these visits she spent three hours daily in her own home, merely on the care of her face and body. She told me with pride about one friend, a clergyman of her own age, who was stooped and bald. To feel the contrast between them was like wine to her.

That case was really unique, for she had neither husband, lover, nor children for whom to be beautiful. She was not doing it for anyone in particular, but just because she wanted everybody to admire and to wonder.

– Helena Rubinstein

BEAUTY SHOP

A woman sees every person she knows en route to the beauty shop. When she comes out, the streets have turned into a ghost town.

– Erma Bombeck

BEAUTY—TEN

I think it's great that so many people say I'm pretty, but I know I'm not that pretty. Nobody is perfect, nobody is a ten really.

– Bo Derek

BED

She's the kind you don't bed unless you wed.

... those people who sleep around helter-skelter. I think it's much more fun to go to bed with friends.
— Sally Rand

BEST-DRESSED

The Duchess of Windsor once said that no woman can be too thin or too rich.

BILL

Interior decorator to stunned client examining her bill: "Don't worry— you'll be giving a party and happily complaining about my fee before you know it."

BIOGRAPHY

Where once biography was devoted to setting up marble statues, it is now devoted, in André Maurois' words, to "pulling dead lions by the beard."
— Barbara Tuchman

BIRTH

The birth of a baby is still the noblest event in our lives.
— Eunice Kennedy Shriver

(On the birth of her first child) It was easier to give birth than to compete in the Olympics.
— Olga Korbut

When, at 41, Alice Roosevelt Longworth surprised everyone by giving birth to a daughter, she commented: "I'm always willing to try anything once."

The three most beautiful sights: a potato garden in bloom, a ship in sail, a woman after the birth of her child.
— Irish proverb

"We just had twins! Boys!" A thrilled eight-year-old Patty announced to a neighbor. "Two brothers. How lovely!" said the neighbor. "I must phone your mother." "Oh, no!" said the youngster, "she knows about it."

BIRTH CONTROL

A doctor's advice to a young bride regarding the use of contraceptives: "Use on every conceivable occasion."
— Sam Levenson

In a TV skit, Susan Ford, daughter of Gerald Ford, was asked, "You don't have White House guards anymore, so what do you use for protection?" Her answer: "Birth control pills."

As a fitting conclusion to the First American Birth Control Conference, a public meeting was arranged at the Town Hall in New York City. The subject chosen for discussion was the ethics of Birth Control. When I attempted to speak, I was dragged off to a police station ... The case was promptly dismissed by the magistrate the following morning ... But the investigation which followed indicated that the police who broke up the meeting had received their orders, not from police headquarters, but from the clergy! The boomerang effect of this performance was indicated by the reverberations in the press. The idea of Birth Control was advertised, dramatized, made the recipient of column upon column of publicity. Only an infinitesimal section of the public had been aware of the first American Birth Control Conference ... The clumsy and illegal tactics of our opponents made the whole country aware of what we were doing ... (Later) There were symposiums, editorials, letters from "constant readers" all of which had the effect deliberately sought by us, of keeping our idea interesting to the public at large.
— Margaret Sanger

BIRTHDAY

What can I say ... except that I am 50 years old, but my heart is 15.
— Princess Grace of Monaco

Seven-year-old Justin Trudeau said of his mother Margaret, "Mom won't be grown up until she gets to be 30."

Women in ancient Greece counted their age from the date of their marriage instead of their birth.

(On her 55th birthday) I feel I'm just starting to come together. I will peak in maybe ten years. I'm just about through with puberty.

— Carol Channing

(Showing a picture of herself on her 100th birthday) I must have been around 85 or 90 ... almost old enough to go in the rocking chair.

— Grandma Moses

Blowing out her candles on her cake, Toni, who had an annoying little brother, Bobby, said, "I wish Bobby will spend next week with Grandma and Grandpa."

When Shirley Temple Black turned 50, she commented she had (movie) prints in storage but doesn't ever look at them. "No need." she said, "I was there."

In 1971 when Nixon gave an 87th birthday party for her in the White House, Mrs. (Alice Roosevelt) Longworth said of her celebration; "So gruesome. Everyone looks at you and wonders if she'll last another year."

— Myra MacPherson

In a speech, Barbara Walters recalled that one morning very early Lyndon Johnson phoned her on her birthday at the NBC studios. "I'm just lyin' here with Lady Bird," he drawled, "and Lady Bird said, 'Lyndon, if you had any guts you'd call her up and wish her a happy birthday."

You can toboggan into old age before 50, or you can glide gently, almost imperceptibly, down a gradual slope of the years into your 70's. But the time for a woman to begin cheating old age is before she begins cheating on the number of candles on her birthday cake. The battle against age must be fought simultaneously and unremittingly on two fronts—the physical and the psychological. The goal of the first is a youthful appearance; the goal of the second, a youthful spirit.

— Clare Boothe Luce

The lady executive, honored with a surprise birthday party, raised her glass of champagne and toasted herself: "Thirty-eight—and still a Virgo!"

Something else I'm getting is not any older. On my seventy-fourth birthday I dreaded looking in the glass. I didn't want any surprises, but I got one. At seventy-four I look better than at seventy-three. If you

make it through seventy-four years, can it be that things shape up?
Think it over.

— Ruth Gordon

BITCH

Bitch is a terribly mean and sexist word ... I don't deserve it ... Men can
become involved in producing, directing and writing and everyone calls
them talented. But a woman who does the same is called power-hungry.
Women are expected to stay on the sidelines and keep their mouths shut
and get along with everyone at all costs ... Well, I'm not like that.

— Barbra Streisand

BLESSING

Humorist Jean Kerr's mother once said what she was looking for was a
blessing that was *not* in disguise.

BOARD MEETING

Woman V.P. to her secretary: "Whether it's all right with the Supreme
Court or not, I say a little prayer everytime I go into one of these board
meetings."

BODY

The body, wrote Cordelia Greene in 1906, is really a fine ocean liner in
which we make the voyage of life. If there is bilge in the hole, if the
furnace is choked or the shaft bent, it makes sailing slow and heavy.

— Dr. Cordelia Greene

BORE

Life becomes a bore only if you lose your appetite for the future.

— Bette Davis

(Speech opening) I can't promise I won't bore you but at least I won't
bore you for long.

— Elizabeth Taylor

BOREDOM

Anthony Newley: "What kills love for you?" Zsa Zsa Gabor: "Boredom."

I've never had a boring day in my life. And the longer I live, the less boring it becomes.

— Sally Rand

I've also been accused of leading an unexciting life. But to me, following the crowd is what's boring and dull. There's nothing more boring than going to a party where all the girls look alike, where everybody is saying the same thing and doing the same thing.

— Debby Boone

BOSS

The average secretary in the U.S. is better educated than the average boss.

— Gloria Steinem

When Don's parents had lunch with their handsome bachelor son, who'd just gone to work for a lady tycoon, Don's mom leaned across the table eagerly and said, "What's your new boss's name, son?... Is she married?"

(On having a woman boss) Yeah. It puts men in a bad spot. I could read their minds, unfortunately, wondering who is this female making this decision, not realizing that maybe I'd consulted six experts first. I'm all wrong as an executive, I feel out of place. I have too many antennae out, I'm too easily hurt and intimidated. But I can make quick surgical incisions.

— Lucille Ball

BOYS

I rode horses every day of my life until I discovered boys.

— Jane Fonda

BRAIN

Are brains a handicap to marriage? I think so, going on the theory that where there's no sense there's no pain.

— Elsie Janis

Its true that women are brainier than men. But we should keep this fact quiet because it could ruin our whole racket.

– Anita Loos

BRAVE

While I think women can be as brave as men, I'm not such a female chauvinist as to expect them to be braver.

– Betty Friedan

BRIDE

As the waiter served the luscious wedding dinner, the bride, looking longingly at the goodies, lamented to the bridegroom, "Oh, gosh—and I'm counting calories!" But suddenly she brightened and said, "I forgot! My dieting days are over!"

BRIDE'S BOUQUET

A columnist advised her woman readers: "Researcher Beverly Norris discovered that in a survey of 30 marriages conducted in Illinois, only 2 out of 30 bridesmaids who actually caught the bouquet were the next to marry. So if *you're* interested in a speedy marriage, don't catch a bride's bouquet!"

BRIDGE

Women should continue to be barred from bridge's Open Championships because they lack "the killer instinct." Men are simply better players, as in other sports. Women do not have the same concentration or physical resistance. In bridge, you have to be strong.

– Omar Sharif

BRIGHT SIDE

She taught us early that the birds will sing when the storm is over, that the rose must know the thorn and that the valley makes the mountain tall.

– Edward Kennedy

BROTHEL QUEEN

Sally Stanford, formerly the "queen" of San Francisco's leading brothel, about her livelihood, "I hope women can learn a lesson from my story ... I came along before food stamps and aid to poverty. We did the best we could with the tools we had."

BUDGET—NATIONAL

When our household is faced with a financial emergency—an operation, a new boiler, a roof that must be replaced—we do not hopelessly wring our hands and say, "There is nothing before us but debt!" We pinch a little harder. We trim. We get along without a new car or a maid or a summer vacation. It could be done in the national household too. Remember that, sir, and tell it to your cabinet and to Congress.

There must be a good many things the government can get along without, to stave off bankruptcy.

— Phyllis McGinley

BUNNY

A girl asked a friend who worked for Hugh Hefner's Playboy Club: "How do Playboy bunnies get to work?" Her friend said, "By rabbit transit."

BUREAUCRACY

Inefficiency is deeply rooted. It's untouched by reorganization at the level where agencies are combined, created and reshuffled. Across-the-board cuts never affect it. Bureaucracy always cuts muscle before fat.

— Sylvia Porter

BUSINESS EXECUTIVE

Description of a hungry tycooness? She only wants what's hers and what lies next to it.

Business executive Beverly C. Lanquist: "You can't always be fair. Honest, yes. But the name of the game is to win, to get the contract, the vote, the deal. Life is not fair."

A mother, president of a manufacturing company, taking eight-year-old Anne, on a tour of the factory, tells her, "Someday, honey, you'll oust me and take control of all this yourself."

If we're going to have men and women in business on an equal basis, with men over women and women over men, we have to develop decent sex morals.

It's very difficult to run an Army if the General is in love with the Sergeant.

— Margaret Mead

Business executive Helen McLane: "In the past 10 years the number of women getting MBAs has grown from a trickle to a substantial number. That means that many companies that hesitated to hire women for the guts of the enterprise are now putting them in slots that are the training ground for tomorrow's chief executive."

Senior law partner Jewel LaFontant: "I don't like to be considered tough. I'm strong. Women will be making a big mistake if they try to pattern themselves to follow the so-called manly way of doing business. As women we're getting in touch with parts of ourselves we used to hide under pink dresses. I don't suppress the different me's. There's some Scarlett O'Hara in me and some Golda Meir."

Rosalind Russell felt that in her films, in which she often played a career woman, she set back Women's Lib by making things look too easy, though she said she always had 12 phones on her desk. By the sixth reel, a leading man was telling her that underneath her cold exterior was a soft feminine woman. "Naturally," she said, "I always turned him down. Leave a business empire—and 12 telephones—for a man and Mexico? Never!"

BUSINESS EXECUTIVE—TIPS FOR

Don't tell your age to anybody ... Don't tell your salary to anybody ... Don't tell the fascinating story of your sex life to anybody ... In the immortal words of Casey Stengel, you don't have to tell nobody nuttin'. Practice smiling. And remember that an unanswered question is stickier for the asker than for the askee.

— Jo Foxworth

Thou shalt try harder; thou need not be only No. 2. Thou shalt know when to zip thy lip and listen quietly. Thou shalt not attempt to hide behind thine own petticoat. Thou shalt speak softly and carry no stick, except lipstick. Thou shalt serve thy lady boss as graciously as thou servest any man. When success cometh, thou shalt not get too big for thy bustle. Thou shalt watch thy language, there may be gentlemen present. Thou shalt not match martinis with the men.

– Jo Foxworth

BUSINESS TRIP

I flew 3,000 miles to make a major presentation and discovered after washing my hair (in my hotel room) that there were no electrical outlets for my dryer. Once reason prevailed, I figured out that where there was a television set, there was probably a plug. But there were mirrors only in the bathroom. So I dried my hair peering into the dark TV screen.

Ariel Angele Allen

CAKE

I'm a great believer in women getting a fairer share of the cake they've baked.

— Glenda Jackson

CALIFORNIA

They say that if you are not an orange maybe you won't like California.

— Lana Svetlana Peters

CAMERA MAN

I told the camera man he had made me look gorgeous in "The Garden of Allah and asked why he hadn't done it in a film we made much later. He said, well, he was eight years older.

— Marlene Dietrich

CAMP

Nine-year-old Cissy, attending a tennis camp, wrote home: "Dear Folks: What is an epidemic?"

CAREER

It never works both ways. My husband's career has to come first.

— Esther Williams

(About her daughter desiring a nursing career) We are ducks ... who have hatched a wild swan.
                                                    — The Mother of Florence Nightingale

I'm starting at the top and working my way down. In ten years, I'll be in the mailroom.
                                                    — Christie Hefner

Headline on an ad recruiting women managers: "What you need is a good swift kick in the career."

(After a comment about her long career): Young man, you make me sound as though I should be stuffed.
                                                    — Lillian Gish

The greatest career a woman can have is in being a wife, the second greatest in being a mother.
                                                    — Ruth Stafford Peale

Actress Mary McCarthy, about her singing/acting career which started in her early teens: "My mother didn't push me. She aimed me."

Any career rests firmly on two pillars—one is natural endowment; and the other, the use one makes of such inborn material.
                                                    — Roberta Peters

It would be nice to have some terrific relationship, but more than that, I think I'd rather have a terrific new play.
                                                    — Lauren Bacall

(Caption under photograph of farm scene with a woman plowing an adjacent field) Back then, the working woman could enter the field of her choice.
                                                    — Virginia Slims ad

I think of my marriage and family as my number one career ... When I fill out applications, I put down "Mother" as my occupation. I feel it's as rewarding for most women as it is for me.
                                                    — Phyllis Schlafly

(About her career) I had stooped to do a thing a woman was not supposed to do, and therefore was supposed not to be quite a nice, refined girl. (A proper young woman) ... was supposed to depend entirely on her male relations.
                                                    — Sister Kenny

CBS White House correspondent Lesley R. Stahl, speaking at a Wheaton College commencement: "Pray that you're not 'discovered' for the first ten years of your professional lives ... What I wish is that you allow your careers to percolate slowly enough to build your competence and confidence securely and firmly. What I hope for you is that none of you becomes a flash in the pan..."

CAREER—SECOND

A new, second career in mid-life can be a glorious adventure. In fact, I cannot overemphasize the message that you should expect and welcome the prospect of two or even three entirely different careers during the course of your working lifetime.

– Sylvia Porter

CAREER WOMEN

Career women frighten me and housewives speak practically a foreign language. Occasionally, when I feel I should like to join their sheltered ranks, my doctor gives me a tonic.

– Hermione Gingold

CHALLENGE

The key to life is accepting challenges. Once someone stops doing this, he's dead.

– Bette Davis

CHANGE

Marry the man today—change his ways tomorrow.

– Shirley Boone

The only time a woman really succeeds in changing a man is when he's a baby.

– Natalie Wood

You can get your face lifted and your nose changed, but unless you keep changing with the times, you'll always have the same old look, no matter what you do.

– Eileen Ford

CHARACTER

Of the mixture of joviality and industry which formed his mother's character, it is almost impossible to speak with exaggeration. The industry was a thing apart, kept to herself. It was not necessary that any one who lived with her should see it. She was at her table (as a writer) at four in the morning, and had finished her work before the world had begun to be aroused. But the joviality was all for others. She could dance with other people's legs, eat and drink with other people's palates, be proud with the lustre of other people's finery. Every mother can do that for her own daughters; but she could do it for any girl whose look, and voice, and manners pleased her. Even when she was at work, the laughter of those she loved was a pleasure to her. She had much, very much, to suffer. Work sometimes came hard to her, so much being required,—for she was extravagant, and liked to have money to spend; but of all people I have known she was the most joyous, or, at any rate, the most capable of joy.

— Anthony Trollope

CHARGE

Father to daughter: "Your mother is a real dynamo—she charges everything in sight."

CHARITY

(About her philosophy of charity) You never saw my name on a charity list (for making a charitable donation), did you?.... but I built whole blocks of buildings in Chicago when the working men there had to have employment.

— Hetty Green

CHARM

(Said of a film star) An actress with such warm charm, glaciers would melt at her approach.

CHEMISTRY

With Clark Gable and me there was just no chemistry, and you can't fight that.

— Lauren Bacall

CHILD

You can have an ex-wife, an ex-husband, an ex-job, but you can't have an ex-child.

My mom loves three things in this world—me, Alan (her husband) and her food processor.

— Suzanne Somers' son, Bruce

A woman handles a child much better with one finger than a man does with both fists.

— Martin Luther

Upon viewing her new-born baby sister, Claudia, through the nursery glass at Good Samaritan Hospital, two-year-old Linda banged on the nursery door and screamed, "Get her out."

A 5-year-old girl got mad at her father and said tearfully, on the way to her room, "How would you like to go to an orphanage for parents?"

— Ina Hughs

The mother of a 30-year-old modern careerist, wishing to become a grandmother, urged her daughter: "Use what Mother Nature gave you before Father Time takes it away."

(On her appetite as a child when at a summer resort) ... finally Mother got to the point where she hung a sign on my back, "Please do not feed this child."

— Betty Ford

Amy, 5, visited her mother and a new sister, at Lying-In Hospital. Through the visitors' glass she eyed the babies lying, sucking their thumbs—some chewing on fists. Then she turned to her mother in amazement and cried, "They're eating their arms!"

It's terribly important for a child to be free to develop what he is. I am a painter. Their father is a musician. But they may not necessarily be artistic. Children so often live in the shadow of their parents. They must feel they can try anything they like.

— Gloria Vanderbilt

I do believe in working women, and I feel so strongly that a child is better off not to have the mother every minute of the time. Children who cling to their mothers—they grow up being babies. And I think it's good for a mother and a child to be separated most of the day.

— Miz Lillian Carter

In an article, writer Robert W. Marks said that when Deborah Kerr's elder daughter, Melanie, was 8, she liked to adopt fanciful roles. One time she decided she was a "mother hawk." Later Deborah asked her how she was feeling. "Not very well," replied Melanie. "It's quite sad. You see, I broke my wing earlier this morning."

CHILD ACTRESS

Mary McCarthy, who was a child actress with Shirley Temple, Jane Withers and Judy Garland, recalled: "At 5 years old, I played outdoors with an ear to the phone inside my house."

CHILDHOOD

Nobody had a happy childhood. It was really reassuring when I found that out.

— Liza Minnelli

(Re raising her children) I'm a teeny bit overprotective ... I try to protect their childhood, I know how fleeting it is ... I want it to be like a storybook.

— Connie Stevens

CHILDREN

In raising children, don't sweat the small stuff ... too much nitpicking.
— Ann Landers

Children are like spring ... full of hope and things to look ahead to.
— Grandma Moses

When she had her twenty-fifth child, Mrs. Jeannie Cyr of Ottawa said: "Papa is crazy about children."

Children are our future, but they're our present too, and they have a birthright to a certain kind of care.

— Marlo Thomas

The amount of respect we give our children when they are young is the amount we get back from them later on.

— Kathryn Murray

Last spring, for example, I didn't get the lead I expected to get in a Broadway play. I called my younger son in Hillsborough and said, "Nathaniel, I'm kind of blue," "Mom," he reminded me. "there'll be time for that. You've got to remember you're still just a rookie." He wants to be a professional golfer, so he's busy now, losing those ten thousand tournaments you have to lose before you can win. My children and I are now all in the same boat together.

— Kathryn Crosby

CHIVALRY

The best-looking and most charming women never are heard complaining about lack of chivalry in men.

— Boston Globe

CHOOSING

In 1918, Florence Leftwich/Ravenel wrote: "The question of the future will be no longer how much shall the woman be permitted to do, for all artifical barriers will have been withdrawn; but rather, first, how far will her own strength of body and mind be likely to carry her in the open road of competition with men on their own ground; and then, and more important still, among the many and diverse tasks and objects proposed to mankind in the great and laborious future, which shall seem most worthy of the woman's choice and pursuit? She may do what she chooses, but what will she choose to do?"

What success means to me isn't people knowing your name and making a fuss over you.... Success means being able to do what you really care about, to choose what you really want to do.

— Marlo Thomas

CHRISTIAN

When Debby Boone was introduced to a group of students as a practicing Christian who didn't smoke, drink or swear, Debby admitted that was almost true: "At least," she said, "I never swear out loud."

CIRCUS

First came the circus. I rehearsed the elephants. I slept with them. I cleaned them and their stable, and I made them go to the bathroom before they went out to perform.

— Geraldine Chaplin

CITY—NEW YORK

I like New York at dawn ... It's something like watching a movie with the sound track off.

— Kim Novak

Why do I live right in Manhattan? So I won't have to get up by yawn's early light.

Woman Advertising Copywriter

Mme. Pandit, as U. N. Assembly president: "Somehow, New York represents nothing but itself; it doesn't even represent the U.S."

New York is great for watching people because nobody looks back at you. You don't feel that you're violating anyone's privacy.

— Lynn Redgrave

Being gracious isn't always that easy, especially in New York. It's probably harder to have good manners here than any place in the world.

— Charlotte Ford

New York is a galaxy of adventure at once elegant, exciting and bizarre. It's a city that moves so fast, it takes energy just to stand still.

— Barbara Walters

Lady Hardwicke, wife of British actor Sir Cedrick Hardwicke: "London is a lover you can trust. New York is the lover you can't trust. Any minute, you expect to get kicked in the pants."

What many visitors discover about the Big Apple is that it's the best city in the world for walking. Just walking, and remaining perfectly anonymous in a sea of people even as you stare. Do you know that in Beverly Hills the police arrest you for loitering if you amble aimlessly? Not in New York.

— Barbara Walters

CITY—PARIS

Paris! City of Love!

— Collette

Always our migrant artists and artisans, unless they return from time to time to regain vigor from the impalpable dust of Paris, to walk her springy pavements, risk seeing the magic wand they thought to take with them turn into a dead twig.

— Colette

CITY—PHILADELPHIA

Feminist lecturer/writer Suzy Sutton describes Philadelphia as the city of "brotherly and sisterly love."

CLASS

The teacher's class was jammed. Her morning attendance report to her principal started off with: "Help! They're all here!"

A teacher reading to a noisy class finally stopped, waiting for the class to quiet down. Quickly a little pigtailed girl raised her hand and said, "Miss Thomas, did you stop because you came to a long word?"

CLONE

Advice columnist Abigail Van Buren says that while she and her twin sister advice columnist Ann Landers are not clones, they have been referred to as cyclones.

CLOSING

(On closing her TV show) I have very mixed emotions ... CBS wanted us back, but I think it's classier to leave before you're asked to leave.
                                                                    — Carol Burnett

COLLEGE

> Princess and women friends set up first women's college:
> Ladies, in entering here, to cast and fling
> The tricks which make us toys of men, that so,
> Some future time, if so indeed you will,
> You may with those self-styled with our lords ally
> Your fortunes, justlier balanced, scale with scale.
>   *— The Princess in Tennyson's* The Princess

COLUMNIST

Columnist Suzy Mengers' self-description: "Champion of the over-privileged."

(Tongue-in-cheek advice for would-be gossip columnist) Be careful what you check, or you may check yourself right off the story.

— Liz Smith

... people lie a lot. Press agents lie. Lawyers lie. Official sources lie. And the subjects of my columns tell some of the most blatant lies of all, about themselves.

— Liz Smith

I function as a red light. I say, "Stop it!" Columnists often become phantom parents to the great...They're looking for people like me to become the mother figure and slap them down.

— Rona Barrett

COMEBACK

(After badly injuring her leg in an air crash) For about four months, I just lay there, thinking not-too-pretty thoughts. Then, one day, I just got to wondering. I wanted desperately to sing; still, I hadn't sung in so long that I wondered whether I could. There was a popular song at that time, about 'a sleepy lagoon, a tropical moon'; the words had a good OO that I could open up on—and so I just did! And it felt wonderful. The people in the hospital thought I'd gone crazy—that the leg pains had worked up to my head—but that didn't matter. I could sing! Whatever else was wrong with me, the breath-bellows and the voice-box were sound, and that was all that counted. Every day, I vocalized and I sang, and it took the I'm ill—I'm out—I'm blue feeling out of me. Pretty soon I got the most pressing urge to go back to work.

In November of 1943, nine months after my accident, I went into a Broadway show.

— Jane Froman

COMFORTER

When Virginia was too ill to go to church, she sent her 8-year-old daughter, "Now, listen, and tell me what the minister said." On returning home, the daughter told her mother the subject was, "Don't worry. You'll get your quilt." "Say that again?" said Virginia incredulously. The youngster repeated what she'd said. Baffled, the mother telephoned the minister, who said his key text had been: "Fear thou not, the Comforter will come."

COMING UP

(About growing older, not being the top star) It's bound to hurt a little bit when you see people coming up and you say to yourself, "but *I* can do *that!*"

— Arlene Francis

COMMITMENT

When you are committed to something, you cannot always take the time to reassess, unless you eliminate the extraneous from your life. I no longer take on more than I can deal with. I've stopped running down so many paths. But friendships just cannot be sacrificed, they are the great wealth, my real security.

— Candice Bergen

COMMON SENSE

One of the cross-stitch designs by Brendan Gardner reads: "Common sense is not so Common."

COMMUNICATION

Sex is a form of communication. And now we are beginning to explore what each of us wants to say.

— Gloria Steinem

COMMUNISM

Don't knock communism if you haven't tried it.

— Jane Fonda

COMPANIONSHIP

Phil Donahue said of his wife Marlo Thomas, "She's what companionship is all about."

She (Mary Tyler Moore) mentioned the time years ago she was in London for six weeks doing a movie for television, with Louis Jourdan, called *Run a Crooked Mile*. She was alone, missed him (her husband)

and was miserable. She did not explore the city by herself. "It was a waste and a shame," she said. "But I have to have Grant's rib to put an elbow in."

— Gloria Emerson

COMPANY

I can tell you with complete honesty that I find the unadulterated company of women tedious beyond belief.

— Glenda Jackson

COMPETENT

My therapist, Martha Friedman, gave me the best advice about coping with success. "It's more important to be competent than to be liked."

— Erica Jong

COMPETING

Competing with other women is a waste of time. A woman should think in terms of competing only with herself...as in golf, where what it's all about is to better yourself. That's the real secret of individuality.

— Polly Bergen

COMPLETE

They told me, "A woman has to have a man"—not so: You have to be whole, complete. And now I am that.

— Evelyn Keyes

COMPLIMENT

If compliments were food, I'd have starved to death 28 years ago.

— Erma Bombeck

(Said to Perry Como) Singing with you is *almost* the most fun a woman can have!

— Lena Horne

At a party for a Pablo Picasso exhibit, CBS board chairman William Paley was introduced to Fran Lebowitz, author of *Metropolitan Life*. Very seriously, Paley said, "Fran, terrific book, terrific book," and

Lebowitz just as seriously answered, "Pretty good network, Bill, pretty good network."

COMPROMISE

(On her husband, country singer Johnny Cash) I tell him what I want and he tells me what he wants, and then we do what I want.
— June Carter Cash

COMRADESHIP

According to the experience of my clients, and according to astrology's teachings as well, it takes about three years for the love of the average man to run its course unless his wife has something new to offer him from time to time.

Incidentally—although it may sound trite—I have learned that the safest and surest thing to offer is comradeship. What a man really wants after the first glamour of love has passed is someone who can enter into his enthusiasm or help him in his work.
Evangeline Adams

CONCEPTION

The aging process begins at conception.
— Maggie Kuhn

Indian matron explaining the fact of life to her daughter: "Stork not bring papoose, it come by beau and error."

We wanted to have a baby for a long time, but it just didn't happen ... I decided to go back to work and start thinking about other things. Sure enough, it worked.
— Peggy Fleming

CONDEMNED

If I am condemned—and I see the fire lit—and the wood made ready— and the scaffold, where they will put me into the fire, ready for me to be thrown into it—and after, when I am in the fire—I shall not say differently from what I have said, but I shall want to maintain what I have said until death.
— Joan of Arc

CONDUCTOR

The only difference I notice when a woman conducts is that you don't
see white shirt cuffs.

— Dominic Cossa

CONFIDENCE

Mary Kay, founder of Mary Kay Cosmetics, Inc., about women's lack of
confidence: "I like to say they're vogue on the outside but vague on the
inside."

I always had a lot of confidence in my ability, though I was not
considered a beautiful actress ... In fact, the joke around Hollywood
was: "Who'd want to win her at the end of a picture?"

— Bette Davis

CONGRESS

A stag Senate, is a stag nation.

— Bella Abzug

What we need in the Senate today is problem solvers, not crisis reactors.

— Lenore Romney

They say a woman's place is in the house. I agree, the U.S. House, the
Senate and the White House.

— Arle Taylor

When she moved from the U.S. House of Representatives into the
Senate, Margaret Chase Smith was asked. "How do you like the
Senate?" Her reply: "It's rather cosy down here."

When running for office, U.S. House of Representatives Leader Gerald
Ford (at the time) suggested to George Romney that his wife Lenore run
for the U.S. Senate. Romney, joking, asked his wife: "Can anyone
imagine anything worse for a guy than having his wife run for a seat in
the Senate?"

After being asked countless times about what it's like to be "the only
woman in the Senate," Nancy Landon Kassebaum joked with reporters:
"There's so much work to do ... the coffee to make and the chambers to
vacuum. There are Pat Moynihan's hats to brush and the buttons to sew
on Bob Byrd's red vests, so I keep quite busy."

The gentlemen of Congress were not all pleased when the House was more and more invaded by female members. They especially resented it when one of them acted "uppity," as if she had just as much a right, if not more, to be there, as they did. For many years these gentlemen felt that the women were there on sufferance. Therefore they were very much upset when the famous Clare Boothe Luce swept into their midst and walked around with her nose in the air. As one of the members kept describing it, "If it had been raining, she'd have drowned."

– William "Fishbait" Miller

CONSUMERS

Consumers will never have a life style of their own choosing until they liberate their budgets from the psychological assaults that may "sell" them more than serve them. Purchasing power and willpower are inseparable.

– Bess Myerson

CONTENTED

There are times (in life) that are not so tranquil, but that are more contented—when you're doing more things, working. There's a better balance.

– Rosemary Clooney

CONTEST

A winner of contests claims she has "Wintuition."

CONTRACT

(After learning Barbara Walters had signed a one-million-dollar-a-year contract with ABC news.) The Barbara Walters news did shake me up at first. There was a first wave of nausea, the sickening sensation that perhaps we were all going under, that all of our efforts to hold network television news aloof from show business had failed.

– Walter Cronkite

CONTROL

When I've been successful, I've been in control. When I've been unsuccessful, I've been controlled.

– Katharine Hepburn

CONVERSATION

In order to be a good conversationalist, one should be a good listener, be really interested in what the other person has to say and be flexible in one's topics.

— Beverly Sills

But the most important lesson I've learned is that what really makes a woman stand out as someone special is what she has to say.

— Joan Fontaine

Prosy talk she (the wife of Emerson) could not endure, and he who could not send the conversational ball back over the net soon knew that, for her, he had ceased to exist. If a visitor tired her she asked that she be read to, and if a companion tried to wax pretentious in conversation she was capable of asking suddenly, "How's your cat?"

— Phillips Russell

COOKING

If he (her husband) wants a hot meal, let him sleep with Julia Child.

— Joan Rivers

A musical director jokes about his wife's inability to cook: "Her favorite dish is kitchens. She burns them down. She's gone through three so far."

Britain's Princess Anne said once she'd like to do a little K.P. "but I got the feeling, having got a cook, that she might resent it if I pottered around the kitchen."

I have never known an egg intimately enough to be able to open it, let alone fry it, but as long as I can still do the buying, I'll sacrifice the frying.

— Elsie Janis

For a fact, home-cooking isn't what it used to be. Nowadays there are so many frozen packages and ready-mixes, and heat-and-serves that bridegrooms never provoke their brides to tears with "This isn't like mother used to make." Nowadays they provoke 'em with "Why don't you buy the same brand that mother used to buy?"

Allison Sanders

Today's emancipated homemaker buys a microwave oven to cook a stew in two minutes and a crock pot to cook it slowly for an afternoon. A lady antique dealer has worked out an interesting technique—she puts her stew in a crock pot, then slides the whole kit and kaboodle into a microwave oven. That way the stew cooks in the old average time.

When enrolled in Fannie Farmer's Cooking School, we had to scrape some meat with a paring knife for an invalid tray. She (Miss Farmer) stood beside me watching. She said, "Miss Strausberger, I can see you've used a paring knife before." That always stayed with me. I thought it was the nicest compliment I ever received.

– Helen Strausberger Nusbaum

Charlotte Observer columnist Helen Moore about Julia Child's program: "I had just watched a segment of 'The French Chef' where she lifted two lids from steaming pans of coq au vin and chicken fricassee and clanged them together exuberantly over her head, like cymballs. Condensed water from the lids splashed down the front of her blouse. She welcomed the TV viewers as she nonchalantly mopped her front with a towel. 'I don't know why I did that,' she says with a laugh. 'It was silly.'"

(This is in reference to parsley, Parmesan, and paprika) The reason for these little garnishes is that even though you hate to cook, you don't always want this fact to show, as it so often does with a plateful of nude food. So you put light things on dark things (like Parmesan on spinach) and dark things on light things (like parsley on sole) and sprinkle paprika on practically everything. Sometimes you end up with a dinner in which everything seems to be sprinkled with something, which gives a certain earnest look to the whole performance.

– Peg Bracken

CORSAGE

(About corsages) I don't like orchids—big things hanging there—unless it's to cover a stain.

– Hermione Gingold

COSMETIC

... taking joy in living is a woman's best cosmetic.

– Rosalind Russell

When a woman doubtingly asked a salesman if a skin-rejuvenation cream really did the trick, he turned to a young girl behind the counter and said, "Hand the lady a jar, Mother."

A cosmetics saleswoman starts her pitch with: "Do you have a mental image of the charming, fun-to-be-around, senior citizen you would like to resemble? But not yet? Then let me tell you about this new wrinkle cream."

COUPLE

Laughter is important between a couple. Tears as well. One without the other is boring.

— Simone Signoret

I think we were the perfect American male and female ... Not idealized. She was a scrapper and tried to boss him around. And he just pushed her off the right moment.

— Katharine Hepburn

COURAGE

I will not be vanquished.

— Rose Kennedy

Courage is the ladder on which all the other virtues mount.

— Clare Boothe Luce

Queen Elizabeth gave a lesson to her cavalry. To stop a runaway 4-horse team and coach, she merely stepped in front of them and shouted, "Whoa."

(When German bombs began to rain on London) I have made up my mind to ignore this completely. I shall have nothing to do with fear, commotion and agitation.

— Clementine (Mrs. Winston) Churchill

COWARD

No coward soul is mine.

— Emily Brontë

CREATION

George Bernard Shaw said that women resent the unequal distribution of the burden of creating life.

Once, at a party, the Brooklyn Women's Bar Association staged a revue called "God Created Adam—Then Corrected Her Mistake."

"So," said the little girl, after a lengthy talk by her mother on God, "how does God find time to make a different face for everyone with all of those other things He has to do?"

A teacher asked her Sunday school class to tell the story of Creation. A little girl stood up and said: "First God created Adam. Then He looked at him, and said, 'Oh, my, I can do better than that.' So He created Eve."
— *Joey Russell*

From Thoreau I learned, "Don't worry when you stumble—remember a worm is the only thing that can't fall down." If you're doing creative work you know how true that is. You must be exploratory, be unafraid of making a mistake or you'll never get beyond yourself.
Bonnie Cashin

I don't pretend to know the exact stairsteps of creation. I'm afraid I don't want to know. It would probably make me self-conscious. The current of thought must flow out as well as in, and self-consciousness is all in-flow. It dams up and causes a short circuit. An idiot before a typewriter, trying to focus a blank stare, describes me when I get self-conscious.
— *Edna O'Brien*

CRITICISM

I don't like adverse criticism—I ignore it.
— *Katherine Anne Porter*

I have had more bad notices ... than Lipton's has tea bags.
— *Glenda Jackson*

The way to take criticism is with your mind, not your emotions.
— *Phyllis Whitney*

CRUISE

They never stop eating on cruise ships. I heard one woman say to her husband. "Hurry up and eat your dessert or we're going to be late for the midnight buffet."
— *Joey Villa*

Jeraldine Saunder, a former cruise director and author of the book on which the "Love Boat" T.V. show is based: "The minute people get on board a cruise ship something beautiful happens. The protective walls we need in the big cities go down. It's like you're at a private party with friends. Everyone feels very warm toward each other."

CURIOSITY

If I had a child and could give her one gift, it would be the gift of curiosity. And that's especially true today, because there is so much to see. I don't understand how anybody could be bored.

— Lillian Gish

CYNIC

It takes a clever man to turn cynic and a wise man to be clever enough not to.

— Fannie Hurst

DANCE

Disco dancing: sacroiliact.

> — *Honey Greer*

Disco is fantasy set to music.

> — *Natalie Cole*

A good education is usually harmful to a dancer. A good calf is better than a good head.

> — *Agnes de Mille*

When asked what was so American about American dance, Agnes de Mille answered, "Humor and robustness ... the twang of it and the salt of it."

(On one occasion she complained to Stanislavsky—actor, author friend—about the visitors who came to see her in her dressing room during intermission.) I cannot dance that way. Before I go out on the stage. I must place a *motor* in my soul. When that begins to work, my legs and arms and my whole body will move independently of my own will. But if I do not get time to put the *motor* in my soul, I cannot dance.

> — *Isadora Duncan*

DANCE—BALLET

Dance is not only ballet. It's everything and everywhere.

> — *Dame Margot Fonteyn*

On returning from ballet practice, the daughter of Shirley MacLaine in the movie "Turning Point" says: "Men dancers sure are conceited. It must be all those mirrors."

Celebrating her 90th birthday, Dame Marie Rampert, founder of a world-famous ballet school, kicked her leg up until her toes were even with her shoulders. She works out like that 30 minutes a day. "It's becoming a bit of an effort now," she admits, "but you must make the effort."

Leslie Caron (as quoted by Cameron Shipp): "Life doesn't really count for dancers...
  And anything in Hollywood is fiction and not to be taken too seriously. As for ballet dancers, suddenly you are feefty, you dance Swan Lake and that is how you have lived."

DANCER—FAN

It's better than doing needlepoint on the patio.

— Sally Rand

DATE

Now women would rather go to dinner with a female friend who's interesting than a man who's not.

— Uta West

(Male in American Express ad) It's time women got their own American Express cards and started taking *me* out to dinner.

DAUGHTER

As is the mother, so is the daughter.

— Ezekiel 16:44

Thou art thy mother's glass, and she in thee calls back the lovely April of her prime.

— Sonnet 3, Wm. Shakespeare

When comedienne Joan Rivers directed her first movie ("Rabbit Test"), she hired her 9-year-old daughter Melissa as associate producer. Her reason? "I just love the feeling of being able to send my employees to bed without supper if they displease me."

I want to work to save money so I don't ever have to depend on anyone—
because I don't *have* anyone I can depend on!

— Helen O'Connell

History has shown us that men have always kept in their hands all
concrete powers; since the earliest days of the patriarchate they have
thought best to keep woman in a state of dependence; their codes of law
have been set up against her; and thus she has been definitely
established as the Other.

— Simone de Beauvoir

Finally, we must be able to join with the men we can now know and love
as friends as well as lovers, and the strangers who will become our
friends. We take our roots with us as we move into the unknown, and I
think we may be strong enough to make it if we admit that we are
unsure and afraid and still need to depend on each other.

— Betty Friedan

DEPRESSION

During the Depression I went from town to town directing plays for
groups like the PTA or Lions Club—this was about the only entertainment these people had. Radio hadn't reached the backwaters yet. The
Lord was good to me. All that time he was leading me by the hand, and I
didn't know it. I began to collect country stories when I was traveling
around, and then I'd give "readings"—we called them readings, they
were really monologues—at various functions if I was allowed to
promote my plays. That was the beginning of Minnie Pearl.

— Minnie Pearl

DESCRIPTION

Cicadas stitching their sewing-machine song.

— Jessamyn West

Barbara Walters—manicurist, pedicurist, guru of kitsch, yenta, maven,
gadfly, blabbermouth and Mother Confessor to the world.

Tom Shales

An admirer once called Jackie Kennedy "the legend of the twentieth
century."

(About Arlene Dahl) She has blue marbles for eyes.

— Mary Tyler Moore

(Actor about his co-star) She's the kind of girl who makes you feel you can stay young forever.

(About Katharine Hepburn) She is a presence. When she's in a room, she takes the stage.

— Morley Safer

(About Evonne Goolagong) Head and shoulders above everyone else—sweeter than Greek pastry.

— A line umpire

(Said to Rosemary Clooney) Yours is the most beautiful speaking voice—like butter.

— Dinah Shore

Carry Nation liked to describe herself as "a bulldog running along at the feet of Jesus, barking at what He doesn't like."

(Speaking of Dewey's defeat) How can you vote for a man who looks like the bridegroom on a wedding cake?

— Alice Roosevelt Longworth

Novelist Virginia Woolf once remarked about Edith Sitwell that she was "...a clean hare's bone that one finds on a moor with emeralds stuck about it."

DESIGN

Talking to her dress designer, Don Loper, singer Dorothy Shay, the "Park Avenue Hillbilly," said: "Show enough of me so they'll know it's me, but not so much as to make 'em sure."

DESTINY

A woman used to feel: "Biology is destiny."

You are the maker and molder of your own destiny.

— Ella Wheeler Wilcox

Anatomy was destiny for a woman when her identity was defined solely as the breeder of the race, as the bearer of children. She had no choice in that matter.

— Betty Friedan

DETAILS

VIDs—that's what I call very important details.

— *Woman Stockbroker*

DETERMINED

Meeting Carlo was the thing that changed my life. But I worked hard to change from an ignorant, unattractive peasant into a real actress. Nobody will ever know how determined I was.

— *Sophia Loren*

DIAMOND

I know the whereabouts and availability of every diamond of consequence on this planet.

— *Elizabeth Taylor*

When you see some young thing wearing diamonds and mink, you can bet your sweet life she didn't get them standing over a kitchen sink.

— *Sophie Tucker*

When Mae West swept into a nightclub in the movie, "She Done Him Wrong," trailing white fox fur and bedecked with dazzling diamonds, the hatcheck girl gasped, "My goodness, what diamonds!" Replied Mae, as she sashayed by, "Honey, goodness had *nothin'* to do with them!"

DIARIES

It's good girls who keep diaries of what they do. Bad girls never have the time.

— *Tallulah Bankhead*

DIET

The simplest diet of all. If it tastes good—spit it out.

— *Audrey Hepburn*

The worst kind of reducing pill is the one who keeps telling you how she did it.

— *Kathryn Grayson*

One woman says: "The diet my doctor gave me is simple. All I have to do is throw away what I like and eat the rest."

(About whacking off 35 pounds before appearing in a movie) It wasn't hard for me to do at all because I wanted to do it.
— Dolly Parton

In an article, writer Laura Bergquist noted that when Gloria Vanderbilt, 5'7", slimmed to 110 pounds, an actor friend commented, "When you put your arms around her there's nothing there."

DINING

One cannot think well, love well, sleep well if one has not dined well.
— Virginia Woolf

Perle Mesta, when she was known as Washington's "hostess with the mostest": "Since men first began to associate with one another ... feasting has always been one of the most pleasant methods of finding out what's going on."

DIRECTED

I don't want to direct anything; I was born to be directed.
— Dinah Shore

I enjoy nothing so much as being directed; to know it's right, that he (the director) likes it, is everything to me. Trying to be the perfect instrument; that's all I want.
— Geraldine Chaplin

DIRECTING

Directing a film, according to actress Jeanne Moreau, is a step up. Says Moreau: "It's as if a woman used to darning goes into fine embroidery."

They told me I couldn't direct a movie because a woman can't be an authority figure. That would certainly come as news to my Brownie troop.
— Joan Rivers

(On being a woman director) There is always some idiot who will come up to you and say, "You're just great for a girl. You think exactly like a man." For Crissake, I always thought intelligence was neuter.
— Elaine May

DISCIPLINE

As plain as the "no's" on a mother's face.

As a mother, I believe in the values of discipline and warm, intense family life.

— Princess Grace of Monaco

DISCRIMINATION

Revere the man, despise the woman.

— Ancient Japanese Maxim

DISEASE

A new name for an ailment affects people like a Parisian name for a novel garment. Everyone hastens to get it.

— Mary Baker Eddy

In these 20 years of work among the people (in Calcutta), I have come more and more to realize it is being unwanted that is the worst disease any human being can ever experience.

— Mother Teresa

I am an optimist at heart and I truly believe that the time will come, notwithstanding the black times we are passing through, when nations will concentrate on forging weapons against the common enemy—disease—instead of atomic bombs and other fratricidal mechanisms.

— Sister Kenny

DISAPPOINTMENT

I think disappointment must be good for me, I get so much of it; and the constant thumping Fate gives me may be a mellowing process; so I shall be a ripe and sweet old pippin before I die.

— Louisa May Alcott

DISHWASHER

When a wife returned to the job market, she bought a dishwasher with her first earnings. Later she filled out a questionnaire and at the question, "What year and model dishwasher are you replacing?" she wrote "Myself—age 36."

DIVINITY

What differs us from plants and animals is that in us is a facet of divinity.

— Elizabeth Kubler-Ross

DIVORCE

Many people felt that my divorce made me more human.

— Ann Landers

Church deals too much with divorce and too little with the divorced.

— Woman Minister

(About her divorce) Never say never, never say always, never say forever—because you never know.

— Ann Landers

Zsa Zsa Gabor is a great housekeeper. Every time she gets a divorce, she keeps the house.

— Johnny Carson

A woman FBI trainee said a divorce prompted her career: "My food was being cut off."

— Pam Proctor

If a divorced woman was starving for sex, as the popular male myth suggests, it was probably while she was still married.

— Irv Kupcinet

Men ... break down more after divorce than women do. They're terribly coddled because women take up all the slack for them ...

— Erica Jong

Two of my women friends went down with divorce fever. I saw them through all the phases of doubt, despair, determination, temper, sadness, and relieved convalescence.

— Sheilah Graham

Just recently I answered my phone and heard a friend's voice say "Hi, Susan." My friend had looked in her address book and called the wrong Mrs. (David) Brinkley. I said, "Wrong wife."

— Ann Brinkley

DIVORCE—APPROVAL OF

Theoretically, I am against it. Practically, it is quite another story.
— Marlene Dietrich

I not only believe in divorce, I sometimes think I don't believe in marriage at all.
— Gloria Swanson

(Pointing out that today's life span is much longer than it used to be). Today, it's ludicrous to expect that two people stay connected for their lifetimes.
Margaret Mead

(When filing for divorce) There's something worse than being by yourself ... It's sitting across the breakfast table from someone for whom you've lost all feeling.
— Shirley Jones

There's a myth about divorced women. The myth says we die a little each day we are alone without a man. The truth is, most of us feel relief. It's terrific to be alone, if you choose.
— Cloris Leachman

DIVORCE—DISAPPROVAL OF

One should never be divorced, because the next (man) is just as bad as the last ... Other girls have love affairs, but I was raised differently. *I get married.*
— Zsa Zsa Gabor

DOCTOR

After an accident, one woman rushed out of the gathering crowd and started to lean over the victim. She was pushed aside by a man who directed, "Step back please! I've had a course in First Aid." The woman stood and watched the man's ministrations for a few minutes, then tapped him on the shoulder. "When you get to that part about calling a doctor," she said, "I'm already here."
— Carolina Country

DOING

I don't want to be a grandmother sitting and rocking my children.
I want to be Auntie Mame, I want to be the Dame May Witty of our
time. I want to keep doing.

— Carol Burnett

DOMESTICITY

(On domesticity) I don't even open the refrigerator door if I can help it.
— Charlotte Ford

DOUBT

Doubt is the mother of intelligence.

— Frank Tyger

DOWAGER

The wealthy dowager drew herself up and said, "Our family's been rich
for so many generations, I'm unequaled in the devastating remark."

DRAFT

(Arguing there is no need to register either men or women for the
draft.) It is a security blanket full of holes. It is a hollow, empty symbol.
Patricia Schroeder

I think we have made so much about equal rights, including me, that
most women would be insulted if they were not asked to register.
— Miz Lillian Carter

DRAG

I don't mind drag—women have been female impersonators for some
time.
— Gloria Steinem

DRESS

Johnny Carson: "Do you dress for women or do you dress for men?"
Angie Dickinson: "I dress for women and undress for men."

Chemical Saleswoman: "I never dress with sexual undertones. How can a man discuss anything rationally if he's looking at my chest or my legs?"

When tennis dynamo Evonne Goolagong left a press lunch, she gathered up a complimentary T-shirt from Avon. A reporter asked, "Why the extra-large size?" "I like to sleep in them," Goolagong replied.

When her dress split down the front just before accepting the Entertainer of the Year Award, Dolly Parton commented: "I guess it's like my Daddy said. You shouldn't try to put 50 pounds of mud in a five-pound sack."

DRESSING

Mitzi Gaynor dances while dressing and never pulls up her stockings as others do. She manages to get the foot of her hose on, then aims her toes toward the sky and is able to pull her stockings down.

DRINKING

Men see in Garbo sober what they see in other women drunk.
— Kenneth Tynam

One reason I don't drink is that I want to know when I'm having a good time.
— Mae West

(Remarking upon a politician whose career was stopped by his heavy drinking, Alice Roosevelt Longworth said) So-and-So would rather be tight than President.

(About living in a "drinking circle" after marriage to Bogey) I had to learn to drink a little in order not to be bored to death and to stay awake!"
— Lauren Bacall

In a tight spot the custom now is to take another drink or a pill. Instead, if they said a "Hail Mary," it would be much better for their figures than an extra drink.

— Rose Kennedy

Since Miss (Bea) Lillie was born with an edge on, she has never felt it necessary to take even one cocktail. The only time she ever broke her rule against spirits was at Sapa Flow, where she went to entertain the fleet shortly after the outbreak of the war. The German planes were coming over twice a day, and after an expecially heavy raid she was persuaded to down a stiff whisky. The next thing she remembers was taking a swift look into the audience as the curtain rose on her show, and seeing a row of German officers staring back at her. Though they subsequently proved to be prisoners of war under guard, she was so shaken that she has never repeated the experiment.

— Barbara Haggie

DRIVING

If you don't like the way women drive, get off the sidewalk.

— Henny Youngman

In Afghanistan, a new law requires a negligent driver to pay $4,895 for running over a man, and $2,447 for running over a woman.

— San Juan Star

A regular customer in a Chicago tavern, asked why he ordered a soft drink: "I never drink when I drive; only when my wife does."

An insurance adjuster asked a Mobile, Ala. woman why she was driving with her left wheels on the center line of the highway. "I always do that," she said, "It makes my tires last longer"

DRUGS

People on drugs are sick people. So now we end up with the government chasing sick people like they were criminals, telling doctors they can't help them, prosecuting them because they had some stuff without paying the tax, and sending them to jail. Imagine if the government chased sick people with diabetes, put a tax on insulin and drove it into the black market, told doctors they couldn't treat them, prosecuted them for not paying their taxes, and then sent them to jail. If we did that, everyone would know we were crazy. Yet we do practically the same thing every day in the week to sick people hooked on drugs. The jails are full and the problem is getting worse every day.

— Billie Holiday

DUES

(To her daughter) And I bet you think you got into medical school just because you're so smart? Fifteen years ago smarts wouldn't have gotten you any place. The women's movement got you into medical school and it's about time you started paying *your* dues.

— Betty Friedan

DULL

"Everything is dull and lifeless when a woman feels dull and lifeless and she doesn't have someone/ (a man) to light her from within."

— Arlene Dahl

DUMB

Now that I've dyed my hair, I've got to learn to be dumb. Men expect blondes to be dumb.

Corinne Calvet

You see an awful lot of smart guys with dumb women, but you hardly ever see a smart woman with a dumb guy.

— Clint Eastwood

Girls have an unfair advantage over men. If they can't get what they want by being smart, they can get it by being dumb.

— Yul Brynner

It doesn't bother me if I'm called dumb, but I resent being referred to as slow. You should see how quickly I learned the way to the bank.

— Charo

Carol Channing said that in life she had practice as a birdbrain: "I was always getting called into the principal's office for something I'd done or, in the case of homework, something I'd not done ... When he'd start to bawl me out, I'd just fall into this asinine girl role and sort of stare dumbly at him."

EARTH

An earth fit for growing children is what every woman should work for.
— *Lillian Smith*

EATING

I don't trust anyone who doesn't like to eat.

— *Kaye Ballard*

Eating is a marvelous thing ... the best thing in life. I was very hungry during the war.

— *Sophia Loren*

As a young newspaper staffer, Margaret Mitchell, author of *Gone With the Wind,* ate snacks in the company lunchroom which she nicknamed, "The Roachery."

ECONOMY

A third economic human right which I would mention is the right to challenge all those at any level who would tell any of us that "all is well, don't you think about it, Papa knows best." Complacency is one of the things I do fear most in our economy today.

— *Sylvia Porter*

EDUCATION

I got all the schooling any actress needs. That is, I learned to write well enough to sign contracts.

— *Hermione Gingold*

Parents lean over like dishwater and college administrators lack
backbone. Let's expel students who disobey the rules.
— Lenore Romney

(Upon being installed as the president of the University of Chicago) It's
too late to be nervous. Now it's time for contemplative resignation.
— Hanna Gray

In 1977, for the first time, Oxford University opened its doors to female
Rhodes Scholars. Out of 32 American students chosen, 13 were women.

The little girl came home from her first day at kindergarten very
downcast. "What's wrong?" asked her mother. "Well," replied the child,
"I was there a whole day and I still don't know how to read or write."

Three times widowed and twice divorced Daphne Rives is opening a
school—for husbands.
  "Women complain about their men's inadequacies as housekeepers,
but women are to blame because they have never taught them," said
Daphne, 86, of Nice, France.
  "I made excellent cooks and housekeepers out of three of my
husbands, and divorced the other two because they were bad pupils."

The editor of this book asked Ariel Durant for permission to quote her
saying that her husband (Will) "was my teacher and my master ... He
wrote on my blank mind." She answered that her husband said he had
"no memory of my ever having a 'blank mind.' His view is that 'Ariel
always had a mind of her own, and it almost always enriched my
thought.' I am still his pupil but we differ on almost everything. This
does no apparent harm to our affection and respect for each other."

EDUCATION—SYSTEM

The education system has moved children along like so many vehicles
on an assembly line, on through the grades and into the streets, ill-
equipped to compete in this society.
— Shirley Chisholm

Education is essential to the upbuilding of human beings, and failure to
advance it is an unpardonable offense. One who allows the beacon of a
lighthouse to go out is justly reproached with the calamities of shipwreck, and those who permit ignorance to continue are guilty of all the
crimes that ignorance commits.
— Helen Keller

(Greece) Education in this country is prehistoric ... The children are crammed with lessons they don't remember and are not taught anything at all about the way to live. My idea is to start a New Modern Greek school, which would run on quite a new system. The present teachers would continue to give book lessons—that is all they know how to give. But there would be new teachers to teach the children how to be decent human beings. They would instill in them a personal responsibility to the community.

– Queen Frederika of Greece

EDUCATION—TEACHING

Eve Arden as T.V.'s Miss Brooks: "Teaching can be a very rich life for a young woman—if she happens to be a very rich young woman."

Anne Frye, associate professor of zoology at Wesleyan University: "I might have dissected a frog five hundred times, but the 501st time I always see something I didn't before—and it's the same thing with teaching students. You always see something new."

ELECTRONICS

(Watching a demonstration of an electronic brain) I can't understand it. I can't even understand the people who can understand it.

– Queen Juliana of the Netherlands

ELIGIBLE

Someone once said: "Men become more distinguished and eligible as they grow older. Grayhaired women just look tired."

EMOTION

(About feeling emotions) I think I'm excessive in everything.

– Elizabeth Ashley

Emotionally is the only way I know how to do anything.

– Lauren Bacall

(About a wearying, hyperemotional woman) She felt in italics and thought in capitals.

– Henry James

EMPLOYMENT

I love to be employed, I hate to be idle.

— Queen Victoria

Daisy Brown, contributor to the Wall St. Journal's editorial pages, gives this definition; "Personnel shuffle: mixed demotions."

Sign in a woman employment agency office: "Overqualified: What you are when they are underqualified to pay you what you deserve."

The new employee entered the woman vice-president's office. "Now, let's not be formal," said the lady veep. "Don't even think of me as a forbidding employer. Just think of me as your good friend—who's always right."

Bernice Fitz-Gibbon, New York department-store advertising director: "It's sex appeal that gets jobs. This may not be high-minded, but you can't fight it. Don't waste a 220-volt girl by putting her in a six-volt job."

On the job keep this in mind—Feminine helplessness is out. Feminine cleverness will never be out.

— FemIron ad

EMPLOYMENT—JOB INTERVIEW

When going for job interviews remember straight-laced is efficient, sexy is dangerous. Frivolous is weak, aggressive is threatening. Once you've got the job, mix and match as you please.

— FemIron ad

Woman editor to woman writer applying for a position: "You are overqualified for this job." (Translation: You are after my job.)

During a job interview, an executive was asked, "Tell me, what is the most important gadget in your house?" He hesitated, thought, and finally answered, "Well, I suppose my wife."

(When applying for a position, the young woman job applicant told her interviewer) "My special talents? Well, last year I won several prizes in crossword-puzzle and slogan-writing contests." The interviewer nodded. "Shows you're bright—but we need people who are smart during office hours." "Oh," said the applicant, "this was during office hours."

ENERGIES

"In the middle ages, women ran the castle and organized supplies ...
Expecting women to concentrate all their energies on their children is
something new. We're ready to go through enormous readjustments to
change that.

— Elizabeth Topham Kenman

ENGLISHMEN

The difference in American and English boys? Well, whatever it is, it's
deliciously unimportant.

— Julie Andrews

Anita Ekberg to Sheila Graham about the Swedish actress's visit to
London: "I like Englishmen. They're very dignified in a dry sort of way.
They could cut your throat and make you feel it's a favor."

ENVIOUS

I am Mediterranean and that means I can admire without feeling
envious.

— Simone Signoret

Writer Sonia Masello, about a woman who was envious of practically
everyone: "She looks at the world through green-colored glasses."

EQUALITY

Show me a retired housewife and I'll show you sexual equality.

When we start honoring mediocre men, we'll have achieved total
equality with men.

— Midge Constanza

Since women make up half the human race, they must now be made
equal so they can hold up their half of the sky.

— Chairman Mao

Victoria C. Woodhull, who ran for president in 1872: "While others
argued the equality of women with men, I proved it ... I boldly entered
the arena."

(On the Stockard Channing TV show "Just Friends") In consoling the job-hunting Susan, Sydney Goldsmith, a young black woman on the show, says: "Honey, let's face it, these days you're not as equal as I am."

ERA

People are not created equal.

— Pearl Buck

When it comes to taxes, women are very equal.

— Carol Burnett

(It's) a step, a stage in human evolution, human liberation.

— Betty Friedan

...As important as antislavery was in the 19th century.

— Jane Fonda

No one should have to dance backwards all their lives.

— Jill Ruckelshaus

Equal rights for the sexes will be achieved only when mediocre women occupy high positions.

— Francoise Giroud

(About the fight to ratify the Equal Rights Amendment) It's time to stop this ladylike nonesense

— Betty Friedan

They (women) are taking a step down (in wanting equality). Superior people should not be equal to (their) inferiors.

— Ashley Montagu

Because women don't know their place anymore, they're on the threshold of new prominence and power—but they'll need both strong goals and a support newtwork to meet them.

Hannah D. Atkins

"I had to practice my belly dancing," apologized Zbigniew Brzezinski, assistant for National Security Affairs in the Carter administration, one time when he arrived late at a social function. "One must be prepared in the age of ERA. You never know when you might be called upon to perform."

(On getting the ERA ratified) You have to be organized, relentless and never let a vote get out of hand. You have to go at it man by man and

Example 107

woman by woman but it's worth it because no matter how much ... (is said), there simply is not equality today.

— Catherine Mackin

ETIQUETTE

Good manners is simply doing what is practical and considerate of others.

— Charlotte Ford

What interests me most are questions about how to build a house wisely, how to furnish it invitingly, how to make the machinery of its management run smoothly, how to fill it with the intangible spirit of home that shall warm the hearts of all who cross its threshold and keep those who dwell beneath its roof in harmony and peace ... These are, to me, the vital subjects within the province of etiquette.

— Emily Post

A few minutes before receiving President and Mrs. Kennedy, Pope John, evincing an air of vague concern, inquired as to the proper mode of addressing the wife of the President of the United States.

"Your Holiness," replied the monsignor in charge of protocol, "can choose either Madame President or simply Madame."

"Ah!" said the Pope with a thoughtful air.

But when John XXIII entered the audience chamber, he spontaneously opened his arms, smiled broadly and exclaimed: "Ah, Jacqueline!"

— Henri Fesquet

EXAMPLE

We're all walking examples. It doesn't matter what you say to children, it's what you do, for better or worse. Sometimes I'm not too pleased about that. Vanessa (her daughter) comes with us very often to our political rallies and things like that, and she hears us talking about democracy and people's rights. Then I come home and I say, "I don't care what you think, Vanessa, you're going to do this, this and this." Then she puts her little hands on her hips, and says, "I have my rights, too. What about democracy at home?"

— Jane Fonda

EXCEL

If I can't be good at something, I don't want to do it.

— Kate Jackson

EXCITING

A woman can look moral and exciting at the same time, if she also looks like it was quite a struggle to make her decision.

— Tina Louise

EXPECTING

It has been said ... that Napoleon's mother read Roman history with absorbed interest during the months preceding his birth.

"Heir-condition," "bow-windowed" and "wearing the bustle wrong" are among the expressions that have been used to describe a pregnant woman.

A couple, expecting their first child, couldn't agree on which sex they preferred. Wife: "Girls are smarter than boys." Husband: "I never heard that before." Wife: "I rest my case."

The most tranquil time of my life was when I was expecting my first baby—staying at home and enjoying it, learning to cook, to be in the garden—the most tranquil time.

— Rosemary Clooney

A minister's wife, who was eight months pregnant, caused a sensation in the Women's Bible Class when she strolled in wearing a T-shirt bearing the legend, "Sow a seed and watch it grow."

— Janet Cardell

It is sad to think that any woman should regard pregnancy as a dreary interlude rather than a heightening of the adventure of life, because an expectant mother ought to be a happy egotist.

— Dorothy Kilgallen

Rumor had it that after nineteen years of marriage Alice Roosevelt Longworth was going to have a baby. Reporters were trying by indirect means to discover the accuracy of the story. It fell to an inexperienced reporter to call her on the telephone and ask: "Why certainly. Nothing to be ashamed of, is it?" came back her reply in her usually frank manner.

— Helena Huntington Smith

EXPERIENCE

As I grow older, it's hurry, do it all, experience everything!
— Judy Blume

A housewife, applying for a job as housepainter, said, "Yes, I've had some experience—climbing walls!"

Women with experience, an amount of living, of maturity, are infinitely more attractive than a vapid starlet.
— Garson Kanin

(Discussing her wish that American actors could get as mixed a bag of acting experience as their English counterparts) I would love to grow up to be Alec Guinness.
— Carol Burnett

When Sally Quinn was interviewed for a reporter's job by Ben Bradlee, executive editor of the *Washington Post*, he asked to look over a few stories she'd written. "I've never written a thing," Sally confessed. "Well," said Bradlee, "nobody's perfect." And hired her.

Conflict and unhappiness are not the worst things that can happen. It depends on the person. Either it can crush you, or build your strength. It's all the experience one has that makes one what one is—the wider the experience, the stronger one's personality.
— Indira Gandhi

... I need to live fast in the fast lane ... I need to do things to excess. I need to go over the edge. I have an obligation to experience the things most people can't experience. The taboos. The things you're not supposed to know or do. That's part of my job. That's why I do it.
— Elizabeth Ashley

EXTREMES

Women run to extremes; they are either better or worse than men.
— Jean de La Bruyere

FAILURE

Failure is impossible.

— Susan B. Anthony

I wasn't afraid to fail. Something good always comes out of failure.

— Anne Baxter

Flops ... are a part of life's menu and I'm never a girl to miss out on any of the courses.

— Rosalind Russell

If a man fails, then his whole life is a disaster. For a woman, a career is still an accessory.

— Diane von Furstenberg

(In paying tribute to pioneering French aviation) It takes as much courage to have tried and failed as it does to have tried and succeeded.

— Anne Morrow Lindbergh

Out of a hundred things you do, you know you are going to fail in at least five of them. But everyone remembers the failures, not the successes.

— Billie Jean King

If you have made mistakes, even serious ones, there is always another chance for you. What we call failure is not the falling down, but the staying down.

— Mary Pickford

FAITH

I think faith is the greatest. It makes everything easy. You wake up in the morning and you think Bobby (Kennedy) is happy in heaven. Heaven is full of surprises, and as long as he's happy, you just go along and go about your business.

— Ethel Kennedy

FAITHFUL

What's the point of looking for a man who will be faithful? If he's faithful, he's sick.

— Zsa Zsa Gabor

FAMILIARITY

Familiarity breeds attempt.

— Jane Ace

When the late Sen. Joseph McCarthy, whom she never liked, kissed her and called her Alice, Alice Roosevelt Longworth said, "The policeman and the trashman may call me Alice. You may not."

FAMILY

The family is above all centered on the children.

— Princess Caroline

Jack called her (Rose Kennedy) the "glue that held the family together."

— Edward Kennedy

(About her director father and her actress/coach mother) If I hadn't been born into this family, I'd ask for membership ...

— Susan Strasberg

When pointing out that she and her husband Carl Dean are not planning to raise a family, Dolly Parton said, "We're sort of each other's kids."

Family life is no longer simply a way to develop human beings but has become the be-all and end-all of our existence. Women want mediocre men and men are working hard to be as mediocre as possible.

— Margaret Mead

The greatest value we can transmit to our children is the value of the family. It is the family—loving, sharing, caring and carrying from one generation to the next the commitment to life—that has enabled humanity for thousands of years to find pride in the past, faith in the present and hope for the future.

— Eunice Kennedy Shriver

(About their family life) You see, we practice what we call "cottage economy." It starts at 7:30 in the morning, with everyone breakfasting together. It sets the note for the day ... In the Middle Ages, a blacksmith's or toolmaker's helpmate kept his forge hot and the children learned the trade at the father's knee. In early America, families linked hands to work a farm, run a village store or small business. Warm companionship developed through striving toward the same goal. These days, cottage economy has all but disappeared. If modern kids are sassy, lack responsibility, treat home as strictly a stopover between dates, and have no respect for earning money, it may be because the old-times ties that bound have been broken.

— Harriet and Ozzie Nelson

FAMILY—IN-LAWS

(On a wall hanging in a museum in St. Augustine, Fla.)
    In-laws are rodents in human guise
    who eate me out of cakes & pies
    o'er hill & vale & rivers & ruts
    they gather for dinner
    I hate their guts.

The only thing that has ever caused any arguments between George Burns and me is my family. For some reason, George thinks my family doesn't like him. That's ridiculous. He's sensitive, I guess, because my mother locks the front door when she sees George coming, but it doesn't mean anything. She does the same thing with my grandfather, but it isn't because she doesn't like him. It's so he'll climb up the rain spout to get to his room.

— Gracie Allen

FAMOUS

It's much more fun being famous than not.

— Barbara Walters

I do wish I had a flair for being famous. That has always been my greatest flaw.

— Helen Hayes

(About her marriage to Picasso) I'm tired of being married to a public monument.

— Francoise Gilot Picasso

(On being a celebrity) I'm getting awfully tired of this chic, slick look. I'd like to wear a pink dress again.

— Margaret Truman

I don't think of myself as famous ... Any time you think you might be overwhelmed by other people's status, think of what they look like in their underwear, and that'll give you a proper perspective.

— Doris Day

Doesn't it strike you as peculiar that a superstar works for years to get people to come and see her, finally achieves stardom, then puts a ten foot electric fence, complete with guard dogs, around her house?

Bette Davis said to Mae West on meeting her for the first time: "You and Garbo were the *only* ones I wanted to meet—and *never* did." Mae West: "I met Garbo ... and now that I've met you, I think I'll go lie down for two days."

FANTASY

I think women fantasize about men as men do about women ... But I will tell you that the main female fantasy is running away.

— Erica Jong

FASHION

She has what it takes to wear the latest fashions—a rich husband.

— Joey Adams

What care I how chic it be, if it be not best for me?

— B. Altman & Co. ad

(Said to Christian Dior) Styles this year are too Oriental for a Persian woman.

Soraya

Fashion is what a her does to a hem to get a him.

— Charles Scholl

Watching a fashion show, French writer Jean Cocteau remarked to Leonard Lyons: "Art produces ugly things which frequently become beautiful with time. But fashion, on the other hand, produces beautiful things which always become ugly with time."

FASHION—DESIGNING

Designing: Show business.

— Mary McFadden

The fashion philosophy of designer Sophie Gimbel: "Sexy elegance."

I like fashion to go down into the street, but I can't accept that it should originate there.

— Coco Chanel

FAT

Close your eyes and think of all the round shapes that mean warmth and light and happiness. I feel we're (fat women) related to heaven and earth. Think of the sun for warmth and light, the moon for mystery and romance, the earth we live on, and the egg, the symbol of life. Now, think of skinny shapes: Sticks, swords, knives, arrows, lightning—all of which suggest destruction. So put all such thoughts of being skinny behind you. Keep thinking BIG, for we are more in tune with the universe.

— Stella Jolles Richman

FATHER

Fathers are a biological necessity and a social accident.

— Margaret Mead

Associated Press writer James Bacon: "Terry Moore is the kind of girl you would take home to mother, if you could trust father."

It's through his father that the child learns to have a will, to face pain and illness, the fight for existence, and the necessity of disciplined work and duty.

— Princess Caroline

In my life I have always wanted to get married and have a family of my own, because in my life that's really what I needed. Maybe because my mother never married my father, maybe this is the reason, I don't know.

But just to feel at home in the situation of life I had to get married and
have children—a family of my own. Maybe this is why I married a man
that was a little older than I was, maybe I always missed my father.

– Sophia Loren

FAVOR

One anecdote out of a thousand sums up beautifully the response of the
Curies to what Pierre called "the favors of fortune." The couple were
dining at the Elysee Palace with President Loubet (of France) ... a lady
came up to Marie and asked: "Would you like me to present you to the
King of Greece?" Marie, innocently and politely, replied in her gentle
voice, all too sincere: "I don't see the utility of it."

– Eve Curie

FEAR

I always thought it was tacky to be afraid.

– Mary Martin

I learned that you can't run away from fear. I learned to face it head-on.

– Ava Gardner

You should always try to do what you're afraid of. As soon as you feel an
apprehension or an anxiety about something, it's that most crystal-
clear signal that that's what you should investigate and explore and
deal with.

– Candice Bergen

There's a lot of luck involved in anything you do. I had a rocky period in
1968 when I did three pictures in a row and the stress told. For a while
no one was willing to take a chance on me.

But I kept going. I had a lot of energy. Always did. I got it from my
mother and grandmother. If I had become frightened I wouldn't have
gone out of my bedroom.

– Ann-Margret

FEAR—PHOBIA

I have three phobias which, could I mute them, would make my life as
slick as a sonnet but as dull as ditch water: I hate to go to bed, I hate to
get up and I hate to be alone.

– Tallulah Bankhead

FEMALE CHAUVINISM

Simone de Beauvoir refused to finish taping a session for the PBS series *Woman* unless all connected with her session were female. The producers dressed the one, indispensable male technician as a female and the taping continued!

FEMININITY

A little girl said to her mother: "Georgie called me 'unfeminine' so I socked him in the gut."

FEMINISM

(On Anita Bryant and anti-ERA leader Phyllis Schlafly) I'd like to take the two of them and make bookends.

— Midge Constanza

If God had wanted me to spend my life in the kitchen, SHE would have coated me with Teflon and given me rubber gloves for hands.

— Suzy Sutton

When Jean Stapleton made her 10-city tour with a production of "Auntie Mame," she would request a woman driver wherever she used a limousine service. However, in Seattle, when she found a limo service that hired only women, she said "I hope that's only transitional, because that's not the goal of feminism. The goal is to forget about it and regard everybody equally under the law."

(Written in 1931) After close to one hundred years of almost steady agitation for what at the start was called the "rights of women," comparative calm has settled on the feminist. Having now what she demanded, she is learning to use it. There is no manner of doubt but that valuable, if unforseen, results are developing—one of the most significant and interesting is the new type of woman produced by a conscious grafting of the acquired "rights" on fine old feminine traditions. It is a broadened, energized, humanized type which if it multiplies and fulfills its promise will justify all the bother of the long and militant campaign which has made it possible.

— Ida M. Tarbell

FICTION

(When Phil Donahue asked if she'd read *Joy of Living*). Oh, yes—I love fiction. The other day I called my husband at the office and said, "If you come home early today I'm all yours." Do you know what he did? He put me on hold.

— Erma Bombeck

FIGHT

Women have not been trained to enjoy a good fight!

— Franklin D. Roosevelt

To get along in this world you've got to fight, fight, fight.

— Elizabeth Arden

Whenever I have the slightest suspicion I'm being used, then I fight like a wildcat. I might look like a sweet old lady to you, but I've always been a fighter, and I still am.

— Helen Hayes

(After the birth of her second son) ... no more children. Never again. I'm a fighter, and I spent years trying to have a child—years of doctors, two miscarriages, eight months in a hotel room without ever going out in order to have my first baby.

— Sophia Loren

FILMMAKING

Actress Thelma Ritter about Hollywood: "I've never been with people who work harder. I once had a permanent wave at six a.m. You haven't lived until you've done that."

For me every picture should be a love affair. I have to fall in love with the script and with everyone I'm working with; otherwise the picture doesn't jell. But that doesn't mean I have affairs with the men I work with.

— Rita Hayworth

FILMMAKING—SCREEN TEST

An MGM executive said of Ava Gardner after seeing her first screen test: "She can't act, she can't talk, she's sensational!"

When Broadway star Helen Gallagher saw her first screen test, she exclaimed: "Good heavens, how I must frighten people who talk to me for the first time."

FIRE FIGHTER

During the probationary period at Engine Company 32, Miss (Sandy) Kupper (fireman) says she was given some bad times, such as having her mask ripped when fighting a dense smoke fire. Once someone turned off the air supply on her backpack oxygen tank during a house fire. "Some of the guys may have thought that was funny—but it scared me and made me angry," she said.

Her only injury of consequence in fighting about 15 house fires was a minor nail puncture in her derriére, suffered while crawling out a bedroom window. "Naturally, everyone wanted to see the wound," she said. "I thought about showing it to them—but changed my mind."

FIRST LADY

In a discussion with first graders, a teacher was told that the First Lady was ... Eve.

The First Lady of the United States is an unpaid public servant elected by one person: her husband.

– Lady Bird Johnson

I had thought I would hate being First Lady. Wrong ... I loved it. I loved it when we rode down the streets in the motorcade and people yelled, "Hi, Betty" or "Hi, First Momma..."

– Betty Ford

FIRST TIME

Anything that happens to you young and for the first time can never be equaled.

– Lauren Bacall

FIRST WOMAN

The first person to receive Nobel prizes in two different scientific fields was Madame Marie Curie.

The *first* commercial pasta factory was started by a woman named Giulia Buitoni in 1827 in Sansepulcro, Italy. Known today as Industrie Buitoni Perugina, it is the oldest and largest macaroni manufacturer in the world.

Now, in her 25th-floor Park Ave. office, she (Muriel Siebert) likes to finger the simple printed badge numbered 2646—the symbol of her Stock Exchange seat—which she bought in January 1968 for $445,000 plus initiation fee. She refers to it as the most expensive piece of jewelry in her collection.

The badge, she explains with a smile, came with a clip on the back to fit the breastpocket of a man's suit. When she took it to a local jeweler, she says, "I complained that he charged me $11.50, but since I had told him what I paid for it, I was in no position to argue."

Miss Siebert is obviously proud of that badge and of her position, and obviously enjoys the good-natured teasing from her male cohorts. As she puts it, "I get a great deal of pleasure out of being first. I havn't gotten sophisticated about it yet."

FITNESS

I'd love to take up jogging because I need the exercise. But I'd give myself a couple of black eyes!

– Dolly Parton

"I'd rather do my exercises at a fitness salon," said a homemaker, "because when I stand on my head at home, I see a lot of places I missed when I was dusting."

A much-married Hollywoodite explains her daily push-ups and rope-skipping at a gym with, "My body has to last a few more years, because it's my only source of income."

I'm a fanatic about staying in condition ... I rattle around on the bedroom floor for 20 minutes in the morning when I get up (5:00 a.m.) doing hip rolls, side bends, 60 sit-ups, touch my toes, kick, jump rope, side straddle-hop.

– Farrah Fawcett

When Carol Channing appeared in a London run of "Hello, Dolly," she visited an antique shop. As she poked around, a heavy bureau drawer dropped on her foot. Despite the pain, she was determined to go on with her performance that night.

A London doctor, who'd been called, decided to give her a mild sedative, so she'd feel a bit more comfortable as she moved actively about the stage. However, since Channing has never used medication of any sort, the slight sedative put her to sleep till after 11:00 p.m.

FOCUS

Unless you develop the capacity to focus in a singular way, you find yourself focusing on nothing—not being very adept or expert in anything ... You must have an area of interest, and develop maximum knowledge in that area in order to be productive and successful.

— Barbara Jordan

FOOD

About airline food

> Anything that's white is sweet
> Anything that's brown is meat
> Anything that's grey don't eat!

— Hermione Gingold

A woman chef once said that eating food with a knife and fork is like making love through an interpreter.

A man in general is better pleased when he has a good dinner than when his wife talks Greek.

— Samuel Johnson

I've tried to teach my children the value of eating good foods. But sometime if it's late and we're going to a movie, I'll suggest getting a hot dog there, and my daughter says, "Oh, Mom, it's got nitrates in it."

— Jane Fonda

Lady Mary Henderson, wife of Sir Nicholas Henderson, Ambassador of Great Britain to the U.S.: "Cooking books should be read for pleasure, tried out for pleasure and then the recipes should be adapted to your own taste. Whatever the dish is, it shouldn't be somebody else's. Make it your own.

"Food should be amusing and be a topic of conversation at the table. It should look attractive, be interesting and taste interesting."

(First panel of cartoon shows woman preparing dinner with organically grown food) The natural, pure nutrients present in organically grown

foods promise to increase your lifespan by twenty years ... (Second panel shows her in hospital bed) ... and the brand of organically grown mushrooms you've been eating is suddenly recalled because of botulism.
– Dean Norman

FOOL

British actress Agnes Bernelle: "No woman really makes a fool out of a man. She merely gives him the opportunity to develop his natural capacities."

FORGOT

(When reminded of cruel treatment once given her) I distinctly remember forgetting that!
– Clara Barton

One of the legendary stories about musical director Sarah Caldwell is that because of many demanding rehearsals she forgot she had a car— and left it for a year in a parking garage.

Drop from view in Washington and you are forgotten before you are gone. A lady in the supermarket stopped me one day with: "I beg your pardon, aren't you the former Barbara Howar?"
– Barbara Howar

FREE

While there is bondage anywhere, we ourselves cannot be fully free. While there is oppression anywhere, we ourselves cannot soar high.
– Indira Gandhi

... being free simply means having the freedom to choose the man to whom I will become a slave.
– Jeanne Moreau

When writer Faith Baldwin interviewed Margaret Mitchell, author of *Gone With the Wind,* Baldwin asked Scarlett's creator what she wanted most in life. The answer, said Baldwin, was "freedom" ... privacy of the spirit and freedom to do what she (Mitchell) wanted to do.

I want to say to a world that has lost its way: The unpardonable sin for you, for me, for every human, is to have more knowledge than understanding, more power than love, to know more about the earth than about the people who live on it, to invent quick means of traveling to far-away places, when one cannot grope one's way inside one's own heart. Freedom is a dreadful thing unless it goes hand in hand with responsibility. Democracy among men is a specter except when the hearts of men are mature.

– Lillian Smith

FRIEND

Woman is woman's natural ally.

– Euripides

True friendship is never serene.

– Marquise de Sevigné

Josephine Baker, international entertainer: "I have no talent—only friends."

The best time to make friends is before you need them.

– Ethel Barrymore

(About her husband King Hussein) His Majesty is my best friend, the one person to whom I can say just about anything.

– Queen Noor el Hussein

(On being teased about always being accompanied by a beautiful young girl) I always like to have a beautiful young female friend—only now I forget what for!

– Georgie Jessel

Friendships between women are as fragile, painful and complex as any love affair between a woman and a man. They need as much care, and offer just as much reward.

– Claudia Weill

The ordinary capacity of woman is inadequate for the communion and fellowship which is the nurse of the sacred bond of friendship, nor does their soul feel firm enough to endure the strain of so tight and durable a knot.

– Montaigne

Oh, the comfort, the inexpressible comfort, of feeling safe with a person, having neither to weigh thoughts nor measure words, but to pour them all out just as they are, chaff and grain together, knowing that a faithful hand will take and sift them, keep what is worth keeping, and then, with the breath of kindness, blow the rest away.

– George Eliot

FRIENDSHIP

Hitherto all my intellectual friendships had been with men, and Vernon Lee was the first highly cultivated and brilliant woman I had ever known. I stood a little in awe of her, as I always did in the presence of intellectual superiority, and liked best to sit silent and listen to a conversation which I still think almost the best to its day. I have been fortunate in knowing intimately some great talkers among men, but I have met only three women who had the real gift.

– Edith Wharton

You probably don't know Jane, but you know someone like her. Someone whom merely to think of brings a smile. When I'm stuck in traffic or listening to a boring speaker or can't get to sleep. I think about Jane ... about the time the lights went out and she reached into her dresser drawer for her face lotion, and when the lights came back on she discovered she'd rubbed blue/black ink instead of skin freshner all over her face ... about the time she called the police to report a stolen car from the shopping center *before* she remembered that her husband had dropped her off ... about the time the exterminator had to come to her house because there was an awful odor in one of the children's closets, and she figured there must be a skunk or a dead rat in the wall, and for $17 the exterminator extracted a green tuna fish sandwich from a red galosh.

– Ina Hughs

FUND RAISING

(On a T-shirt) Fund raising is the perfect housewife retread.

FUNERAL

At Martha Mitchell's funeral, one wreath read: "Martha was right."

(Commenting on the funeral of her husband, Bing Crosby) He hated funerals ... I'm sure he didn't plan to come to this one at all.

– Kathryn Crosby

FUNNY

Whatever you have read I have said is almost certainly untrue, except if it is funny, in which case I definitely said it.

– Tallulah Bankhead

FUTURE

I am not a has-been. I'm a will be.

– Lauren Bacall

I'm not a reflective person. I live for the future.

– Hermione Gingold

Where will I be five years from now? I delight in not knowing. That's one of the greatest things about life—its wonderful surprises.

– Marlo Thomas

The Japanese used the term monsai, meaning "a toast to ten thousand years." That, indeed, is looking forward. The Gray Panthers are futurists, too. As we look ahead, you can be sure of one thing: We're not going to be living in the past.

– Maggie Kuhn

GADGET

Despite all the new household gadgets, the handiest one to have around the house is still a husband.

— Denise Lor

GAIETY

Must one be at all times in deadly earnest in order to count as a serious person? To my mind, both earnestness and gaiety should balance each other out in equal measure.

— Soraya

GAMBLING

(When visiting Las Vegas) Blackjack has infiltrated my whole being. I'd go broke if I lived here.

— Miz Lillian Carter

GAME

When a child, India's Prime Minister Indira Gandhi liked dolls ... but played with them differently from most little girls. She liked to line them up as men and women engaged in insurrections, battles and other political activities.

GARAGE SALE

Women's bumper sticker: "We Brake for Garage Sales."

GARDEN

I had a fabulous rose garden. You know, most people think of a garden as a quiet, peaceful place. Mine was nothing of the sort; it was a battleground. I fought aphids and everything else.

– Mary Welsh Hemingway

Gardener's Report

Though everybody knows
That plants mature from seedlings
Weeds appear full-grown—
There's no such thing as "weedlings."

– Rosemarie Williamson

Lady tourist: "I say—how did you get the grass so thick and green?" Woman gardener: "Nothing to it, ma'am. Just seed, feed, weed and mow—about 400 years."

– Conversation overheard on an estate in England

GAY

We (entertainers) owe our acts to gays. We owe much of our music, our dancing, our costumes, plenty of everything to gays.

– Shirley MacLaine

(About two young men she, Emily Kimbrough, met at a party in Paris) They were so different from the men I know ... although they were very pleasant. They laughed a lot and they seemed to be wonderfully good friends. I sat between them and they kept leaning across, and talking so eagerly to each other.

Father, who had been reading the theatrical newspaper *Commoedia,* at this point looked up over his glasses. Emily Kimbrough, encouraged by his interest, continued, "Wasn't it odd? They both had rouge on and eye shadow." Father made an odd choking sound. "But then I learned that they were from the theatre. I imagine they must have just come from a matinee and hadn't bothered to take off their makeup. You know," and Emily turned on Father her most social smile, "you've probably done the same thing lots of times yourself."

– Cornelia Otis Skinner

GENERATION

I must resemble the whole of my generation, and that's why they have adopted me so nicely.

— Brigitte Bardot

GENIUS

Of course, a genius in this field (acting) or in any other will succeed. But the genius does not have to seek a profession; it seeks her.

— Ella Wheeler Wilcox

GIFT

(As reported by Earl Wilson) "I don't take gifts from perfect strangers—but then, nobody's perfect.

— Zsa Zsa Gabor

Hugh Carey, as Governor of New York, gave Anne Ford Uzielli a garnet birthstone, inscribed: "The Guv, with Luv."

Tennis star, Martina Navratilova, was given a diamond necklace, which has a check mark to which was attached a diamond-studded "X". "Ex-Czech," smiles Martina, "which is what I am!"

(On a TV talk show she was answering a jibe about daughter Zsa-Zsa accepting such outrageously expensive gifts from men) What would you expect a man to give a woman like my Zsa-Zsa—one perfect rose?

— Jolie Gabor

Said of Alice Roosevelt regarding the acceptance of gifts while her father was President: "Alice will accept anything but a red-hot stove, and she'll take that if it doesn't take too long to cool off."

— Helena Huntington Smith

I tell myself that God gave my children many gifts—spirit, beauty, intelligence, the capacity to make friends and to inspire respect ... There was only one gift he held back—length of life.

— Rose Kennedy

We have an English proverb that says, "He that would thrive must ask his wife." It was lucky for me that I had one as much disposed to industry and frugality as myself. She assisted me cheerfully in my business, folding and stitching pamphlets, tending shop, purchasing old linen rags for the paper-makers, etc. We kept no idle servants, our table was plain and simple, our furniture of the cheapest ... For instance, my breakfast for a long time was bread and milk (no tea), and I eate it out of a twopenny earthen porringer with a pewter spoon. But mark how luxuries will enter families and make a progress in spite of principle. Being called one morning to breakfast, I found it in a china bowl with a spoon of silver! They had been bought for me without my knowledge by my wife, and had cost her the enormous sum of twenty-three shillings, for which she had no other excuse or apology to make but that she thought *her* husband deserved a silver spoon and china bowl as well as any of his neighbors.

— Benjamin Franklin

GIRL SCOUT

A woman speaker asked: "What's the difference between the WAACS and the Girl Scouts?" Quickly a WAAC in the audience answered, "The Girl Scouts have adult leadership."

A telephone call marks the historic beginning of Girl Scouting in the United States: "Come right over, Nina, I've got something for the girls of Savannah and all America, and all the world, and we are going to start it tonight." That was the way that Juliette Low, the Founder of the Girl Scouts in the United States of America, announced the beginning of the movement in March, 1912.

— Girl Scout Handbook

America's first Girl Scout—Daisy Gordon Lawrence—didn't want to be a Girl Scout. Though her aunt, Juliette Gordon Low enrolled Lawrence when she organized the scouts in 1912 in Savannah, Ga., Lawrence always felt she was a flop at scouting and didn't even bother to attend the first meeting. Later, though, Lawrence attended meetings because it allowed her to study first aid, a great interest of hers.

GIVEN UP

I entertain for senior citizens—and some of them are younger than I am!...because they've given up.

— Hermione Gingold

GLASSES

If you wish to accomplish something, don dream-colored glasses.

— Cathy Handley

Columnist Earl Wilson, quoting D. O. Flynn: "The glasses that make a woman look most attractive to men are those recently emptied."

GOAL

Do not aim lower than your potential. Few people have ever attained a higher level than the one to which they aspired.
— Patricia Harris

I'm a sucker for men's looks ... But what I liked most of all was that he (her husband) seemed to be the kind of person who would always be a bachelor. It became a goal to capture him.
— Nancy Lopez-Melton

If I had one wish for my children, it would be that each of you would reach for goals that have meaning for you as individuals.
— Miz Lillian Carter

You have to make a decision, "I am going to be such and such," even if that is not, in the end, the great answer. You have to set your sight on a goal to get anywhere.
— Mary Wells Lawrence

The solution (to choosing lifetime goals) ... is to refuse to substitute one generation's imperatives with another's—to finally invent our own individual ideal of the Full Life, and our own means of getting there.
— Letty Cottin Pogrebin

Marjorie Bell Chambers, National President, American Association of University Women, in a speech delivered at Mississippi University for Women: "Reach out to a far horizon and chart your course to get there, so that you can purchase a future, wherein, you will play a role to enable this nation to be seen once more as a 'City upon a Hill'—a beacon in the darkness ... a light unto all the world! You can do it IF you will but recognize that genius is the ability to light one's own fire. Do it and light up this world as it has never been lit before."

And you're in the trap called *here*. But you can get out of it. You *can* get there from here. The goal, the objective—the dream!—they are all attainable. The first step is to *take* the first step—raise one foot off dead center. You're not compelled to achieve your aspiration by one soaring flight, not even by giant steps, only one foot at a time. After the first footstep, the second is easier, the third is surer, the fourth is faster. Suddenly the miracle happens. Your mind is off the footsteps and only on the dream. Only you're not dreaming the dream anymore—you're living it. Winning. Getting the best of yourself.
— Katherine Nash

GOD

I see God in every human being.

— Mother Teresa

I have learned, ... that God is able to bring positive good out of any so-called tragedy.

— Catherine Marshall

I often think of God as a fireball—friendly—who just rolls by. If you're lucky you get a slight glimpse of him.

Annie Dillard

Somebody said recently that Congresswoman Jordan is exactly the way God looks if God is black and a woman.

— William "Fishbait" Miller

God put music in my heart, and a voice in my throat. I serve Him when I serve music.

— Lotte Lehmann

First of all, I hold that a firm faith in God is life's greatest blessing.
— Ernestine Schumann-Heink

Dr. Phillip J. Boyer, former professor of theology: "Modern feminists have been insisting that God is not necessarily a man; He could be a She. And they could be right."

(About changing courses at Georgetown University in Washington) I switched from French to theology ... because I discovered God was easier to understand than French.

— Pearl Bailey

GOOD

When I'm good, I'm very good. When I'm bad, I'm better.

— Mae West

GOSSIP

There are some women who do not like passing on gossip. They are content with inventing it.

— Juliette Greco

A homemaker says that gossip is like grapefruit—the juicier the better.

We were brought up to believe gossip was dirty journalism—trivia about trivial people. And you had to read it in your bathroom.

– Rona Barrett

If we could channel all this gossip into energy, we could solve all the problems in the U.S. with gossip power.

I depend a lot on innuendo. Frequently, I simply report the rumor. The words "they say" should make it clear to everyone that even *I* don't know whether it's true or not.

– Liz Smith

Writer Carolina Maria de Jesus: "I can't stand these (Portugese) favela women, they want to know everything. Their tongues are like chicken feet. Scratching at everything."

Writer Bill Fay said that when Fran Allison of the Kukla, Fran and Ollie TV show needed a pithy description of a neighborhood gossip, Fran's mother suggested, "There was a woman back home who was just about the talkingest person I ever met. She could stay longer in an hour than anybody else could in a whole afternoon."

Time (magazine) invited me to have lunch with her (Martha Mitchell): "Martha," I said, "tell me how you feel about the gossip that you have a weakness for whiskey." She said, "You tell me first about the gossip that you have a weakness for Henry Kissinger!" "That particular passion is overestimated," I said. "So is mine for alchohol," she replied.

– Barbara Howar

GOVERNMENT

You cannot have national welfare before someone has created national wealth.

– Margaret Thatcher

I came to Washington to work for God, F.D.R. and the millions of forgotten, plain, common workingmen.

– Frances Perkins

GRANDCHILD

Bette Davis told her 8-year-old grandson about an upcoming movie "Witch Mountain" she'd just made. The youngster exclaimed, "Grandmother Davis is a star at last."

A little girl was visiting her grandmother. On seeing her get out of the tub after her bath the granddaughter said: "Grandma, God made your skin too big."

GRANDMOTHER

Anne Morrow Lindbergh's grandchildren call her "Grannymouse."

Elizabeth Taylor once called herself a "semi-retired grandmother."

Feminist lecturer Suzy Sutton describes herself as a "glamorous granny."

She used to raise children with a firm hand and a logical heart, but that was before she became a grandparent.

— Erma Bombeck

(Husband to his wife) You're not allowed to be a grandmother anymore; you're a "grandperson."

Queen Elizabeth, the Queen Mother, is not only known as the "Queen Mum" but also for her delightful "Granny" personality.

Grandma was babysitting her daughter's five-year-old son for a few hours. She phoned her daughter to ask, "When do you want me to bring Tommy home?" Without hesitation, the daughter replied, "When he's grown up."

As I look back over my life, I see two great obvious mistakes. First, I tried so desperately hard never to give my husband's children the impression that I was their stepmother that I hardly dared take care of my own babies ... Years later I made the same mistake all over again with the grandchildren. Now I hope I have awakened in time.

— Maria Von Trapp

GRANDMOTHER—LIVELY

After watching his attractive wife serve at tennis, a grandfather said, "Nowadays you can't tell a grandmother by looking at her."

Clarice, a grandmother who manages to juggle her job, her 18 grandchildren, her church work and her hobby of making oil paintings of people's homes for fees, is often asked how she does so much. "Well, you see," she answers, "I really don't live in this century. It's too limiting. I live in another age—that I call the Age of Adventure. When you're adventurous, you can get an awful lot done!"

Myra, walking down her neighborhood block, met her friend, a white-haired grandmother, and her little granddaughter roller skating companionably along on the sidewalk. The grandmother stopped and said, "Myra! We're having more fun! Last week I taught my granddaughter to tap dance. Almost everyday my son says to me, 'Mother, be your age!' But I always answer, 'The nursing homes are filled with old ladies being their age—I'll be any age I choose!'"

GRANDPARENT

When Marian McQuade, mother of 15 and grandmother of 14, visited nursing homes, she saw older people who were sometimes forgotten by their families. This prompted her to write to government officials and members of Congress. As a result of her work, in 1977, the first Sunday after Labor Day became officially Grandparents Day.

GRAVEYARD

And I say, if she'd ha' died, Ethan might ha' lived; and the way they are now, I don't see's there's much difference between the Fromes up at the farm and the Fromes down in the graveyard; 'cept that down there they're all quiet, and the women have got to hold their tongues.
— *Mrs. Hale, character in* Ethan Frome
by Edith Wharton

GREATNESS

The touchstone of human greatness lies in cooperation and collaboration, the antitheses of domination and exploitation of one people by another.
— *Madame Chiang Kai-Shek*

GUEST

Joyce Grenfell talking about the weekend guest of her aunt, Lady (Nancy) Astor: "The company was varied and it was not unusual to meet a duchess, with or without her duke. MP's of all parties, an international banker, a Christian Science lecturer, all mixed up with friends from Uncle Waldorf's English youth and my aunt's American girlhood;

and there were younger married couples and, often a lonely man or woman whom no one seemed to know and whose identity was never discovered throughout the week-end. My mother always believed it would be possible for an adventurer to stay at Cliveden undetected, because Aunt Nancy would expect he'd been asked by Uncle Waldorf or *vice-versa*; it could be supposed he was a friend of one of the children's."

GUIDANCE

One wants a kind of guidance. That's why one looks for a mentor, and most of the people who are accomplished and wise seem to us to be men. Of course, the whole sexual charge makes it much more exciting. There, I think women love the sense of being chosen by men—and we're terrified that at any moment of our lives we may not be being chosen.
– Mary Gordon

GUILT

I'm devoting my life to writing a book, *Guilt Without Sex*.
– Marilyn Sokol

After a visit home, a woman college professor commented her mother had a very busy schedule. "After all," said the professor, "mother's the southwest distributor of guilt."

HAND HOLDING

I (am) proud of the women in our administration who don't hold office but hold hands of the men who do....

— Richard M. Nixon

HANG-UP

Father, about daughter: "If she has any hang-ups, it's certainly not the telephone receiver."

HAPPINESS

Women are capable of greater happiness and of greater unhappiness than men.

— Joyce Brothers

Happiness is not a station you arrive at, but a manner of traveling.

— Margaret Lee Runbeck

A mature single man says: "You know immediately on meeting her if a woman is happy. The vibes are there."

The favorite saying of a homemaker who makes her own slipcovers and bric-a-brac is, "Happiness is homemade."

When I'm pushing myself, testing myself, that's when I'm happiest. It's a great reward system.

— Sissy Spacek

The older you grow and the more you are exposed to in the world, how the hell can you be happy?

— Lauren Bacall

... Happiness does not depend so much on circumstances as on one's inner self. But I have always found in practice that theories are of little comfort.

— Jennie, Lady Randolph Churchill

In the office of writer Frances Lear, and that of her writer/TV producer husband Norman Lear, hang identical framed inscriptions by an anonymous early Greek philosopher: "Happiness is the exercise of one's vital abilities along lines of excellence in a life that affords them scope."

I've seen very few happy stars and I was determined that that wasn't going to happen to me. The plums hang so high and the vampires beckon and I know that if I fell for it I'd be as unhappy as the other ladies in Hollywood. Ambition doesn't go too well with age or companionship.

— Vivian Vance

I should have liked to feel that such prodigious success, a scientific reputation without precedent for a woman, had brought my mother (Marie Curie) happiness. That this unique adventure should have made its heroine suffer constantly seemed to me too unjust, and I should have given a great deal to find at the end of a letter, in the midst of a confidence, some movement of selfish pride, a cry or a sigh of victory.

It was a childish hope. Marie, promoted to "the celebrated Mme. Curie," was ... happy at times, but only in the silence of her laboratory or the intimacy of her home ... in order to escape from those who would have dragged her onto the stage, to avoid being the "Star" ...

— Eve Curie

HARD TIMES

(When a TV talk show host asked if she'd had hard times) Hard times? five flights walk-up, plenty of baked beans!

— Chita Rivera

HATE

(About a movie star) When she hated, she hated hard.

HEAD

I worked my head to the bone.

– Jane Ace

HEALTH

Talk health. The dreary, never-ending tale of mortal maladies is worn and stale. You cannot charm or interest or please by harping on that minor cord—disease. So, say that you are well, and all is well with you. And God will hear your words and make them true.

– Ella Wheeler Wilcox

Take one brisk walk to a library. Take any book by a tried-and-true writer. Take a brisk walk home and read with all attention. The exercise plus the tonic of the book will provide all physical and mental requirements for good health.

– Helen Hayes

During the times we are discussing, the woman shopper (like her allegedly better-protected sister today) had to be careful about commercially made hair dyes, cosmetics, and powders that were likely to destroy the hair, blotch the face, and rot the teeth. More homely ingredients such as wheat bran, marshmallow powder, almond meal, and bean meal were apparently safer to experiment with.

– Daniel Aaron

HEART

... in my personal life I am very vulnerable. I believe in broken hearts.

– Kate Jackson

HEAVEN

In heaven, there were two lines. One line had a sign over it: "Stand here if you are a man dominated by a woman." The line was long, perhaps 100 men. In the other line, there was a sign overhead which said: "Stand here if you are not dominated by women." Only one man stood under that sign. When St. Peter asked the man why he was in the second line, the man answered: "I don't know; my wife told me to do it."

HERS

My husband is my hero. Some say I'm the one who makes all the decisions, and that I am the mastermind. That's not correct. I want to be Mrs. Ronald Reagan. If he were selling ball bearings, I'd be out there pushing ball bearings.

– Nancy Reagan

HERSTORY

Delilah was the first woman barber.

HIM-PECKED

One militant woman can drown out a thousand normal females who glory in domineering husbands.

– Margaret Fishback

HOLIDAYS

(During the holiday season) the fragrance of a family, fragrance of a holiday, is a sensual thing.

– Virginia Graham

HOLLYWOOD

Commenting that as soon as you get to the top, Hollywood waits for you to take a fall, Liza Minnelli added, "Well, keeping my balance is the best part of my act."

... the people here (Hollywood) are not so much evil as simply children. They do not have a parent, setting values. There are no leaders. Everyone is nervous and uncertain.

– Rona Barrett

A woman, describing a friend's wedding at sunset on a Hollywood hill, said, "It was a conservative wedding. The bride wore an heirloom veil ... so long it almost covered her slacks."

In London, they kept saying, "Learn to be an actress." In Hollywood, they say you're great when they mean you're good, and then say you're good, when they mean you're awful. I prefer the Hollywood method.

– Joan Collins

Broadway star Helen Gallagher said: "I'll go to Hollywood when they want *me*. So far, all you movie people have wanted to take me out there and change the way I act, change my hair, my clothes, change everything. I can be had, but not for a remodeling job. I'll stay the way I am."

HOME

Women have twice as much power and influence on the home atmosphere. I liken it to a light bulb and its candle power. Men have 100-watt influence and women have 200 watts.

– Dr. Herbert Spaugh

Asked what a woman's contribution to a better world should be, she (Madame Curie) replied that it began at home, then spread to those immediately connected, her immediate friends, then the community in which she lived, and if the work proved to meet a need of the world at large it spread there. But the important thing was the beginning, and that beginning, Madame Curie insisted, was in the home, the center of small things.

– Ida M. Tarbell

HOMELY

There are no such things as homely women—only lazy ones.

– Deborah Kerr

HONOR

India, in bestowing highest distinction on the Roman Catholic nun, Mother Teresa of Calcutta, named her, "Jewel of India."

When she was honored by UNICEF and presented with a silver tray, Miz Lillian Carter examined it and quipped, "It's just large enough to hold three martini glasses."

(Said when she was finally recognized with respect and greeted with roses from eight doctors when landing at Madrid airport in 1946) It is very gratifying to receive flowers from doctors while I am still here to smell them.

– Sister Kenny

(An ode written in honor of Nadia Boulanger, teacher of noted musicians, and recited by Markevitch on Boulanger's 80th birthday) If all your friends' voices were to be heard together, you would be deafened by the sound, and if they were to speak to you one by one, this lovely evening would last 100 years. With your vitality, your spiritual strength, and your imagination, if love did not exist, you would have invented it.

HOPE

... uncertainty has its charm and though in his heart every man may think he prefers the sweet home-loving, mother-of-his-children type, he is likely to forget his vulnerability to the shingled, dive-adoring, shaker-of-the-shimmy Delilahs. And so hope springs infernal in the human unrest.

— Elsie Janis

There are no hopeless situations—only people who are hopeless about them.

— Dinah Shore

HOSPITAL

The doctors and nurses were all so, so good to me ... As I was leaving, I asked, "Oh, how in the world will I ever be able to repay you all? And they told me, "By check, money order or cash."

— Donna Fargo

A hospital is good for the seriously ill alone—otherwise it becomes a lodging-house where the nervous become more nervous, the foolish more foolish, the idle and selfish more selfish and idle. For two of the elements essential to a Hospital are want of occupation and directing the attention to bodily health.

— Florence Nightingale

When Fran Allison, who played the role of Aunt Fanny in the Breakfast Club, returned to the program after an appendectomy, Master of Ceremonies Don McNeill said, "Well, well, it's good to see you again, Aunt Fanny. Did the doctors find out what you had?" "No," Aunt Fanny replied. "but they came within three or four dollars."

HOT-TUBS

To tell the truth ... I don't like to do anything that more than two people are doing. I'm suspicious of it.

— Louise Lasser

HOT WATER

Hot water is my native element. I was in it as a baby and have never seemed to get out of it since.

— Dame Edith Sitwell

HOUSE

(An embroidered sampler) A clean house is the sign of a wasted life.

One woman's advice: "If you want to make your old home seem more attractive, just price a new one."

In a career woman's house is a sign: "This is an equal-opportunity kitchen."

Once you let a man put you in the kitchen, it's curtains, and he'll even have you washing those by hand.

— Paulette Goddard

Busy writer Lady Antonia Frazier, one day while walking down a hallway of her home gestured toward a door and said to a visitor, "rumor has it that is the kitchen."

HOUSEHOLD DRUDGE

Lady to friend (as they played bridge while her husband cooked dinner) "If George thinks he is going to make me into a household drudge, he has another think coming."

HOUSEWORK

Housework's the hardest work in the world. That's why men won't do it.

— Edna Ferber

A woman who likes housework is a woman with a maid.

A career woman said to one of her husband's friends who phoned: "Jim will call you back as soon as he finishes his vacuuming."

In Japan, a government survey showed that women do housework for about six hours a day and men for about six minutes.

A woman should be as proud of her success in making her house into a perfect little world as the greatest statesman of his organizing a nation's affairs.

– André Maurois

The house husband, writing a novel and keeping house while his wife worked, proved to be a good cook but a poor housekeeper. However, one day, caught up with his writing, he thoroughly cleaned the house, That evening, his wife, going into the den to make a business phone call, shouted in dismay, "Honey, where's the dust on the desk? I had a phone number written on it."

HUMAN

In 1911, Olive Schreiner, South African writer and feminist, predicted: "It is quite possible, in the new world which is arising about us, that the type of human most useful to society and best fitted for its future conditions, and who will excel in the most numerous forms of activity, will be not the muscularly powerful and bulky, but the highly versatile, active, vital, adaptive, sensitive, physically fine-drawn type."

HUMAN LIFE

Too soon, too soon came the bridal veils, the jewels, the breast bands and the narrow shifts; too soon the marriage bed, the seeking hands, the bloody sheets. And what was after? The house keys, the cradle, the distaff and wheel, old age and the old, old crackle, the nodding white head, and death. What god made a human soul for this? Or what demon?

– Sappho

HUMAN RACE

There is only one race—the human race.

– Pearl Bailey

The human race was not destined for mechanical efficiency but rather for the efficiency of the mind and the spirit.

– Frances Perkins

Now, ... the dominant attitude toward the human race is not one of pride. You see that in literature and art. The figures are all antiheroes.

The beginning of the "ugh" period of literature—meaning "horrid"—began after World War I.
— Barbara Tuchman

During those years since Peter's death, I had found that life is people—wonderful people, dear people, God's people. Could it have been that I —who had so valued solitude that I had fled up the back stairs to find it—had had to be stripped, released to aloneness, to discover how much I needed people, wanted them? Out of loneliness I had found love. Out of the heart's need, I had crept humbly back to acknowledge that need and to rejoin the human race.
— Catherine Marshall

HUMAN RIGHT

"We demand as a human right a full voice and role for women...."
— Declaration of American Women,
Houston convention, 1977

HUMOR

A beautiful girl without a sense of humor is too much trouble.
— Flo Ziegfeld

Totie Fields recounted pulling this practical joke on her friends Steve Lawrence and wife Eydie Gormé. When Lawrence was appearing in Las Vegas, Totie was visiting him in his hotel suite. While there, she furtively counted the stack of clean undershorts in his drawer, and rubbed her lipstick in a smear on (the fly of) the pair that would be uncovered the first day Steve got home (counting one pair per day). Later she phoned to ask innocently, how was his homecoming? She roared at hearing of Eydie's explosion and Steve's protest of outraged innocence—and confessed she was the culprit.

HUNTING

The late Lady Phyllis Sopwith of Britain, along with her husband, loved hunting and other outdoor sports. Some years ago Lady Sopwith required a pacemaker for her heart. Her family recalled that she instructed it be inserted on her left side so that she could put her shot gun up to her right shoulder.

A husband took his wife on her first deer hunt. Tucked into her stand, she raised her gun, fired several shots and "connected." But when she saw another hunter trying to make off with her animal, she ran over to him and said, "Stop it! That's my deer, that's my deer! You get away from my deer." The plaid-shirted man looked shaken and said, "Okay, ma'am, it's yours. Just let me pull off my saddle."

IDEA

(Expressing an idea) So I discovered that one of the sweetest compliments you can have is to advance an idea that you believe in—not as advice—but as your own feeling. Then wait and hear it echoed back, not with you as the source, but as an acceptable idea.

— Lady Bird Johnson

IDEAL

Columnist Bertha Shore: "The ideal will be reached when all women are married and all men are single."

IDENTIFIABLE

It's not a good idea to be identifiable, though it's reassuring. It feels safe and that's bad, because it means that you're accepted, and once that happens that's where you stay.

— Diane Keaton

IDENTITY

Jean Kerr, explaining her denial of identity: "It was simply ... that there I was in a fourteen-ninety-five Tall-Gal dress from Lane Bryant's with a rip in my sweater and hair in my face, and I don't want anybody to think Jean Kerr looks like *that*."

In a patriarchy having everything assumes that you start off with your basic stick-to-the-ribs wife/mother identity—and the rest is liberated gravy.

— Letty Cottin Pogrebin

... Women whose identity depends more on their outsides than their insides are dangerous when they begin to age. Because I have work I care about, it's possible that I may be less difficult to get along with when the double chins start to form.

— Gloria Steinem

IDOL

We, the public, are very hard on our idols.

— Barbara Walters

IGNORANCE

The only real tragedies in life are the ones where you don't learn something. I always look forward, not backward.

— Susan Strasberg

IMMORTALITY

I really do believe in a hereafter. I do not know it's location or appearance but it is somewhere.

— Lady Bird Johnson

IMPORTANT

There are three important people since time began, Christ, Spinoza and me.

— Gertrude Stein

INAUGURATION

(On her husband's inaugural day) I felt as though I had been turned into a piece of public property. It's frightening to lose your anonymity at 31.

— Jacqueline Onassis

INCOME TAX

I declared $60,000 on my income tax for makeup. They called me down (for a tax audit), took one look at my face and allowed the deductions.

— Joan Rivers

INDEPENDENCE

I can't be a rose in any man's lapel.

— Margaret Trudeau

Men don't want you to be independent because you will escape them.

— Bianca Jagger

I have always lived life through men. Now I realize I can't do that anymore.

— Jacqueline Onassis

Some women want to depend on a man; I don't like to depend on *anybody*. I want my life depending only on me.

— Gina Lollobrigida

(Puzzled by the fact that men say they want a liberated, independent woman till they meet one) ... (then) they're so threatened by her independence that they run away. I'd push my mother down the ramp of the Guggenheim Museum in roller skates for a good marriage.

— Candice Bergen

If a woman is independent she alienates men and ends up alone, unhappy and bitter. A woman's role is to complete her man. Her happiness is to love someone and take care of him. Being married is the best prison for a woman. It could be a marvelous jail.

— Pierre Cardin

INDIVIDUAL

I was born an individual. I don't choose to live vicariously through a man. I am somebody on my own.

— Ester Rolle

Seated in a box at a Republican convention or on a couch at a posh capital party, Mrs. Alice Roosevelt Longworth would sit cross-legged, her legs hidden by her skirt.

INDOMITABLE

(About Sister Kenny) The average among us breathe youthful fires and cool as we age and harden into old, average patterns. She never gave up.
                                                        – Victor Cohn

INEQUALITY

Wilma Scott Heide, President of the National Organization for Women: "The basic human inequality throughout time has been sexual inequality. Once the *idea* of human inequality of rights and freedom was sanctioned and institutionalized in law and practice, other kinds of racial, religious and class inequalities were predictable. The legal and social model for non-white slaves brought to this country was the legal and social status of women. We do not accept the white patriarchal model of family or nation or state to be either desirable or viable. I would hope my black and brown and other sisters and brothers recognized the white male system has produced racism, poverty and the exclusion of nearly all women as well as minority men from decision-making and societal value judgments including law-making."

INFERIORITY

According to French actress Marie Daems, the cure for a women's inferiority complex: "All you have to do is go to bed for a day while your husband takes charge of the household."

In Japan, during the first half of the 11th century a remarkable coincidence occurred. Virtually every fine author, whether a novelist, diarist or poet, turned out to be a woman. This fact is even more extraordinary since women at this time were assigned to a status of "irremediable inferiority," as one latterday historian put it.

INFIDELITY

Married to the director of the Folies Bergere, Mme. Paul Derval said: "I do not worry about my husband. A pastry cook never has a taste for cakes."

I'm a secure enough person, that if my husband was unfaithful with someone else, I would say, "Buster, that's a no-no!"—but I would stay with him.
                                                        – Elke Sommer

INFINITY

You make the choice of days yourself, You mark the calendar at the end of a certain segment of time—the end of March, the end of a week. You put an X on that day, not to cross it out but to make it sacred. In infinity, nothing is sacred. Too much distance, too much time.

— A character from New Heaven, New Earth
by Joyce Carol Oates

INFLATION

One neighbor woman to another: "I went on a steak diet and took off $118.00 in 14 days."

Sign in women's dress shop window: "Without inflation we wouldn't be able to afford today's high prices."

I do not understand why there is not a nationwide howl of protest against the ever-rising cost of living in our land in the past 18 months. I do not understand why there has not been a torrent of editorials asking just why the general consumer must pay and pay and pay as the big unions gain wage increases for their members and big businessmen protect their stockholders and obtain money for their own plant expansion by passing on the costs to us. I do not understand the still widespread indifference to built-in inflationary forces which are constantly eroding our dollar's value.

— Sylvia Porter

INSULTS

The insults to a working woman for being a woman are simply unperceived by men. "You think like a man. You write like a man" are deeply wounding words to hear.

— Shana Alexander

INTELLECTUAL

French playwright Marcel Achard: "An intellectual is a man who doesn't strike up a conversation with a pretty girl on a train because she is reading a book he doesn't approve of."

An earlier day woman physician, Dr. Murray, advised, "If your face lacks intellectuality, the only way to remedy it is by exercise of the mind." She recommended hobbies. The collection of spoons and teapots awakens interest, extends observation, and widens the scope and powers.

– Daniel Aaron

INTELLIGENCE

Columnist Abigail Van Buren has pointed out that no matter how bright a person is, there's somebody brighter.

INTEREST

Work has been my sideline—*men* have been my main interest in life.

– Britt Ekland

Nothing is interesting if you're not interested.

– Helen MacInnes

I found that people who are all wrapped up in themselves can't enjoy others because they use up all their energy wondering: "What will people say?" or "What will people think?" I discovered that when I got interested in other people, I wasn't afraid of being laughed at.

– Ava Gardner

IRELAND

Mother of Winston Churchill, Lady Randolph: "I have been three years in this country (Ireland) and never found a dull man."

I sometimes wonder what shape our (Ireland's) history of today will have taken upon the hillsides after another fifty years. Will England at last have fallen out of the saga? On what names will the praises rest or the blame? I think of a tale told to A. E. a score of years ago in some remote district. It was a woman who lay dying and whose two sons went out to stand on the road east and west to keep Death back from coming to the door. But when they returned to the house they found her dead, and each accused the other of having let Death pass him, and they struck at one another in anger and each killed the other. Was this wild story a foreshadowing, a symbol, of what is happening today? And if it is love of country that has led to present angers, must they not be in part forgiven? For now, as ever, all right is not on one or the other side, and why should those quarrel whose faces are set, as I think, towards the one city, to the attainment of Plato's dream?

– Lady Augusta Gregory

IRON CURTAIN

(About visiting Czechoslovakia) One of the Czechs said to me, "Sister, we will always leave a crack in the Iron Curtain for you to creep through to us." I replied, "I would be happy to creep through that crack whenever my help should be needed—so long as it is left open for me to creep out when I want to."

– Sister Kenny

JAZZ AGE

(Remarking that the popularity of her father F. Scott Fitzgerald lasts) Because he was writing about youth, his daughter Scottie Fitzgerald Smith said: "He was a PR man for the jazz age."

A jazz band is responsible for more marriages and divorces than even prohibition. The results of both are apt to be total blindness.

– Elsie Janis

JEALOUSY

I'm *very* jealous ... I can do anything I want but when my man looks at another woman I get hysterical.

– Zsa Zsa Gabor

It is said that jealousy is love, but I deny it; for though it may be procured by love, as ashes are by fire, yet jealousy extinguishes love, as ashes smother the flame.

– Margaret of Navarre

For aspiring barristers, a legal textbook gives advice for a lawyer defending a female—try not to have any woman about her own age on the jury. Why? Because unconsciously many women are jealous of another female in their own age bracket.

Before they were married, Kathy Crosby revealed, her husband, Bing, fell in love with his costar, Princess Grace, in Country Girl. "I've been jealous of you," Kathy later told Grace. "Bing always loved you." After Bing's death, when Grace rearranged her busy schedule to make a guest appearance on a TV Special, The Best of Bing, Kathy sent Her Highness a huge bouquet of flowers and a card signed "With love and jealousy."

JOG

I like to jog—because it helps my love life—I meet lots of guys that way!
— Brenda Vaccaro

Walking is for people who like to dream. Jogging is for people who like to compete.
— Emily Herring Wilson

Joggers aren't very friendly. They pant rather than speak. If you get in their way, they run over you rather than stop their stride, or they stand impatiently, moving their legs up and down and shaking their hands. Joggers don't have time to talk to each other. Joggers can't help you get the rock out of your shoe. Joggers are intent on *finishing*.
— Emily Herring Wilson

JOURNALIST

I'm not one of those journalists with a staff. I don't even have a secretary. I act as a sponge. I soak it up and squeeze it out in ink every two weeks.
— Janet Flanner

JOY

Joy seems to me a step beyond happiness—happiness is a sort of atmosphere you can live in sometimes when you're lucky. Joy is a light that fills you with faith and hope and love.
— Adela Rogers St. Johns

JUMP

Several years ago, I went to interview photographer Philippe Halsman, whose notable achievements include a charming book containing photographs of celebrities jumping. The jumps are quite revealing in a predictable sort of way. Richard Nixon with his rigid, constricted jump, the Duke and Duchess of Windsor in a deeply dependent jump. And so forth. In the course of the interview, Halsman asked me if I wanted to jump for him; seeing it as a way to avoid possibly years of psycho-analysis, I agreed. I did what I thought was my quintessential jump. "Do it again," said Halsman. I did, attempting to duplicate exactly what I had done before. "Again," he said, and I did. "Well," said Halsman, "I can see from your jump that you are a very determined, ambitious, directed person, but you will never write a novel." "Why is that?" I asked. "Because you have only one jump in you," he said.

— *Nora Ephron*

JUNGLE

My feeling is that if one takes care of himself and takes precautions he can keep out of trouble in the jungle as well as anywhere else.

— *Osa Johnson*

Cannibals seem to be more ritualistic than malicious about killing and eating their victims. Like other peoples on this sorry globe, those tribes have their enemies and are usually at war with some other tribe. Some taboo is violated or some insult given, or one tribe wants another's land or property or "place in the sun." And there is a certain virtue in killing—a man is not regarded as being a he-man until he has killed someone and thereby shown his superiority.

When a man kills another he eats his victim, not because he is necessarily hungry or lacks meat but because by eating the other fellow he thinks he acquires his victim's strength. But a man never troubles to eat a woman; she is weak and inconsequential. So the men eat the men, and the women eat the women.

— *Osa Johnson*

KIDNAP

On the back of Patty Hearst's T-shirt was a message: "Being kidnapped means always having to say you're sorry."

Weren't you once personally involved in a political kidnapping?

No, I was not. What happened, when the son of the leader of the Socialist party was kidnapped, Guido De Martino, is this. A fascist communique was sent to the newspapers and it said that they would accept only Fallaci as intermediary. I had to answer if I accepted or not, and this is how I did it. "Granted that I do not recognize this vile kidnapping and these negotiations, neither any kind of kidnapping and negotiations; granted that I would never permit anyone to negotiate for me should I be kidnapped; considered, however, that it is not my life that is in danger but the life of another citizen, I put myself at the disposal of the bastards who demand my intercession while insisting that I shall not accept any imposition or blackmail, and reserving the right to spit in their faces." Of course nobody called anymore. However, the episode clarifies my attitude on the matter: If I am kidnapped, consider me dead. I said it on various occasions. Don't negotiate. Don't give up. Of course it's easier to speak courageously when death seems far away, but I like to believe that I wouldn't surrender. Sometimes in order to live we have to die.

— Oriana Fallaci

KING

There is no king who has not had a slave among his ancestors, and no slave who has not had a king among his.

— Helen Keller

KISS

When women kiss it always reminds one of prizefighters shaking hands.

— H. L. Mencken

John Adams once jested he had given his wife Abigail two or three million kisses for each received from her.

I think it's disgusting. Sex has always been with us, but never so flamboyantly as it is today. I don't approve, never did. I was known as the "kissless star." My leading men used to say, "What's the matter with me, do I have bad breath?" I said "No, but I'm against kissing on the screen." In a way, a kiss is a promise, and I didn't want to create the wrong impression.

— Mary Pickford

KNOCK 'EM DEAD

(On the musical "Call Me Madam") And then, when the curtain went up, it was the old, old Merman story—Ethel took command, kept command and left 'em cheering. One lady in the audience of 1,657 veteran playgoers was heard to say, "Isn't it wonderful how much she's improved since Annie Get Your Gun?"

Her escort replied, "That's like saying, 'My, hasn't electricity improved since last year?'"

— James Poling

KNOWLEDGE

The time ain't far off when a woman won't know any more than a man.
— Will Rogers

LADDER

The career woman pointed out that the way to go up the ladder is, "Type for play, not for pay."

Couldn't it have been, ... that I made it because my head was better than most men's heads?

— *Sue Mengers*

If you want to go up the ladder, it is more important to do the right job than to do the job right.

— *Woman Personnel Manager*

Barbara Walters: You never have to step on anyone (to go up the ladder).

Joan Rivers: Well, you do—but I have a manager for that.

Going up the ladder on your head may seem more difficult than making the trip on your back, but in the long run it's more emotionally rewarding.

— *Jo Foxworth*

If you do every little thing you can do in your own modest position, one thing leads to another. So do it and be it and write the letters and make the phone calls and get on with it.

— *Helen Gurley Brown*

LADY

Pro golfer Carol Mann: "A lady is an attitude; a woman is a biological fact."

One good thing about being a lady is that she is entitled to be as trashy as she wants, whenever she wants.

— Lena Horne

Being ladylike is a matter of control ... and I don't have that control. I try finesse and tact, but I always come out badly.

— Rita Moreno

LANGUAGE

Language is the vehicle of expression of thought and emotion, and it should be treated with more respect.

— Ethel Barrymore

Claire Booth Luce, as quoted by columnist Leonard Lyons, speaking to a group of Italians: "I am now going to talk a language that's not mine. And when I do, you'll probably think it's not yours either."

LAUGH

I must laugh ... laughter is like air and water to me.

— Rosalind Russell

Laugh and the world laughs with you. Cry and you cry alone.

— Ella Wheeler Wilcox

Comedian Phyllis Diller's laugh is described as "an old Chevrolet starting up on a below-freezing morning."

Being able to laugh with and at each other in romantic relationships is the most important thing.

— Eydie Gormé

When things get really gloomy ... I close my eyes and move myself a mile away from my trouble, where I can get a good look at it (and laugh) ... And you can't be troubled when you laugh.

— Helen Traubel

To me romance means hysteria—I mean *laughter!*

— Eydie Gormé

(When speaking at a Rosary College graduation) I have one wish for all of you. Something that will sustain you throughout your whole lives. Something you can afford. I wish you laughter in the bad times.

— Erma Bombeck

LEADERSHIP

(About the Egyptians) It is contrary to reason and nature that women should reign in families—but not that they should govern an empire.

– Montesquieu

LEARNING

How the Holmes women loved learning! Women, who John Calvin—if not Scripture—taught were the mouthpiece of the Devil, women had been the instrument, in the Holmes family at least, of keeping the flame of culture alive in those rude pioneer settlements. Grandmother Hewet, for instance. Abiel remembered her, at eighty-five, pink and pretty, with gentle manners and a spicy way of talking. She had taught herself to read Latin back in the times when you might wake any black night to find a tomahawk quivering in your cabin door. "When I was a girl," she had told Abiel, "I begged to go to school with the boys. But the elders were angry, and said Latin was not for women's head. Go home, Tempy, they said, and learn to spin and weave ... So I taught myself to read Vergil..."

"Forsan et haec olim meminisse juvabit..." said Grandmother Hewet softly, in her light old voice. "Abiel, I still find it beautiful."

– Yankee from Olympus
by Catherine Drinker Bowen

LEG

(Regaling audiences with a description of the ugliness of her new artificial leg)—and then I put it on, and would you believe it looked exactly like the other one?

– Totie Fields

LEGAL

When a woman lawyer passed the D.C. bar exam, her husband, a judge, gave her a memento to mark the occasion—a sign reading, "Honest lawyer—one flight up."

Cornelia G. Kennedy, the first woman chief judge of a U.S. District Court in the 189-year history of the court system, speaking of women lawyers: "You don't need great physical strength. You need stamina and I think women have the stamina to keep going and work harder."

LEGEND

(About being a legend) I don't think anyone feels like anything. I always felt they were out to get me, and that I'd better be good.

— *Katharine Hepburn*

LESSON

Barbara Jordan's grandfather, John Patten, repeated this statement to her: "Just remember the world is not a playground but a schoolroom. Life is not a holiday but an education. One eternal lesson for us all: to teach us how better we should love."

LIBERATED MALE

Her husband liked to say he was a "liberated" male. So one night his wife went to a club meeting, left no dinner and a note: "Tonight, the part of the wife will be played by the husband."

LIBERATION

If liberation means that women will make the same arbitrary demands of men that men have for generations made of women, it will be a sorry outcome for the human race which is not universally young, vigorous and beautiful.

— *Germaine Greer*

LIBRARIAN

(Accepting the American Library Association's Laura Ingalls Wilder Award for contributions to children's literature)
    In the name of Miss Bodanker
    I thank you for this award
    If that librarian hadn't launched me
    I would never have been aboard.

— *Dr. Seuss (Theodore Geisel)*

LIFE

You only get out of life what you put into it.

— *Ethel Merman*

Life is the best party I've ever been invited to.

> — *Arlene Francis*

Life is what happens to you when you're making other plans.

> — *Betty (Mrs. Herman) Talmadge*

Life is searching, growing, learning, being alert to opportunities.

> — *Patricia Harris*

... the qualities of our later life will be determined by the life we have already shaped.

> — *Rose Kennedy*

All the great minds never solved the mystery of life ... You can't really reach what it is.

> — *Louise Nevelson*

No life is so hard that you can't make it easier by the way you take it.

> — *Ellen Glasgow*

Life often seems like a long shipwreck of which the debris are friendship, glory and love.

> — *Madame de Staël*

I will not just live my life—I will not just spend my life—I will *invest* my life.

> — *Helen Keller*

I believe life is a continuous thing—it doesn't start at any particular age and it doesn't end at any particular age.

> — *Cloris Leachman*

Actress Isabell Adjani said in a press interview: "Life is worth being lived, but not worth being discussed all the time."

Cross-stitch motto by Brendan Gardner: "Life is like a round of golf. When you get out of one hole, you head for another."

But warm, eager, living life—to be rooted in life—to learn, to desire to know—to feel, to think, to act. That is what I want. And nothing less.

> — *Katherine Mansfield*

Life was always a puzzle to me, and gets more mysterious as I go on. I shall find it out by and by and see that it's all right. I can only keep brave and patient to the end.

> — *Louisa May Alcott*

LIFE—ENJOYMENT

(About Ruth Gordon) She enjoys life every day—she embraces life.

> — *Garson Kanin*

LIKE

Chris Evert Lloyd's mother: "There have been boys that Chris has been fond of in the past, most of them tennis players. I could tell if she liked them, ... because she'd hit the ball into the net a lot when she played them. I think she's smart."

(Said to Art Buchwald) When we (the British) were on top, we never cared who liked us. But since you people (the Americans) have been on top, you are very sensitive to what people think of you. You would be much happier if you didn't care.

— Nancy Mitford

LION

It's better to be a lion for a day than a sheep all your life.

— Sister Kenny

LIVING

I come from a long line of women who were on their feet until the end.

— Claudette Colbert

I believe in living your life positively instead of negatively.

— Lauren Bacall

Actress Alexis Smith likes to live for the moment. If you can do that, she says, "... without allowing your head to do trips about the past or future, you can really live fully."

LIVING TOGETHER

A woman film director said that living together can be nice if it's "as a partnership, not as ownership."

LOATHED

At the age of 86 she (Alice Roosevelt Longworth) revealed there were two things she loathed: Going to funerals and going to parties with anyone her own age.

— Myra MacPherson

LOOK

People hurried by me. Something in my face must have attracted them, because they glanced at me—that look men give to women, startled, recoiling a little as if looking into a beacon, too much unwanted light, and then going neutral again, very civilized.

— A character from The Goddess and Other Women
by Joyce Carol Oates

LOOKING BACK

I don't want to look back at my movies ... It's too soon. You just want to do things differently. It's a waste of energy. What you put down was right at the time.

— Doris Day

LOSING

After a surprisingly successful run at Wimbledon, was Andrea Jaeger, 15, downcast at losing? "Disappointed? Oh, no. If you get disappointed when you reach the quarter-finals and lose to someone who has won Wimbledon, what are you going to do if you lose to someone who is ranked No. 67?"

LOVE

My life has been saved by love.

— Virginia Graham

Love is the passport to a longer, happier life.

— Rosalind Russell

If love is the answer, could you rephrase the question?

— Lily Tomlin

French movie star Martine Carol once defined platonic love as, "The period between being introduced and the first wink."

I believe that exhibitionists are repressing feelings of shame ... For me, love needs mystery, secrecy, silence. It is a very private affair.

— Brigitte Bardot

I think it's very important for a woman today to know she's with a man
for the right reasons—not because, oh, ... I've got to get married; but
because I'm fulfilled in one area and not the other....
                                                            — *Sue Mengers*

Winners of the Honolulu-Star Bulletin "Love Is .." Contest: Under 10
years of age: "Love Is ... eating Mom's cooking even when it's yukkey";
10 to 18, "Love Is ... riding his skateboard home from a date"; 18 to 40,
"Love Is ... an occasional pat on the fanny."

LOVE AFFAIR

My first love affair led to marriage. It was ridiculous!
                                                       — *Hermione Gingold*

When the engagement of Queen Elizabeth was announced with much
fanfare, her sister Princess Margaret said: "Poor Lil! Nothing of your
own. Not even your own love affair."
                                                       — *Natalie Gittelson*

LOVE—FALLING IN

To fall in love is awfully simple, but to fall out of it is simply awful.
                                                          — *Bess Myerson*

                            Oops!
           I slipped on a piece of love
              and fell through the floor
                          of sanity.

                                                         — *Sue Hogshead*

Women don't want to fall in love with the tough hero, but rather with
the child in the man.
                                                          — *Bianca Jagger*

In Paris, when a girl does not know love by the time she is 20, it means
one of three things—she is not pretty, she has led a sheltered life or she
is a Communist.
                                                        — *Francoise Sagan*

We met at a party in Hoboken and George (Burns) has always said it
was a case of love at first sight, but it wasn't really. I'll admit we loved
Hoboken, but it wasn't the first time we'd seen it.
                                                           — *Gracie Allen*

It would be impossible to fall in love with someone who would want me to give up my career. What is love but an extreme case of like? And why would I even like a person who isn't interested in my fulfillment?

— Marlo Thomas

Behold before you a monster—Frankly, for the last few years I have fallen madly in love with myself. And I'm not quite sure, but it may be the best relationship I've ever had. Trying to be as objective as possible, I think the secret to my whole being is that what I am as a woman is what I hear in the actual sound of my voice.

— Leontyne Price

LOVE—FREE

I advocate free love in its highest, purest sense, as the only cure for the immorality, the deep damnation by which men corrupt and disfigure God's most holy institution of sexual relations. I have the inalienable constitutional right to love whom I may, to love as long or short a period as I can, to change that love every day if I please, and with that right neither you nor any law you can frame have a right to interfere.

— Victoria Woodhull, 1872

LOVE—MARRIAGE

But love is the dearest thing in life, and I'm a woman who lives for love and longs for marriage. When you're in love, you're living.

— Rita Hayworth

LOVEMAKING

… a woman who has just made love sparkles. I always sparkle …

— Zsa Zsa Gabor

I've given up on lovemaking. It's become a gymnastic exercise—and I've never been keen on sports.

— Germaine Greer

To help stimulate our love life, I put a mirror on our bedroom ceiling but it didn't work. Now my husband shaves in bed.

— Joan Rivers

One evening, when they were going out, Pierre (Curie) contemplated Marie's outlines with unusual attention—her free neck, her bare arms, so feminine and noble. A shadow of regret passed over the face of this man made stoop-shouldered by science. "It's a pity," he murmured. "Evening dress becomes you!" With a sigh, he added: "But there it is, we haven't got time."

— Eve Curie

LOVER

We've had 17 husbands among us. But my girls don't play around. They're old fashioned—they marry their lovers!

— Jolie Gabor

We have been so crippled by the American myth about machoism and strength, that many men can't function with the sensitivity and generosity that is needed to make a good lover.

— Jane Fonda

LUCKY

I am lucky and I believe in luck—it can't all be hard work or intelligence.

— Simone Signoret

(Because of her radio show Tallulah Bankhead could not get to the ballpark .. and was watching the game on television in her hotel suite) A waiter had come into the room just as the ball game took a favorable turn for the Giants. He did not get out again. "You're lucky! You're better than my rabbit's foot!" Tallulah yelled richly. She sat him on the piano bench and made him stay there until the game was over. Through no wish of his own he was a star-kissed influence. The Giants won.

— John Lardner

LUST

I told (Jimmy Carter) that if he is pressed to be more specific about his list of women he has lusted after in his heart, I would certainly appreciate being mentioned.

— Barabara Howar

MAIDEN

If all maidens stayed maidens there'd be nobody left.

– Malcolm Forbes

MAKEUP

I am absolutely in favor of women doing anything they can to bring out their good features, but when they paint each one a different color they bring them out so far that I for one would like to push them back in again.

– Elsie Janis

MALE

(On interviewing George Wallace) Unfortunately, like every other slick-tongued southern male bigot in my life, the Governor got the best of me and may again in the future. It was not that he backed me down or changed my mind; it was that I could not back HIM down or change HIS mind. When the happy day comes that I can convert the male symbol of my childhood, I will have arrived.

– Barbara Howar

MALE CHAUVINISM

I think that women should be abolished.

– Richard Burton

Actress Constance Towers: "If a man asks me to fix his breakfast, I'll do it; if he *demands* it, I won't do it."

Woman was made from man's ribs, which, as any butcher will tell you, isn't the best cut.

— Robert Orben

According to lecturer Suzy Sutton, male chauvinism started with Adam and Eve; after all, Adam asked Eve to sew the leaves, because "that was woman's work. That," said Mrs. Sutton, "was the first apron."

My idea of a real woman is someone who can make a young man feel mature, an old man youthful and a middle-aged man feel completely sure of himself. Unfortunately, I have never met her.

— Cary Grant

MALE CHAUVINIST PIG

(About Groucho Marx) He's a male chauvinist piglet.

— Betty Friedan

When Diane Nafranowicz was not allowed to enter the Iowa pork-cooking contest because it was to promote pork on the cookout grill by men, Ms. Nafranowicz indignantly changed the name of her entry. She said: "It was called cranberry stuffed pork but I'm changing the name to roast chauvinist pig."

MAN

All your life you wait around for some damn man.

— Dorothy Parker

I prefer an outdoor man with an indoor temperament.

— Ann Miller

The first thing I notice in a man is his eyes. If you're a phony, your eyes are the giveaway. I hate phonies, so I always look into a man's eyes.

— Lauren Bacall

I have to be with a man who is superior to me in every way, as Robert (Bolt, her husband) was. My dream is a man with no boundaries. It will never happen—unless I meet a madman.

— Sarah Miles

... you can't always gauge how conventional a man's heart is by the clothes he wears. Or his conversation. But the conventional idealist will always give himself away by his inability to let you be yourself. He simply can't resist attempting little surgical operations on your personality.

– Margaret Bourke-White

(In an article in *Forum*, Margaret Fishback wrote) The old Charlot's Revue ballad, so feelingly rendered by Beatrice Lillie, aptly expresses the feminine emotional viewpoint. It goes something like this:

Blue eyes don't fill me with dreams of delight,
Youth never thrilled me with love at first sight.
But he who'll enchant me from now till I die
Is he who can plant me a lovely black eye.
Oh! to be taken unawares,
And kicked down a
whole flight of stairs!

Chorus

I want a man to insult me,
To beat me, ill-treat me.
I want a man with some vim and some punch,
Who bruises me at breakfast, and lynches me at lunch.
I want a man who can wrestle,
As catch-as-catch-can as can be—
A regular smiter, a fighter, a biter,
Rough stuff ... that's me!

MANAGE

The silliest woman can manage a clever man, but it needs a very clever woman to manage a fool.

– Rudyard Kipling

Dorothy M. Simon, vice-president-research, AVCO: "Men tend to lead by asserting authority, but women manage through the participative mode, by helping people develop their capabilities and solve problems. Now men are beginning to do the same. In science and engineering you *have* to manage participatively because your staff knows more than you do."

MARCHING

Now we have women marching in the streets! If only things would quiet down!

– Arthur Burns

MARRIAGE

I walked out of my Daddy's arms into my husband's arms.
— Loretta Lynn

... if you work your marriage like you work your business, it will be a success.
— Pearl Nipon

I love marriage. A woman by herself is a perfectly asinine way to live.
— Bette Davis

(Marriage) ... is the supreme test, fantastic and beautiful ... A woman, I believe, is not put in the world to live alone.
— Brigitte Bardot

(On marriage) Neither of us is a dependent. I'm not his child and he's not my child ... though we both have childish moments.
— Suzanne Somers

Many a man who is in love with a dimple makes the mistake of marrying the whole girl.
— Stephen Leacock

I do not think that a home is necessary to happy marriage. All that is necessary is that a man and wife should be together.
— Audrey Hepburn

I don't believe there is such a thing as a marriage without its ugly, very ugly, aspects.
— Elizabeth Ashley

Nobody knows what anyone's marriage is like except the two of them—and sometimes one of them doesn't know.
— Ann Landers

Johnny Carson asked Betty White, "What advice would you give to a young couple contemplating marriage?" White answered, "Wait until you've lived together through at least one cold that each of you have had."

My generation, men and women now in their 40s and 50s, is the last one that fully, really believed in marriage. We may even have worshipped it to death. For the sorry truth is that we, the parents of the baby boom, are also the plaintiffs of the divorce boom.
— Shana Alexander

The wife of Marty Feldman, the British comedian-actor, is from a family of butchers. Feldman has said that "it was not the idea of their Catholic daughter marrying a Jew that shocked them. It was the idea that the daughter of a family of butchers was marrying a vegetarian ... I mean, how would a butcher understand a vegetarian?"

— Coleman McCarthy

I am no marital expert either but I have been through an experience that perturbs a large number of young married women today. I have had to plot, scratch and connive to hold a husband. I lost him once and got him back. Both of us have been sickened and frustrated many times by conflicting careers. And we had been married more than ten years before we finally managed to have our first child.

— Lucille Ball

Senior Editor Nan A. Talese, wife of Gay Talese: "The one most overwhelming surprise in my life was marriage. What I'd feared in marriage was being trapped. I thought I'd feel encumbered, suffer a loss of independence. But once the ceremony was over, I had the most amazing sense of freedom ... and I have it to this day. It is now nineteen years later, and I still have a sense of freedom in being married."

MARRIAGE—ANTI

Man: "You're a pretty girl. How come you're not married?" Woman: "Sheer luck."

There's something totally archaic about marriage. It's like being enclosed in a box.

— Jacqueline Bisset

Marriage is against nature because the person to love and to be loved by forever doesn't exist, unless you lie or you bend for convenience and hypocrisy and fear of loneliness.

— Oriana Fallaci

Marriage is a prison where the first prisoner is the woman ... Marriage is against nature because sentiments get worn down like hoes that continuously must be mended.

— Oriana Fallaci

But I don't believe in marriage or children. I have nothing to contribute as a wife or mother, and those labels would put me in a box and ruin a perfectly beautiful relationship.

— Jacqueline Bisset

MARRIAGE—ARRANGED

The (French) marriages were arranged by the parents, almost always. I think it worked as well, that system, as does the modern way of marrying for love. Love is so blind, you see. But the sharp eyes of a French mama and papa could be trusted to pick a good man, who could make a living. Love was supposed to come later. And sometimes it did. But if it did not there was no great tragedy, no scandal, no divorce. Sometimes both wives and husbands had sweethearts, but the sanctity of the home remained secure and love affairs on the side were only a matter of recourse.

– Lilly Daché

MARRIAGE—CONGENIALITY

To get a wife is easy enough, but to love her with constancy is difficult, and he who can do that may well be grateful to our Lord God. For the mere union of the flesh is not sufficient. There must be congeniality of tastes and character.

– Martin Luther

MARRIAGE CONTRACT

(About the courtship of Hetty Green) Edward A. Green had once been a poor boy in Bellows Falls, Vt., but subsequently made a fortune in the Philippines as an exporter. The story is told that Mr. Green, one Valentine's day, bought a valentine to send to his sweetheart, but by mistake addrest and sent her the wrong envelop—one that contained a receipted bill for a cheap suit of clothes. This, it was said, so strongly appealed to Mrs. Green's love of economy that from that time he was her accepted suitor. Before marrying, however, she insisted on Mr. Green's signing a contract by which he agreed that his wife's fortune should not be liable for his debts and that he should support her just the same as tho she were without wealth. This contract was ever strictly enforced.

– New York Sun

MARRIAGE—DIFFERENCES

Don't be alarmed if you differ about some things. Marriage is a partnership, not a merger of identities.

– Ruth Stafford Peale

MARRIAGE—ECONOMICS

The most popular labor-saving device in the world is still a husband with money.

— Phyllis George

My wife sure knows how to spend money ... She's extravagant. I mean, who tips at toll booths?

— Rodney Dangerfield

Custom decrees that a woman may not accept money from a man unless she's married to him, when it's a case of winner take all.

— Boston Globe

But mistress, know yourself. Down on your knees, And thank heaven, fasting, for a good man's love; For I must tell you friendly in your ear, Sell when you can!

— Character in As You Like It,
William Shakespeare

I don't need a man around the house to do chores, fix electrical outlets or the plumbing. I learned how to do all that myself. And I'm capable of supporting myself. I don't believe in marriage as a means of lifelong support.

— Jacqueline Bisset

MARRIAGE—FIGHTING

My wife (Elizabeth Taylor) and I have reached a state of detente. We have agreed to disagree.

— John Warner

(In response to his question, she asks a reporter if he's married ... he is) Then you don't have to ask me what a marriage is like. You know then that it's a combination of fightin' an' lovin'.

— Loretta Lynn

MARRIAGE—HOMEMAKER

Homemaker: "He gives the orders, but I'm the boss."

Ella Grasso: "I'm having trouble managing the (governor's) mansion. What I need is a wife."

I do not refer to myself as a "housewife" for the reason that I did not marry a house.

— Wilma Scott Heide

It's tough being a housewife. Want to goof off? There's no place to stay home from.

A homemaker to her analyst: "I've never told this to anyone before but I *like* being a housewife."

Writer John Gunther said that in North Africa, a lady married ten years, quarreled bitterly with her husband because he would not take another wife—a nice strong No. 2 wife who'd do the chores.

I think housewives are the world's best managers, and their jobs shouldn't be downgraded. In the course of the day a housewife really accomplishes an important feat: She takes care of the children, cooks, cleans, shops and sometimes even fixes the plumbing.

— Nancy Kissinger

When I first started to write about the homemaker, she was a stereotype in every sense of the word. She had no name; at her own suggestion she was called Justa Housewife. Everyone accepted that: "Do you work—or are you Justa Housewife?"

Justa was the proverbial bad driver; she was flat-chested and she never got Bill Holden in the end. She ironed towels, and in television commercials she discussed her irregularity with her next door neighbor. Her children came back from school each afternoon, looked her squarely in the face and asked, "Is there anyone home?" If she was aware of the irony, she never mentioned it.

— Erma Bombeck

MARRIAGE—HUSBAND

It is better for a woman to marry a man who loves her than a man she loves.

— Arabian Proverb

The best way to get most husbands to do something is to suggest that perhaps they're too old to do it!

— Anne Bancroft

And then there was the mother who advised her daughter not to look for "Mister Right." "Look for Doctor Right," she admonished.

Why does a woman work 10 years to change a man's habits and then complain he's not the man she married?

— Barbra Streisand

Though supportive, Denis Thatcher, the husband of England's Prime Minister, Margaret Thatcher, likes to refer to himself as "the most shadowy husband of all time."

A wife was asked whether her busy husband believed in life after death. "I don't know," she replied, "but as far as I can tell, he doesn't believe in life after dinner!"

I'm caught in the trap of feeling that a man should be above the woman. In my case, I want James's (her husband's) career to be a teeny bit better than mine.

— Carly Simon

I think that if a woman has 50 years of her life to give to marriage, she would be much better off having 5 husbands—each for 10 years—than one for 50 years.

— Ingrid Bergman

(When someone remarked to her about her being 15 years older than her husband Max Mallowan, the archaeologist) That's the wonderful thing about being married to an archaeologist; the older I get, the more interesting I am to him!

— Agatha Christie

An old maid was anxious to find a husband, so she went into the woods to pray about it. Suddenly she heard a voice from the tree tops say: "Whoo! Whoo!" She replied, "Anybody, Lord, Anybody."

They (suavely sophisticated men) lack perhaps the most important ingredient that any woman needs in a husband. That is a *boy* quality. This boyishness is an outreaching for human help. It gives the wife the feeling of basic usefulness. It is where *our* ego comes in.

— Rosalind Russell

MARRIAGE—HUSBAND (APPROVAL OF)

(Talking about marrying her husband Pat Boone) He wasn't always a 10.

— Shirley Boone

(About her husband Prince Albert) At last, I have found someone I can really trust.

— *Princess Grace of Monaco*

(One girl to another) I see lots of men every day who would make wonderful husbands. Trouble is, they already are.

Carl (her husband) works the farm, he does contracting and sells real estate. He wants to be an ordinary person, and he is, in an extraordinary way.

— *Dolly Parton*

A wife we interviewed says, "A husband is the person who changes 'I' into 'we,' 'me' into 'us,' and living into loving.

— *Richard and Helen Exley*

MARRIAGE—INTERRACIAL

It's not that you just have to be with a black woman if you're a black man, or white woman, white man, it's whoever you enjoy being with as people. If you're not right for that man, whatever color, you're just not going to be with him anyhow. I don't think there should be any separation whatever. Then, that's what the world's trying to get at, isn't it? Aren't we trying to blend and mix together as one, as God's children?

— *Diana Ross*

MARRIAGE—LASTING

It used to be when we said, " 'til death do us part," death parted us pretty soon. That's why marriages used to last forever. Everybody was dead.

— *Margaret Mead*

Chains do not hold a marriage together. It is threads, tiny threads, which sew people together through the years. That is what makes a marriage last—more than passion or sex. It is the threads.... But those threads should never become chains.

— *Simone Signoret*

MARRIAGE—MULTI

Marriage is too interesting an experience to be tried only once or twice.

— *Eva Gabor*

MARRIAGE—PARTNERSHIP

Gloria Steinem, speaking in Houston, Texas: "... for the sake of those who wish to live in equal partnership, we have to abolish and reform the institution of legal marriage."

There is no possible doubt of the basic fact that marriage, today more than ever, must be a partnership. And what sort of partnership can exist where one of the members has not the least idea whether the business is running at immense profit, or total loss; where not one detail is discussed, where no judgment is asked, where no say in any decision is permitted? Every day, certain men in seemingly modest circumstances die, leaving their widows in utterly untrained control of millions; while others, who have sheltered their wives behind every protecting luxury, leave them to the equally unprepared necessity of earning their daily bread. I can name a number of the first, and a score of the latter, among my personal friends. And I confess that the latter have achieved a distinctly better average of success than the first.

— Emily Post

MARRIAGE PLUS CAREER

The juggling act is a gender-specific hype: it is meant to occupy and silence the New Woman, that colossal complainer with her trouble-making Movement. And the New Man isn't standing in her way: Let's give her what she wants. Let her do it all. Why not?

— Letty Cottin Pogrebin

Debbie Reynolds (asked if she thought a career could be successully combined with marriage) "Every case is different but I feel that a marriage and a career can work out as long as the woman's career does not interfere with her marriage. The first and most important thing is that the marriage be a happy one and if the career does interfere then you should try to work out whatever problems are in the way. If it means giving up the career—if it's that much of a problem—then it should be given up."

MARRIAGE—ROLES
Ike fights the wars; I turn the lamb chops.

— Mamie Eisenhower

It's a good marriage if he makes the living and she makes the living worthwhile.

Don't let anybody tell you that marriage is a two-way street. Marriage is a one-way street, and it better be his.

— Eileen Ford

I believe the male should rule the roost. I like my man to be captain of the home ship. But I feel the harmony in the home is the woman's responsibility.

— Julie London

In marriage there is assumed superiority on the part of the husband, and admitted inferiority with a promise of obedience on the part of the wife. This subject calls loudly for examination in order that the wrong may be redressed. Customs suited to darker ages in Eastern countries are not binding upon enlightened society.

— Lucretia Mott, (1849)

MARRIAGE—RULES AND RECIPES

One wife's recipe for staying successfully married: "Don't 'keep book' on your husband."

I have nothing against marriage, but I do if it's a rule, like you simply have to be mated up.

— Marlo Thomas

Remember to respect his work. When you marry a man, you also marry his job.

— Ruth Stafford Peale

Use your talents. If you can design, decorate, write, cook or whatever, use that talent. It will expand your marriage.

— Ruth Stafford Peale

Dr. Herbert Spaugh's wife gave him framed rules for marriage he has passed on to others during his long-term career as minister and counselor. Advice to wives:

"When you marry him, love him. After you marry him, study him. If he is secretive, trust him. If he is sad, cheer him. When he is talkative, listen to him. When he is quarrelsome, ignore him. If he is jealous, cure him. If he cares naught for pleasure, coax him. If he favors society, accompany him. When he deserves it, kiss him. Let him think how well you understand him. But never let him know that you manage him."

MARRIAGE—SUCCESSFUL

(About his wife Clementine) It would have been impossible for any ordinary man to have got through what I have had to get through, in peace and war, without her devoted aid.

— Sir Winston Churchill

My marriage was the most fortunate and joyous event which happened to me in the whole of my life, for what can be more glorious than to be united in one's walk through life with a being incapable of an ignoble thought.

— Sir Winston Churchill

People are always asking couples whose marriage has endured at least a quarter of a century for their secret for success. Actually, it is no secret at all. I am a forgiving woman. Long ago, I forgave my husband for not being Paul Newman.

— Erma Bombeck

To love and cherish a man as long as life lasts, this is the great soul-satisfying role of a wife. And never make the mistake of thinking it a secondary role. Where the ship of matrimony is concerned your husband may be the engine, but you are the rudder, and it's the rudder that determines where the ship will go.

— Ruth Stafford Peale

What surprises me in life are not the marriages that fail but the marriages that succeed. Individuals are so different. We all have different goals, needs, environments, memories. I'm inclined to believe in people—sometimes that has proven a mistake, there are men who capitalize on that. But the mistake stems from the fact that I'm in love with life. I always will be.

— Rita Hayworth

MARRIAGE—WIDOW

(About Mary Hemingway, Ernest's widow) The earthly Muses of literary men tend to follow a certain succession. The first wife gets to bear the babies. The next wife or two come in on the money and the fame. The poor last wife is left to serve as practical nurse to the Great Man's aches and pains and, as widow, play keeper to his flame.

— Melvin Maddocks

A woman said she married a man 10 years her junior because: "Younger men don't leave widows."

Statistics show that older men tend to have living wives; most older women are widows.

Nobody wants to sit around with someone who sheds tears over a lost life ... people like to be with people who make them laugh.
                                                                    — Sylvia Porter

(After her husband's death) My great advantage was my career—it was there to protect me like a wonderful life preserver keeping me on top of it all, keeping me from sinking. A career is a good tranquilizer for the spirit when a woman is alone. I've seen other women without the advantage of a job or a career, who have chosen the more obvious tranquilizers, like the bottle or the bridge table.
                                                                    — Helen Hayes

MARRIAGE—WIFE

Take my wife ... please!
                                                                    — Henny Youngman

Better be happy old maids than unhappy wives.
                                                    — Mrs. March in Little Women
                                                                    by Louisa May Alcott
She (Gloria Vanderbilt) invariably refers to her childhood friend, Oona O'Neill Chaplin ... as an example of "the perfect Arab wife."
                                                                    — Laura Bergquist

When Sir Noel Bowater was London's Lord Mayor he said: "The happiest wife is not the one who marries the best man. She is the one who makes the best man out of the one she married."

Women's natural role is to be a pillar of the family. It's their psychological job. Women only want to work to get off the hook and avoid their responsibilities.
                                                                    — Princess Grace of Monaco

Newspaper columnist Kays Gary: "Surely there is a better way, a way better than roses or poems, for a man to say that in his deepest oafish heart his wife is, in every way, the reality of impossible beautiful dreams."

He (Emerson) was content to devote himself to his writing and to his bride. As they became better acquainted, he began to call her "Mine

Asia" and "Queenie." Her native wisdom, serene and gently uttered, sometimes astonished him. "I, as always," he wrote, "venerate the oracular nature of woman. The sentiment which a man thinks he came unto gradually through the events of years, to his surprise he finds woman dwelling there in the same, as her native home."

— Phillips Russell

Yoko's first marriage (before she married "Beatle" John Lennon) immersed her in a different sort of situation, hardly less frustrating. "It was hard to make people understand that I was an artist too," she says. "My husband was famous in his own circle, around Juilliard and John Cage and those people. He was just a very nice and well-balanced guy who was taking prizes every year, like the Copland prize. I was having affairs and things like that to compensate, so our relationship deteriorated."

Yoko began to think that she was taking intolerable advantage of her husband. "In New York," she says, "I was always having abortions. I was too neurotic to take precautions. I was always having trouble, messed up, always having abortions. I would go out and have an affair and come back, and oh, I'm in a mess, and my first husband was very kind." Finally she told him, "Why don't you go back to Japan and make it on your own because I'm being such a bad strong wife to you?" He did go, and he did make it. Yoko still thinks the decision was a good one.

— Charles McCarry

MARRIAGE—WIFE (SECOND)

The second marriage when the first marriage was not happy must be a great thing. You can do all the things your poor husband had been deprived of, and you can really glory in being bigger and better every day of your life. However, if the first marriage has been a very happy one, then it is not that easy.

— Maria Von Trapp

MARRIAGE—WIFE SUPPORTED

On being asked if he didn't want to talk about how he made his living—after Lillie, his wife, was made an honorary member of the Society of Industrial Engineers—Frank Gilbreth said: "Well, from now on I'm going to make it from the sweat of my frau."

MARRIAGE—WIVES' UNION

According to writer Nanette Kutner, a family friend said of Mamie Eisenhower's refusal to tolerate anyone's straying husband, "Bless her, she's a charter member of the wives' union."

MARRY

Every man should marry—and no woman.

When asked if her brother actor/director Warren Beatty ever will marry, actress Shirley MacLaine replied: "I doubt it. Warren likes to do his own shirts."

MASTER

If you survive, you become a legend. I'm a legend because I've survived over a long period of time. I'm revered rather like an old building. And I still seem to be the master of my fate. I'm still paddling the boat myself, you know. I'm not sitting being paddled by anybody. Now, it may just be a canoe, but nevertheless I'm paddling it.

— Katharine Hepburn

Throughout history, females have picked providers for mates. Males pick anything.

— Margaret Mead

MATHEMATICS

Marcel Achard, distinguished French playwright: "Women have a passion for mathematics: They divide their age by half, double the price of their clothes and always add at least five years to the age of their best friend."

ME

I don't pretend I'm something I'm not. Even when I danced with John Denver on television—he wore safety shoes—I was me.

— Erma Bombeck

The first thing people always think when they meet me is that I'm much smaller than they had thought ... I don't get indignant when people say they think I'm cute. I accept it. Every actor has a different package. Some are too short, others are too tall. And I long ago decided that I was going to be the best me I could be.

– Sally Field

MEDIA

Elizabeth Ashley refers to women media reporters as "mediaettes."

There's the saying in (covering) news, if you take too long a breath, people will get there before you.

– Barbara Walters

(After making a book promotional tour and talking to the media) Media is my new ... sort of pet hate.

– Elizabeth Ashley

(To a newspaper reporter who criticized her for her lack of cooperation in being interviewed) You're getting paid for this—I'm not.

– Althea Gibson

(About what she learned from the more aggressive women reporters) They taught me that you have to be opinionated ... even if you don't have an opinion.

– Phyllis George

Helen Thomas, who as a United Press International member covered many news conferences with presidents, was the first woman to end a presidential news conference with the traditional closing, when she told then President Kennedy, "Thank you Mr. President."

My general conclusion after thirty years in journalism is that women (TV journalists) are no worse than men ... There are fewer klunkers among the women because, until recently, it's been harder for them to get where they've got.

– Harry Reasoner

MEDICINE

(After her son, Jimmy Carter, took medical doctors to task for high fees) If I get pregnant again, I'm going to have a midwife.

– Miz Lillian Carter

MEETING

A woman executive, a former teacher, addressing a trade meeting: "Good morning, gentlemen. Now, before I get into my talk on tips for purchasing heavy machinery, I'd like you to all sit up straight, button your coats, straighten those papers in front of you—and no gum chewing!"

(Mme. Francoise Giroud, France's first and only Minister of Women's Affairs): One morning during the course of a cabinet meeting, she passed a note to Mme. Saunier-Seite, the state secretary for universities. "Did you, Dear Alice," the note read, "imagine cabinet meetings could be so boring?" Mme. Saunier-Seite wrote back: "Yes, Dear Francoise, because I've always observed the inexplicable childishness of men."

MEMORIES

Memories are everyone's second chance at happiness.
                        — *Britain's Queen Elizabeth, the Queen Mother*

MEMORY

A computer hath no memory like a wife.

                                                          — *Art Buchwald*

A generous gentleman donated a new loudspeaker to church in fond memory of his wife.

                                                      — *V.F.W. Magazine*

I was early persuaded that a good memory was essential to success and accomplishment whether in the White House, the laboratory, the courtroom, house and garden, aviation, navigation, writing poetry, Wall Street bulls and bears, or quarterbacking the Stanford Indians. From Plato to Johnny Carson no man could be tops in his field without it.
                                                  — *Adela Rogers St. Johns*

MEN

I like difficult men.

                                                      — *Lauren Bacall*

Men are the funniest things since silly putty.

— Florence King

Men are the same wherever you go—attractive.

— Eva Gabor

The men in my life are the men who in some sense I wanted to be.

— Elizabeth Ashley

(About men) I don't have any list of the top ten.

— Elizabeth Ashley

Women who spend their entire lives pleasing men, end up hating themselves.

— Mae West

Every woman wants a man in her corner. That's so common it ought to be written on the bathroom wall.

— Barbara Howar

Through celebrated, at times, and respected, the men I knew weren't very worthy, and the day always came when I proved to have more balls than they.

— Oriana Fallaci

Mae West philosophied in the movie "She Done Him Wrong," "It ain't the men in your life that counts, it's the life in your men."

American women like a man who's hard to get. A man who's all over you, who wants him? And then when you get them, you don't know what the hell to do with them.

— Zsa Zsa Gabor

Once, I seemed to spend all my time around men of great affluence. Then I went into my poor period, when I was with men who were seekers after truth—usually in shabby coffee bars. Now, I realize a man can be a seeker after truth and own a jet plane as well.

— Dyan Cannon

All at once men have become the salted peanuts of the social sciences. While academics are emerging with studies of them, news magazines discuss their predicament in cover stories, and now along comes a book by a hardcore feminist psychologist who explains that not ideology, not psycholanalysis, not Marxism, not Existentialism, or even feminism, could sufficiently answer her questions about men's psychological nature—so she wrote a book to try to understand them.

— Gail Sheehy

MEN—APPEARANCE

(On moving from California to New York) I like 'em (men) in ties and three-piece suits.

— Linda Ronstadt

I'm a sucker for men's looks. When I'm playing, I concentrate. But when I'm practicing, I check out the guys.

— Nancy Lopez-Melton

MEN—OLDER

In this wild century that has taken us by the shoulders and shaken us in myriad directions, these men (born at the turn of the century) still follow through, giving what they have..... They conform only to something inside themselves. And with all this, they remain men; they never appear to be anything more than human beings. I don't know what magic potion was brewed up at the turn of the century, but I wish there were some left so the young men of today could have a little sip.

— Lauren Bacall

MEN—TREATMENT OF WOMEN

The most sympathetic of men never fully comprehend woman's concrete situation.

— Simone de Beauvoir

You've got your two basic types of men: the kind that pretend a woman is a little girl and the kind that like to think she's their mother.

— Harold Robbins

All men are the same, whether they are French, English, Italian, American. There is no difference—just that some think they can conquer a woman quickly, and others like to woo her slowly.

— Gina Lollobrigida

Business vice-president Margot Sherman: "In all institutions, there are men who are insecure around women. They have been brought up to think of women as wives and nurturers, and when they look upon women who want executive jobs, they get afraid. I worked with terribly secure men. All they wanted were ideas, and ideas have no gender."

MIDDLE AGE

The really frightening thing about middle age is the knowledge that you'll outgrow it.

– Doris Day

Noting that the child-bearing years were a block to creativity, Margaret Mead once observed, "Menopause relieves so much anxiety."

MILITARY

The first time I came into close contact with women in the military, not counting nurses, was in Texas in World War II.

... Social contact with the WAC officer candidates was what you might call potluck. You would go into one of the dormitories and say to the non-com on duty in the gathering room, "Anybody loose?" ... The one I wound up with was in fine shape. As soon as we got in the car she flexed her bicep and said, "Feel." I had to admit it was hard as a rock.

While I was still buttering my potato, she went through one of those monstrous steaks they serve in Texas. I asked if she wanted another one and she said, no, they had eaten supper before we arrived.

We had some rotgut called "Singing Sam" that you could cut with about five parts of water and squeeze in half a dozen lemons and it still felt like an iron claw trying to tear out your throat. My date drank it straight from the bottle, chasing it with a cigarette, not even catching her breath.

During the evening she pinned me four out of four falls. We were parked near the football field and I was tuckered out from arm wrestling, having lost every matchup. She wanted to go down to the track and run me a fast 880.

– Jim Shumaker

MIND—NARROW

She's got such a narrow mind, when she walks fast, her earrings bang together!

– John Cantu

MINISTER'S CHILD

It's like being raised in the diplomatic corps.

– Joan Mondale

MIRROR

They don't make mirrors like they used to. I can remember when I used to look in a mirror and I looked almost like a schoolgirl. Those were the days when they knew how to make mirrors.

— Jane Ace

MODEL

"My biggest years?" asked the model, "My lean years."

Top fashion model Charlotte Payne said: "To be successful you need a streak of iron, the hide of an elephant, the endurance of a plow horse, and the ego of a peacock."

Grace Downs who ran a school for models and air hostesses in New York: "Everything a fashion model shows belongs to the manufacturer. Everything an artist's model shows belongs to her."

Why have I become so popular after all these years? I don't know. I think because I've become more Japanese than ever. Japanese women used to model themselves after foreign women. Now I remain Japanese, and the French women model themselves after me.

— Sayoko

Modeling's a no-nonsense, no-excuse business and a girl must be willing to devote her life to it. Models today are really dead serious about their work. The girl 20 or 30 years ago had a different mentality. She saw herself as a glamorous woman. It's hard to find models who think that way today—business is on their mind. There's a lot at stake and the dollars are big.

— Eileen Ford

You know I'm our fitting model. I know this sounds strange because I am not very tall, but I guess I'm like rubber. I pull myself in ... and up ... and suddenly I'm five-feet-eight. Interestingly enough, every model on Seventh Avenue fits into the same clothes. When I put something on, if it feels good, I know it's a winner. If it doesn't feel good, it doesn't make the line. I believe that one of the most important things for today's woman is to feel comfortable as well as pretty.

— Pearl Nipon

MODESTY

Persons who use their brains, tongues and pens for the improvement of their kind are those of whom biographies may profitably be written. The grand things their tongues and pens have said are accessible and form a living inspiration to others, but I,—I know nothing remarkable I have done. The humdrum work of my everyday life seems to me quite without incident.

— Clara Barton

MONEY

Woman executive: "All work and no play makes jack."

Writer Aline Thompson: "I'm not one to make a dollar go a long way, but I sure can make it go fast."

I cannot permit money to disrupt my life or interfere with my happiness.

— Joan Baez

There may be wonder in money, but, dear God, there is money in wonder.

— From National Velvet
by Enid Bagnold

(To columnist Earl Wilson) Maybe you can't take it with you, but where can you go without it?

— Pearl Bailey

For myself, I loathe money. It's really terribly boring. But it's even more boring to have none.

— Barbara Cartland

I won't say my previous husbands thought only of my money, but it had a certain fascination for them.

— Barbara Hutton

I could write my own check, but I like him (her husband) to give it to me. Money is sexy.

— Helen Gurley Brown

Ivy Baker Priest, former Treasurer of the U.S., commenting on not having her picture on paper money: "We women don't care too much

about getting our pictures on money as long as we can get our hands on
it."

From birth to age eighteen, a girl needs good parents. From eighteen to
thirty-five, she needs good looks. From thirty-five to fifty-five, she needs
a good personality. From fifty-five on, she needs cash.

– Sophie Tucker

The cream of the joke is, that we made our own money ourselves, and no
one gave us a blessed penny. That does soothe my rumpled soul so much
that the glory is not worth thinking of.

– Louisa May Alcott

MONEY—COUNTERFEIT

One day, miser Hetty Green (who when she died, left her two children
an estate valued at over 100 million dollars) boarded a street car in New
York and gave the motorman a fifty-cent piece. He realized it was
counterfeit and returned it. Green, who had no other money in her
purse, was vouched for by another rider. Later, she went to the office of
the trolley car company, plunked down a nickel, kept her finder on it till
she received a receipt ... and about this same time loaned the City of
New York $4,500,000.

– Richard McKetchum

MONEY—MANAGEMENT

While there are exceptions to the general rule, this business of keeping
an eye on the dollar, putting it through its paces and never letting go of
it till we've got a hundred cents' worth in return isn't up to Ferdie and
Fred. It's the job allotted to Mary Elizabeth and Irene. The man earns,
the woman spends—for the family, for herself and, much more frequently than most business executives seem to think, for her husband
as well. Yet nothing in her formal education has ever prepared the
blushing bride to make those wily little bits of green paper jump
through the hoops of married life. Which is one reason—perhaps the
biggest and gravest—why the hoops get smashed, up to and including
the little hoop of gold or platinum that adorns the fourth finger.

– Betty Thornley Stuart,

MONOGAMOUS

I'm monogamous. The only time I ever fooled around was when I was married, and I wasn't happy.

— Barbara Howar

MONTH

During the month of July, the WNET series, "Great Performances," celebrated a month of great women. During the month, they featured fine programs by strong, unusual women. However, August was not named "Month of the Man," because, said feminists, ordinarily every month is.

MOON

Two frog sisters jumped on the moon's forehead. They spoiled his looks forever.

— North American Indian tale

Boy Moon was so fond of his mother, the Sun, that he followed her constantly across the sky. Sun Mother did not like this. Once, while washing the dishes, she became so annoyed that she threw a dirty discloth in his face. The stains it made on Boy Moon's face remain.

— Turkish Tale

MORALITY

I'm simply not going to play a part in anything which offends my sense of morality. If I've learned any one lesson from life, it's this: If you don't stand for something, you will stand for anything.

— Ginger Rogers

No, my dear sir, do not make the mistake of thinking woman is going to bring herself down to man's level of immorality; instead, she is slowly but surely bringing him up to her standard.

— Ella Wheeler Wilcox

MOTHER

I do wonder how old I'll be when it no longer matters what Mother says.

— Farrah Fawcett

I like my mother a lot; it's unusual these days.

— Madeline Kahn

The only mothers it is safe to forget on Mother's Day are the good ones.
— Mignon McLaughlin

The mother's heart is the child's schoolroom.

— Henry Ward Beecher

It is not in the nature of the mother's back to let the baby fall.
— African proverb

The most important thing a father can do for his kids is to love their mother.

— Kirk Douglas

She never quite leaves her children at home, even when she doesn't take them along.

— Margaret Culkin Banning

(About her daughter Caroline) I hope we have love and respect for one another, and I think we are friendly enough that we can discuss almost anything, but your mother's not going to be your best pal.
— Princess Grace of Monaco

I think of my marriage and family as my number one career. When I fill out applications, I put down "mother" as my occupation. I feel it's as rewarding for most women as it is for me.

— Phyllis Schlafly

There were times when I hated the role of "mama," but I couldn't admit that to myself. Now, when I wake up and realize I don't feel like being "mama," I yell down the hall, "Hey, kids! Your ma is checking out and Rosemary is checking in—and she expects to be treated like a guest." I've learned it's okay to be a person first.

— Rosemary Clooney

MOTHER-IN-LAW (PROSPECTIVE)

A young couple, university students, were overheard talking about their relationship. "I don't mind having your mother live with us," the fellow was saying. "But I do wish she'd wait until we get married."
— Lufkin Industries ROUNDUP

MOTHER—JOB DESCRIPTION

What is a mother's job description any way?

A mother is a person who can carry a caterpillar in her pocket all the way home from the church picnic and then forget about it until her blouse gets laundered. Then she goes out in the yard even after dark to find another worm and helps poke holes in a jar with an ice pick.

(A mother is a person) who thinks the girls who go after her son are forward and the ones that don't are stupid.

She takes out the garbage, feeds the fish, sets the table, makes the beds, picks up the toys under the bed even when it's not her turn and doesn't always deduct it from the allowances like she said she would.

She sometimes threatens to wring necks or cut out tongues, to change her name from "MOM" to Zelda or Tallulah, or to take the fastest slow boat to China ... but, she never does.

She's all bark and no bite. Her hard head is only a heartbeat away from her soft lap. And, she's never too tired or cross or sleepy or preoccupied to stop by each bed at night and smile and be grateful, to pull up the covers and stoop over to give a kiss.

– Ina Hughs

MOTHER—STAGE

Stage mother: "I don't push my daughter—she pulls me."

Mr. Disney was there all the time, supervising everything. He wouldn't allow any mothers on the set, and that was wise. He very shrewdly built a special room for mothers to wait in.

– Annette Funicello

(After one of his stage performances) I shook her. "Mama, it's me, Milton. Tell me what happened."

I held her until her breathing slowed a little. "All right, you can let go now. I was sitting next to that guy, and I felt a hand on my knee. I push his hand away, and it's right back. Then he starts to feel the side of my leg and he tried to put his hands under my dress! No matter what I did, he was there with the hands, right from the beginning of the show all the way through!"

It didn't make sense to me. "Mama, I'm on for fifty minutes. When did this happen?"

"When you first came on—while you were doing your opening monologue."

I asked, "Why did you wait for forty-five minutes?"

Mama said the classic line: "I didn't want to miss a cue!"

— Milton Berle

MOTHERHOOD

Motherhood, no matter how joyously undertaken, can no longer give woman justification in society for most of the years in her life.

— Betty Friedan

(Motherhood is) the greatest role a woman can have. Some people find it rather dull but I think it's quite challenging to think that you have this precious little baby and what you say is going to influence him for the rest of his life and for eternity, and he in his turn is going to influence other people.

— Rose Kennedy

MOUNTAINS

Charlotte Observer columnist Harriet Doar: "We got lost looking for Tater Hill, but it doesn't matter if you get lost in the mountains. You just discover a new range of views. The mountains are a midsummer dream of flowering banks and green depths, and any place is the right place for creative loafing."

MOVE

The time has come when women must no longer be armchair citizens, sitting back and criticizing all those individuals who are trying in some desperate fashion to make the dream come true. I think it is time for women to really move out in this country.

— Shirley Chisholm

MOVIES

Movies are still a man's medium. But I'm happy to support any man.

— Angie Dickinson

... most of us would like to see a good movie, but there are so many "super-films" it's hard to find a good movie.

— Elsie Janis

They've made everybody like the girl next door. And you're not going to the movies to see the girl next door—if you can go next door.

— Joan Bennett

MS

The expression Ms. really means misery.

— Phyllis Schlafly

MUSIC

And my music doesn't come and go with elation or sorrow; it is always there, faithful in its way, as an old lover or an overnight guest. It can take care of itself, with a little help from its friends.

— Judy Collins

Piano Virtuoso Walter Rommel: "When I saw her (Queen Elizabeth of Belgium) a few days ago, her right hand was in a bandage and it required great art to kiss the royal hand. 'I have just strained my thumb by practicing too energetically; I now have to remain six weeks without playing.' She continued modestly, 'It is too bad as I wanted to play some sonatas with you and thought you would find my playing improved.'"

More than any other art, music is appreciated by the uneducated, for almost everyone has an acute sense of the beauty of melody and harmony. Music was never meant for the educated alone; its most direct appeal is not to ideas but to human emotions. Music does not incite to argument or even to a desire for learning it; it awakens a desire to receive, to follow, to obey. The strains of a country's national hymn do not offer an elaborate definition of patriotism—but they quicken the heartbeat of every patriot to deeds of daring.

— Evangeline Booth

MUSIC—DIRECTOR

(After being invited to exchange podiums with a Soviet woman orchestra leader) I'm a conductor, not a woman conductor.

— Sarah Caldwell

MUSIC—ROCK

Actress Yvette Mimieux once owned and ran a school called Ye Olde Rocke Conservatore in Hollywood Hills—which she explained was the Juilliard School of rock music.

MYSTERY

Like sex itself, nudity is more exciting, more turning-on, when there is mystery and illusion.

— Sally Rand

Years after her prime, Mary Pickford fans were still saying: "We loved you, Mary Pickford." It made her feel marvelous. "After all these years!" she said. "And I'll tell you why. I'm still a mystery to them. I never let the public in. If you do magic, don't tell how the trick was done. The role of a star is never to reveal yourself."

— Gene Shalit

(When an interviewer commented that in her books she gave her readers both hope and despair, anger and love) I guess, I must stay faithful to art. I get in my little canoe and paddle out to the edge of mystery; it is unfortunately true that words fail, reason fails; and all I can do is to create a world which by its internal coherence makes a degree of sense. I can either do that or hush. And then I learn to make statements about that world, to furrow deeper into mystery.

Every single thing I follow takes me there, to the edge of a cliff. As soon as I start writing, I'm hanging over the cliff again. You can make a perfectly coherent world at the snap of a finger—but only if you don't bother being honest about it.

— Annie Dillard

NAME

Picasso and Le Corbusier selected their mother's maiden names for professional use. (Their last names were "Ruiz" and "Jeanneret.")

It's a terrible name, but I look exactly like an Erma. The only other thing Mother could possibly have called me would have been Iodine.
— Erma Bombeck

New York City Council President, Carol Bellamy, taking a telephone call, replied to the greeting she received, "Call me 'Carol' do not call me 'dear.'"

Her name used to be Margot, but Margaux Hemingway explains: "... I found out from my parents that I was conceived on a bottle of Château Margaux, a good French wine, so I decided to change my name."

When Emerson married his second wife, he asked her to change her name from Lydia to Lydian. His reason? So that a consonant would come between the vowels *a* and *e* when she took his name. She agreed to his request and immediately became "Lydian Emerson."

Sarah Caldwell, Boston muscial director, *not* an avid woman's libber, was in a photographer's studio in the Big Apple when Gloria Steinem came in and asked, "Where's the john?" Caldwell replied, "When are you going to start calling it the Mary?"

By naming their daughter Molly Miranda Jong-Fast, feminist writer Erica Jong and her husband, Jonathan Fast, felt that she has many options for the future. Jong-Fast explained: "... (she) can call herself

Molly Fast if she becomes an atomic scientist, Miranda Fast if an actress or, say, M.M. Jong-Fast if she opts for mystery writing."

NATION

Happy nations and honest women have no story.

— French Proverb

There is a pervasive desire among Americans to lead a useful life, to correct the defects in our society and make our nation greater than it already is.

— Rosalynn Carter

By permitting activities subversive to democratic ideals that nation denies to itself the right of self-defense, while those who think that chaos lends charm to democracy deny to democracy the right of self-preservation.

— Madame Chiang Kai-Shek

NATURE

Because I, too, am a woman. I must pause to marvel at you. You're the life force that makes the world what it is. And me what I am. Nature. You're a free spirit man has yet to conquer. I have never seen you, but I see you. When I look up at the sky. When I walk in the rain. When I hold a newborn baby. The world is your offspring. And I am one of them. For I am nature's child. As a woman, I am one with nature.

— Redken Ad

NEIGHBOR

The morning we moved into a tract house in a subdivision, I opened the door and there was this lady, standing there with a coffeepot. "Hi," she said. "I'm your neighbor and we have coffee klatches every morning." God! I just panicked. I thought, This is what my whole life is going to be—and I knew I couldn't stay in that marriage. I knew I had to have more.

— Suzanne Somers

NEUROTIC

All the most successful people seem to be neurotic these days. Perhaps we should stop being sorry for them and start being sorry for me—for being so confounded normal.

— Deborah Kerr

NEW YEAR'S RESOLUTION

I'm going to give up cursing. I don't curse so I'll be able to feel virtuous all year.

— Joyce Brothers

I'm going to give up skydiving and mustard shakes. Most resolutions should be taken with a grain of salt and two aspirins.

— Phyllis Diller

I resolve never to sleep in the Lincoln Bed again when I visit the White House. It's too hard.

— Miz Lillian Carter

It takes so much work and so many years to get your life the way you want it, you don't change it for anyone's little old new year.

— Carol Channing

I don't need to make resolutions—I'm already the best. But when the boys get ready to break their resolutions, have them come up and see me sometime.

— Mae West

Helen Gurley Brown, editor of *Cosmopolitan*, said her New Year's resolutions were, as usual, to improve her posture and "not fuss with busy making chores (that somebody *else* can do)" while postponing the more difficult things.

NEW YORK PUBLIC LIBRARY

In explaining why he couldn't work at the New York Public Library, a writer said: "Too many old women are rustling paper bags."

NEWS

Dead news like dead love has no phoenix in its ashes.

— Enid Bagnold

Margaret Sanger's mother used to say a decent woman only had her name in the newspapers three times during her life—when she was born, when she married, and when she died.

To you people who say there is never any good news in the papers, I have an answer: You are very astute readers. There is no doubt that the handbasket we are riding in is burning rubber and screeching around corners on its way to the fire and brimstone. The head of the family is now the color TV. If you ask a 10th grade kid to count his feet, he has to get out his pocket calculator. The dollar (if it is shiny enough and silver) is now inflated several thousand percent in a hundred years. We turn to the funny papers for solace. And what do we get? Aha. Here is the evil doctor about to murder Eve Jones ... Oh no! He is thwarted! And that glow we got from burning the Sunday funnies in disgust was not warmth, we read later, when our vision cleared, but lead poisoning.

– Dot Jackson

NICE GIRL

The line "nice guys finish last" is bitter but it reflects some truth: nice guys or girls never dazzle, astonish, revolutionize, go further, fly. They are never stars. Niceness plods, works hard, covers every inch of the ground, takes no chances, plays it safe and by the rules and finishes second. (Come to think of it, second place is probably the nice-girl object: It's so much *nicer* than first.)

– Amy Gross

NIGHT CLUB

Helen Traubel, when she began playing night clubs, often told night club audiences that she greatly enjoyed "being in the saloon business."

NIGHT PERSON

Imee Marcos, daughter of Ferdinand and Imelda Marcos of the Philippines: "Like most theater people, I am the proverbial night animal. Clear morning air is fatal for my health, the rosy fingers of dawn clutch at my throat, and if bothered before lunch, I guarantee violence."

NONVIOLENCE

People who think nonviolence is easy don't realize that it's a spiritual discipline requiring a great deal of strength, growth and purging of the self so that one can overcome almost any obstacle for the good of all without being concerned about one's own welfare.

– Coretta King

NOSTALGIA

What bores me are stories that smother me in nostalgia. I am not yesterday's magic. I am not lonely. I have friends I've known forever and I make new friends wherever I go.

– Rita Hayworth

NURTURE

Women, in contrast to men, possess a certain innate nurturing instinct. We nurture by nature and have a need to be needed.

– Liz Carpenter

OFFICER

A newspaper account about female officers who would start working regular shifts at New York City's East River toll crossings for the first time in the 40-year history of the Triborough Bridge and Tunnel Authority was headlined: "Tollhouse cookies on way."

OLYMPICS

The Olympics are a joke ... All the amateur athletes you are reading about are taking money under the table. The Olympics should be open. The athletes should compete for prize money.

– Billie Jean King

OPEN MIND

Columnist Bertha Shore: "Trouble with the open mind is that most anything can be thrown into it."

OPERA

If you approach an opera as though it were something that always went a certain way, that's what you get. I approach an opera as though I didn't know it.

– Sarah Caldwell

Musical director Sarah Caldwell said that opera was "worth the effort for one simple reason: it produces a marvelous product that can easily become addictive."

OPPORTUNITY

(On new opportunities for women) Sure she can rearrange the chronology, redesign her life span, persuade herself that she's got it under control. As long as there are no tremors beneath the status quo; as long as men don't have to give up their political supremacy, good jobs, hot dinners, casual fatherhood, sexual services, birthright power.

— Letty Cottin Pogrebin

OPTIMISM

I love the highs and no matter how low the lows I know I'll be up high again.

— Dinah Shore

OPTIONS

Options are a lot easier than decisions. You're living in a time when women are being told they can have it all, and we know we can't.

— Ellen Goodman

ORGANIZER

When she was president of the General Federation of Women's Clubs, Helen Chapman did a monumental job in helping organize their community efforts. One of her subordinates said: "If I end up in an old ladies' home and Helen is there, too—it sure will be organized."

OUTSIDER

The trouble with me is I'm an outsider. And that's a very hard thing to be in American life.

— Jacqueline Onassis

OVEREXUBERANCE

I am full of curiosity and overexuberance ... and overexuberance is something I hate in the aged.

– *Alice Roosevelt Longworth*

PACKAGING

Writer Sonia Masello:

"Two shoelaces and two cheap pens needed ... Shoelaces came six to the package, or none at all. Each pair ... encased separately in its own stiff plastic coffin, all of them mounted on a large cardboard and covered with an airtight plastic skin ... pens packaged similarly....

As I ... launched my customary attack on them, I reflected through clenched teeth that it not only takes the strength of King Kong to open those transparent tombs, it takes King's mentality to package them that way in the first place."

PAIN

(When her husband Freddie Brisson would ask her how she was feeling during her final illness) The pain, Freddie? ... It's a pain in the derriere.
— *Rosalind Russell*

PANTS

A magazine ad says about today's woman: "The fact is today they (husband and wife) both wear the pants. It's just that hers fit better."

PARADE

Embroidered on a bordello-keeper's pillow: 'If they're trying to run you out of town, get in front of the crowd and act like it's a parade."

PARENT

If you've never been hated by your child, you've never been a parent.
– Bette Davis

I feel we should put in equal time with the kids ... Right now I have to be around more because I'm nursing. When I'm ready to work James (Taylor, her husband) has to take care of them. That's a must.
– Carly Simon

PARKING

A sunbelt meter maid says her favorite excuse for a parking violation was that of a business man, who said, he parked in a loading zone so he could buy his pregnant wife a hot dog. The sentimental meter maid tore up the ticket.

PARLIAMENT

Acts of Parliament ... were not like women, the worse for becoming old.
– England's Duke of Buckingham

PARTNER

Give me my tennis racquet and my horses and the fresh air and a handsome man as a partner and you can have the tennis racquet and the horses and the fresh air.
– Angie Dickinson

I am not concerned about whether or not my children choose "blue-blooded" partners ... (I hope Albert, my son) will choose a woman with the character and attributes that would be appropriate for her job as the future princess of Monaco .. I cannot say whether these strengths are to be found in a princess or a country girl.
– Princess Grace of Monaco

PARTY

Parties I leave airly—eef you don't enjoy before 12, you won't after 12.
– Lily Pons

Mrs. A.F. Irvine in *The Star:* "My child was permitted to sit on the stairs for a short while to watch our rather noisy cocktail party. The next day, when asked what she thought of the party, she replied. 'Well, it kinda sounded like being on the school bus.' ”

PASSES

“Why do today's men make passes at lasses who wear glasses?” asks the woman optician. “Perhaps it's due to the stylish frames.”

PASTRY

Pastry! Sinning sweetly.

— Ad for Town & Country

PATIENCE

I've been thinking of the problems I've had these days. I can take the ups and downs of life. If I can't store up courage to live, I've resolved to store up patience.

— Carolina Maria de Jesus

PAY

If you pay peanuts you get monkeys.

— Woman Boss

Working is nothing new in life. I just never got paid before.

— Charlotte Ford

Once I got a check for $2,000 after I made a speech … but I sent it back because Jimmy (Carter) wouldn't have allowed it. It's too bad—I could have used the money.

— Miz Lillian Carter

(Mentioning her salary to his maid, Florence) At these prices, I want to see some fancy maiding.

— George Jefferson in TV's ”The Jeffersons”

PEACE

We've gained from the wars a lot of trouble and hatred and bitterness … Women are for peace always. They are for peace by nature.

— Jehan Sadat

PEACEMAKER

She was one of those who have the blessed nature of a peacemaker by
default. They are unable to handle rage.
> – *Character in* A Glorious Third
> *by Cynthia Proper Seton*

PEDESTAL

People thought everything a lark for me. Fan magazines painted a false
image of all of us. They eliminated all of the problems in our lives. Put
us on pedestals. That was all bull.
> – *Doris Day*

At a Washington benefit for the Women's Campaign Fund, writer
Francine du Plessix Gray pointed out that being put on a pedestal could
sometimes prevent a woman from becoming successful. Women, according to Gray, are "the only exploited group in history who have been
idealized into powerlessness."

PEDESTRIAN

Eve Arden, to columnist Frank Farrell: "If there's anything I can't
stand, it's pedestrians. Why don't they get cars like everybody else and
defend themselves?"

PERFECTION

(On piggybacking career responsibilities onto what society considers
woman's first responsibility: marriage) Most important perhaps, we
must ask why it is that our struggle for survival in an unjust system is
countered not with political change, but with upping the ante on female
perfection.
> – *Letty Cottin Pogrebin*

Description of Babe Didrikson Zaharias by her husband, George: "She
could hardly do anything wrong, and if she did, she would work until
she made it right. Competition was her life, but not competition against
her opponents—competition against the game itself. Every stroke had
to be perfect. She had to be perfect in everything she did. She walked
like a gazelle, she dressed perfectly in the way she wanted to dress. She
had perfection in golf, in wearing clothes, in driving a car, in building

the house we built later in Tampa. I knew her better than anybody else ever knew her, and I can say she was perfect in everything she did. She was the best."

PERFORM

I love to perform, I love to sing.... When I first went on, the excitement was so great, it was like sex.
— Dolly Parton

I think I perform better without having been overrehearsed.
— Dinah Shore

(On being a lawyer) It still may be that for a woman to do as well as a man she may have to do a little more and a little better. But my advice is to do that little more and do it better.
— Cornelia G. Kennedy

PERFUME

Readers of the *Ladies' Home Journal* (of Feb. 1906) were told by Editor Bok that "women of good birth and breeding long ago discarded the use of perfumes. No well-bred woman will exhale any other scent than that indescribable pure sweet aroma which is the result of the daily bath and clean linen."

PERSONAL COMMENT

I don't care what is written about me so long as it isn't true.
— Katharine Hepburn

PERSONAL LIFE

Flo (Polly Holliday) in the TV series, *Alice*—explaining how she's streamlined her life and lives in a small apartment in order to concentrate on acting—said, "I do my personal life easy."

PERSONALITY

British actress Diana Dors: "I have only got personality to sell—so I may as well wrap it up as decoratively as possible."

PHILOSOPHER

Pearl Bailey once described herself as "more of a philosopher than an entertainer."

You go either of two ways in this world; you either take the challenges that present themselves, or not—and none of us has any guarantees. I remember this cab driver I had once—I was running like mad because it was raining and I said to him, "Thank God you're here; it's such a lousy morning," and he turned to me and said, "Lady, there is no such thing as a lousy morning; you are not *owed* today."

— Muriel Siebert

PIANO

But before the authors gave me the script, they observed, in a matter-of-course manner, "Of course you play piano? You'll have to sing to your own accompaniment in the piece." As these alarming tidings were in the course of being made, I caught a bewildered look in my mother's eyes, and so I spoke up before she could. "Certainly I play piano," I answered. As we left the theater, my mother sighed. "I hate to see you start under a handicap," she said. "What made you say you could play piano?" "The feeling that I *will* play before rehearsals begin," I said. We went at once to try to rent a piano; couldn't find one; and ended by buying one. I began lessons at once, practiced finger-exercises till I could no longer see the notes—and began rehearsals with the ability to accompany myself. Since then, I have never lived too far from a piano.

— Helen Hayes

PICTURE

(About wanting to look good in *Playboy* mag's sexy picture of her) I told 'em they could use an airbrush; I think they used a blowtorch!

— Dolly Parton

The lady attorney and her manufacturer husband, on a round-the-world trip, were dining in a fabulous Hong Kong restaurant. Suddenly his wife said anxiously, "What's happened, Henry? You look like your passport photo!"

(About her pictures being used in *Playboy*) If I were to sue *Playboy*, I don't really want money. What I would really like is a private nude photo session with Hugh Hefner, and I would like to have complete control and ownership of the photos to sell to whomever I want.

– Suzanne Somers

PIGEONS

Pigeons on the grass, alas!

– Gertrude Stein

PILL (THE)

A divorced woman airlines executive, when she speaks to young career women's groups, likes to say, "By the way, we had the Pill in the 1950's." She pauses. "In fact, I married two of them."

Dr. Carl Djerassi, father of "the pill": "Just because I was involved in oral contraceptives, they (people) are assuming that I'm basically a male chauvinist. And I think I'm basically a feminist.

"If I could say that there was anything I was sorry about … it's that I wasn't a woman. It would have been so much better if a woman had carried this out."

PLACE

Pro golfer Linda Craft, when asked where in Texas she was from: "Jacksboro," she says, and then waits for the inevitable "Where's that?"

"Well, I'll tell you. I went out to my front porch one day, raised my arms and said, 'God, help me.' And God, He looked down, and He said, real bewildered like, 'I would. But where are you?'"

– Vivian Gornick

PLANNED PARENTHOOD

Faye Wattleton holds three firsts. When she became president of Planned Parenthood, she was the first woman, first black and the youngest president in Planned Parenthood's history.

PLUMBER

People keep asking me why I'm doing a man's job. This is not a man's job. It belongs to anybody who can do it right.

– Woman plumber

POLITICAL POWER

We are told it is economic conditions, reinforced by discriminatory attitudes, that keep women out of political power, ... Yet, we must realize that without political power, women will not be able to change the socioeconomic conditions that oppress them.

— Bella Abzug

POLITICIAN

A politician should be born a foundling and remain a bachelor.

— Lady Bird Johnson

Just say the word "politician," and I think of chicanery.

— Lucille Ball

I have always felt that politicians and Mafia people are the same, excluding the violent acts.

— Judith Exner

I am a professional politician. I didn't get here by being black or a woman. I got here by working hard. My life is my work.

— Barbara Jordan

Karen Ahrland, a Swedish parliament member, said at the United Nations World Conference on Women: "Over at the general conference ... we used the male politician's language, which means we spent a lot of time saying nothing."

Politician Louise Young: "To succeed as a politician you need to be a man plus a woman. You have to play hard ball. If you play girls' rules, you will sit on the side lines and that is what a lot of women do."

The sister of Adlai Stevenson, Elizabeth "Buffie" Ives, said: "I like politics.... It makes me so mad when the word 'politician' is used as an epithet. By sneering at politicians we drag down the whole fabric of political business."

(About Congresswoman Jeanette Rankin who voted "No" to going to war in WWI): Women who are scorned and ridiculed—women like Rankin and Eleanor Roosevelt—if they live long enough, are idolized and revered in a far greater share than others who were not so controversial.

— William "Fishbait" Miller

POLITICS

Politics: The "King of Sports."

> — *Cornelia Wallace*

There are no personal sympathies in politics.

> — *Margaret Thatcher*

It is the fate of the great in political life to be criticized, condemned and hated. It is the mediocre who are popular.

> — *Carrie Chapman Catt*

Chicago's Mayor Jane Byrne: "I think it's the law of the jungle in politics. You don't have friends, just allies."

I am politics. If my husband does not keep me acting, I am all politics!

> — *Melina Mercouri*

There aren't many women now I'd like to see as President—but there are fewer men.

> — *Clare Booth Luce*

No one who has been in that terrible limelight (living in the White House) would ever seek it again.

> — *Mamie Eisenhower*

Sometimes things go wrong and I get a bit edgy. Well, Denis (her husband) is sort of a shock-absorber.

> — *Margaret Thatcher*

(About women delegates at a political convention) You could see they took their politics seriously—they were on the plump side.

> — *Male Newspaper Reporter*

I remember Senate campaign speeches when he (U.S. President John Kennedy) would say over and over that the Greek word for idiot meant one who took no part in the affairs of his state.

> — *Jacqueline Onassis*

It's necessary to have a super ego in politics ... the politician has to go before people shouting like Muhammad Ali, "I am the greatest."... and that's ego.

> — *Barbara Jordan*

Fusae Ichikawa, 87, who had just won her fifth six-year term to the upper house, Japan's House of Councillors: "Women themselves need to become more interested in politics.... I so often find that women whom I think would make splendid legislators just don't want to get involved."

Writer Barbara Wendell Kerr once said about women entering politics: "... when they do have something to contribute, they must persuade, cajole, charm or, as a last resort, shoulder their way into party inner sanctums. No one will ask them in; they must open the door themselves."

When Queen Frederika of Greece was talking more about Greek politics than a Senator thought fitting, he asked: "Madam, where were you born?" Queen Frederika answered: "I was born a full-blooded barbarian and I came to Greece to be civilized." The Senator was enchanted.

POLITICS—CAMPAIGNING

I don't know much about politics, but I can shake hands and remember names.

— Margaret Truman

I never felt it was good taste to go out and electioneer for my husband.

— Eleanor Roosevelt

It's one of the things that a husband and wife can do together.... Campaigning is better than sitting home nights alone.

— Martha (Mrs. Robert A.) Taft

Too many elected officials become professional campaigners. They keep their eyes on the public-opinion polls and rarely risk leadership.

— Nancy Landon Kassebaum

(When campaigning for her brother Ted Kennedy) A lot of you have said I look like my mother. And I do, because I have been campaigning for five months, and I look 90 years old.

— Pat Lawford

Senator Bob Dole delighted in introducing his wife, Federal Trade Commissioner Elizabeth Hanford Dole, on the campaign trail. To a business group he might say: "This is my wife, the Federal Trade Commissioner. Anyone here who isn't being sued by FTC?"

— Advertising Age

How does a woman feel about her husband becoming president of the United States? Nellie Connally, whose husband John was seeking the Republican nomination, said that she didn't mind sharing her husband with the state or the country, "but I don't want to give him away."

The other day we watched the movie Coal Miner's Daughter, the story of how Loretta Lynn broke into show business ...

Edna Langford, an old friend who is son Jack's (Carter) mother-in-law and I were sitting on the floor watching. When the movie showed how Loretta piled her babies in a car and took off toward radio towers in search of stations, we both started to laugh. We were rolling on the floor, hysterical.

I never knew anyone else ever did that. I thought it was an original idea of mine how to get on some radio talk shows when Edna and (White House aide) Tim Kraft and I traveled from town to town doing that. One night I was sleeping in the back seat when the car lurched and stopped. We had run out of road and the car was perched on railroad tracks, smack up against a chainlink fence surrounding a big field with a lonely radio tower sticking up in the middle. We knew then it was time to quit for the night.

— Rosalynn Carter

The Trumans had a small routine that they would use at every train stop during the campaign of '48. At every station, whether early in the morning or late at night, Mr. and Mrs. Truman would emerge from their car together. Truman would say a few words, point to his wife and say: "My boss." Many newsmen often added that they saw her blue-penciling Mr. Truman's speeches as she sat by the window of the train, waiting for another stop somewhere down the line.

POLITICS—CANDIDATES

(About a group of U.S. presidential candidates) God: The country that produced George Washington has got this collection of crumb bums!

— Barbara Tuchman

Melina Mercouri, running for election to the Greek parliament: "They (the voters) trust me not as a star, but rather as a woman with dynamism who knows how to fight, how to go on strike. I want to be a thorn in parliament."

POLITICS—CONSERVATIVE

Writer Mary Austin: "Besides, women are seldom really liberal. They are radical for the things they have definitely made up their minds about, and conservative about the rest."

POLITICS—CONTRIBUTION

Barbara Wendell Kerr, a magazine public affairs editor, once described an unusual political situation in which U.S. House Speaker Sam Rayburn and Senator Lyndon Johnson, both Texans, wanted to recapture Texas for the Democrats. "This meant ... beating (Allen) Shivers' delegation at the precinct level. As in many 'forlorn hope' situations they turned to a woman.... Kathleen Voigt, who had heretofore worked only at the precinct level herself, became executive secretary of the newly formed Democratic Advisory Council. She started in a small office with $1.57 in her pocket and a list of 126 possible donors. A year later she had parlayed that to $75,000 and a statewide organization of 20,000 supporters. They beat Shivers to a standstill."

POLITICS—HOLDING OFFICE

(On being Governor of Connecticut) I've also learned how to listen, to hear what is said and what is left unsaid, and only then to make a decision.

— Ella Grasso

After three years in the California legislature, a former businesswoman said: "Business is a piece of cake compared to this."

(On serving 3 years in the House of Representatives) There is such a heavy responsibility to make the right decision. Each time you vote, there are only three buttons to press: yea, nay and present. There isn't any maybe.

— Shirley Pettis

When Charlotte Whitton was Mayor of Ottawa, capital of Canada, she refused to tolerate special consideration because she was a woman. When an alderman referred to her as "the lady present," she leaped to her feet with the blunt announcement, "Whatever my sex, I'm no lady."

(About a U.S. President's term of office) Americans will understand more than they ever have that a president can have all the good intentions in the world, can have a good personality and a deep faith and commitment and a great deal of integrity—and in the end it's not enough. The president has to have a program.

— Jane Fonda

POLITICS—REELECTION

When a politician said to a gathering of U.S. Senators that Senator Margaret Chase Smith should be thinking about her upcoming reelection in the next year, one of the Senators remarked, "Mrs. Smith doesn't have to think about elections, she thinks about people."

POLITICS—SPEECH

But I have little sympathy for those women who say, with a deep sigh, that they "simply had to give up everything when the babies arrived." I know, for example, that it is possible to write a political speech with one hand while dishing up breakfast food for two healthy youngsters with the other. Often the speech was not finished until far into the night, after the children were in bed and my fingers were too numb to hold a pencil. But there was something in that speech which I felt should be said, and which was more important than an easy night's rest.

— Helen Gahagan Douglas

POLITICS—VOLUNTEER

Volunteerism comes from the heart ... When you're paid, it's too commercial. You volunteer because you love your country, your people, and because it makes you feel good. So many women can't work full-time; volunteerism gives them a chance to be useful with the hours they can afford. In volunteerism, it is your heart that is speaking, and it's listened to. It's working with people on a one-to-one basis.

— Patricia Nixon

POLITICS—WATERGATE

If it hadn't been for Martha (Mitchell), there'd have been no Watergate.

— Richard M. Nixon

POLITICS—WOMEN

It is women who can bring empathy, tolerance, insight, patience, and persistence to government—the qualities we naturally have or have had to develop because of our suppression by men. The women of a nation mold its morals, its religion, and its politics by the lives they live. At present, our country needs women's idealism and determination, perhaps more in politics than anywhere else.

— Shirley Chisholm

Political development is like all other development. We must begin with ourselves, our own consciousness, and clean out our own hearts before we take on the job of putting others straight. So with politics. If we women put our hands to local politics, we must begin with the foundations. After all, central governments only echo local ones; ... Let us make that constituency so clean, so straight, so high in its purpose, that the representative in Washington will not dare to take a small limited view about any question, be it a national or an international one.

— Nancy Astor, M.P.

Friends used to ask, with lifted eyebrows, whether I thought that politics was really a suitable activity for a woman. My answer is that politics is a job that needs doing, by anyone who is interested enough to train for it and work at it. It is like housekeeping: Somebody has to do it in our homes, and somebody has to do it in our communities, in our states, and in our national capital. Whether the job is done by men or women is not the important thing, but only whether the job is done well or badly.

— Helen Gahagan Douglas

POLLYANNA

I try to keep up with the changes in the world, even though I don't like a lot of them ... I'm a Pollyanna.

— Arlene Francis

POOL

When a wealthy Texan bought a posh estate, he wired his college daughter Samantha to come home for a weekend. As he showed her around, they stopped at a giant swimming pool to watch several muscular and handsome young men dive from the board. "Oh, Daddy," said Samantha, "You've stocked the pool! And for me!"

PORNOGRAPHY

Feminist-actress Marie-France Pisier: "I think the women's lib movement has done a great deal to cut the throat of the pornography business."

Silence is a form of consent—and so I intend to be as opposed as I possibly can.

— Princess Grace of Monaco

Pornography ... is essentially sentimental, for it leaves out the connection of sex with its hard purposes, disconnects it from its meaning in life and makes it simply an experience for its own sake.

— Flannery O'Connor

It (pornography) is a problem that exists all over the world. If I'm in Paris or in America and I pass a store that sells and promotes pornography, I simply walk in and tell them what I think about the subject.

— Princess Grace of Monaco

Pornography is to women what Klan literature is to blacks or Nazi propaganda is to Jews ... Pornography is the product of woman-hatred, marked by cruelty or violence and shouldn't be confused with erotica, which is rooted in the idea of free will and love.

— Gloria Steinem

Pornography and health are very closely connected. I believe that if a person cannot become aroused without having pornography and obscenity, then that person is not healthy, and it all comes back to food, you see. A person who eats well does not need pornography ...

If you fed a dog like most men are fed these days, the Royal Society for the Prevention of Cruelty to Animals would prosecute.

— Barbara Cartland

Right now ... the only popular connection between the pornographic uses of women and children is a patriarchal connection of blame. If women weren't becoming so rebellious, the reasoning goes, we would continue to satisfy man's "natural" need for sexual dominance—and then men wouldn't become desperate enough to turn to children. In other words, child pornography, like so many other social ills, is somehow the fault of women.

— Gloria Steinem

POSSESSIONS

Actress Sada Thompson: "I don't really think material things are important. If you get so involved in possessions ... you won't go anywhere."

POSTER

(To Johnny Carson) How come I never showed you my poster? I showed you everything else!

— Angie Dickinson

A best-selling feminist poster drives the point home with a photograph of Golda Meir and the caption, "But can she type?"

POVERTY

Zita Potts, rural poverty fighter: "Bein' poor is no shame. It's just real unhandy."

British movie queen Diana Dors: "I would much rather be unhappy in luxury than unhappy in poverty."

We need to tell the poor "that they are somebody to us, that they too have been created with the same loving hand of God, to love and be loved."

— Mother Teresa

(When accepting the 1979 Nobel Peace Prize) Our poor people are great people, a very lovable people. They don't need our pity and sympathy. They need our understanding, love and respect.

— Mother Teresa

Too many people are acting as if the war on poverty is over. I'm not sure if that means we won or it was a tie. Unfortunately nobody's gotten around to telling the poor people this good news.

— Rep. Barbara Mikulski

Our (the people of Northern Ireland) place is not on the bottom, saying, "Thank you very much and please, can we have tomorrow's dinner?" Our place is ending the system whereby we have to be on the bottom. I hope that what I did was to get rid of that feeling of guilt, of inferiority that the poor have; the feeling that somehow God is or they are responsible for the fact that they are not as rich as Henry Ford.

— Bernadette Devlin

POWER

Achieving power is a combination of timing, luck and hard work. Plus one other ingredient women overlook a lot. That's wanting power ...

Race, don't walk, when you see an opening you can fill. Wanting power is half the secret of getting it.

– Jane Trahey

PRAISE

After Barbara Stanwyck saw the film Jezebel, she couldn't wait to write Bette Davis—she had to phone. The maid said Miss Davis was sleeping. Barbara called next day; Miss Davis was out. After the fifth call—Miss Davis was napping—Barbara left a message: "When Snow White wakes up tell her I think she was marvelous."

– Frank S. Nugent

PRAYER

More tears are shed over answered prayers than unanswered ones.

– St. Teresa of Avila

But woman, once she really understands, is content to say, "Prayer is simply being with God and knowing it."

– Mary Lou Lacy

Everything that has happened to me, I attribute to God. During all those slack times, I was bending His ear.

– Isabel Sanford

When times would get tough, I'd get down on my knees and cry out to the Lord—and things would always get better.

– Isabel Sanford

Two nuns, who'd been shopping, were debating who was to drive back to the convent. One said, "You drive, Sister Theresa, and I'll pray." "*You* pray?" Sister Theresa asked. "Don't you trust MY praying?"

PRESENT AGE

As a matter of fact: In what age before have we seen women so energetic and so vital and so dynamic? So full of muscle and movement? For themselves—not simply, as in the past, to be strong helpmates. In what age before have we questioned the ways in which we are bringing up little girls? In what age before have we thought that they might become something more than simply *big* girls?

– Sey Chassler

PRINCE CHARMING

In their attack on marriage and the home, the women's liberationists
tell young women that *Cinderella* and all fairy tales in which the girl
meets her Prince Charming and they "live happily ever after" are a
myth and a delusion. One thing is sure. If you make up your mind that
you will never find your "Prince Charming," you won't. If you decide in
advance that it is impossible to "live happily ever after," you won't. It all
can happen to you, however, if you make up your mind that it *will*
happen. I *know*—because it happened to me.

– Phyllis Schlafly

PRIORITY

When you find yourself being pulled at from every direction ... you have
to just sit down and decide what you *must* do, then you set your
priorities and be very firm about not adding a lot of other things.

– Coretta King

You have to establish priorities if you want a career that's really
successful. You have to establish what comes first and eliminate the
other things and not regret them.

– Mary Wells Lawrence

The worst thing about the movement is that it is distracting the
attention of thousands of women from more urgent and important
questions. They should get their priorities straight. Instead of yapping
about men treating them as "sex objects" (and, personally, I have always
liked being treated as a sex object), they might better devote themselves
to more socially useful protests: against the war in Indochina, against
nuclear, chemical and biological weapons, against environmental pollu-
tion, to name a few of the more obvious.

– Helen Lawrenson

PRIVATE

You have to learn how to remain private in public ...

– Susan Strasberg

I'm a very private person and I think it's an interesting business that
most people aren't interested in a thing until they learn it's none of
their business.

– Audrey Hepburn

There are people who are so immature and insecure that they have to spill everything. They use the public as analysts. I think they share too much. I don't owe anything to the public but my performance. My private life is my private life and I will keep it so.
– Mary Tyler Moore

In trying to maintain her personal privacy, model Suzy Parker instructed her mother not to reveal any details of her life to the press. One day Suzy, Pitou (her new husband) and her mother, walking along a street, bumped into a friend of her family, a Baptist minister. According to Parker, her mother said: "Pastor, I've just taught Suzy to make caramel custard for her husb, er, ah, man—no, friend."

PRIVILEGE

The claim that American women are downtrodden and unfairly treated is the fraud of the century.... The truth is that American women have never had it so good. Why should we lower ourselves to "equal rights" when we already have the status of special privilege?
– Phyllis Schlafly

PROBLEMS

Early in my career I learned I had to take these problems (of her readers) seriously—but not personally.
– Ann Landers

PROCRASTINATION

Dannye Romine, book editor of *The Charlotte Observer:* "If procrastination is a habit you've resolved to kick this year, think again.... Here is an example: Joan's college roommate, it seems, had a sweater drawer always in a rumple and a jumble. If she knew she had to settle down for some serious studying, she would immediately flail her arms and cry out, 'Oh! My sweater drawer, my sweater drawer. There's not a thing I can do until it's straightened out.' Of course, Joan was on to her ruse—as was the roommate herself—but not one to pass up a good thing, Joan adopted the trick, and to this day when she must tackle an unpleasant chore, she throws her arms and wails, 'Oh! My sweater drawer, my sweater drawer. There's not a thing I can do until it's straightened out.'"

PROFESSION

His profession was women.

PROFESSIONAL

The only difference between a woman amateur and a woman professional is that the amateur gave up.

PROFESSOR

The female students in sorority meetings refer to romantic old professors as "retreads."

— Jim Bishop

PROGRESS

Virginia Y. Trotter, of Department of Health, Education and Welfare: "The seesaw—or the escalator—is an excellent image in that as the new gains and setbacks take effect, the sexes will only hamper progress if they see themselves at opposite ends of a seesaw, one falling as the other rises. It is recognizing our mutual stakes in abandoning stereotypes that we can turn the seesaw into an escalator for lifting everybody as it goes along."

PROPERTY

Patricia Schroeder, U.S. Congresswoman from Colorado: "I find men more interested in acquiring and possessing territory than women. I assume the difference is because women look at property differently— as something they have to clean."

PROPOSAL

I get proposals all the time. Some of them might even be considered honorable.

— Elsa Martinelli

They (Hollywood men) will propose to you after a cocktail party and two dinners. At times, I was rather insulted.

— Joan Greenwood

(When Hemingway proposed marriage soon after first meeting) ... Don't be idiotic. We're both married and we don't know each other. What nonsense!

— Mary Hemingway

English writer Thomas Hardy, proposed to his second wife, Florence Hardy, in the family graveyard. As they strolled among the tombstones, he pointed out to her a spot available for her own grave close to his first wife's.

(Speaking of her proposal from the Baron) If he had only asked me to marry him I might not have said yes, because at that time I really truly was not in love. I liked him but didn't love him. I loved the children, and so in a way I really married the children.

— Maria Von Trapp

As they sat in the car, looking at the moon, a young man proposed to the pretty girl and she promptly said, "Gerald, dear, how sweet. But I don't want a little cottage with a rose-covered fence, I want my own designing firm with a first-rate security fence ... and a guard dog."

PROSTITUTE

A former congressman, who made headlines because of a romantic involvement, said: "Hell hath no fury like a prostitute with a press agent."

PROTEST

Jeanette Rankin, the First United States Congresswoman, said about women, for whose rights she labored a lifetime: "They've been worms. They let their sons go off to war because they're afraid their husbands will lose their jobs in industry if they protest."

PROTEST MARCHES

Popular English singer, Lulu: "With their protests, they are trying to say they care. What a marvelous message. And isn't there something wrong with us if we don't listen?"

PSYCHIATRIST

French comedian Jean Rigaux: "A psychiatrist is a man who goes to the Folies Bergère to look at the audience."

I'm not putting psychiatry down. I just don't want to spend that much time with myself. I'm pretty content. I mean, I'm here. I survived. If I go to a shrink, he might tell me some things I hadn't thought of that I might not like about myself and I might not wake up the next morning.
— Liza Minnelli

PUBLIC AFFAIRS

Writer Mary Austin: "Less and less, as they emerge into public affairs, women show themselves attracted by the glittering generality or the vague altruistic gesture. When their chief business in life was being pleased with what men had to offer, they sat and smiled at the peacock plummage of oratory and fine sentiment; but secretly most women are convinced that a man's stake in his country, the world, the future, is not any different, nor to be handled in any other way, than his stake in his town and his street and the business by which he makes a living.

"This is probably what they mean when they express themselves as favoring a 'business man' for a chief executive."

PUBLIC WOMEN

We are the public women. We make a career of sharing what we know. We have the voice and the amplifiers, and we stand at the portals of the public consciousness. And we could ... lead women into the future they deserve.
— Marlo Thomas

PURE

Tallulah Bankhead once remarked: "I'm pure as the driven slush."

PUT-DOWN

She (Barbara Jordan) is also capable of swift put-downs when irritated. At a meeting of the Texas Congressional delegation, a fellow member was talking endlessly about some problems involving fertilizer, until Jordan finally broke in to say, "I can't tell you how refreshing it is to hear you talk about something you're really into."

– Irwin Ross

QUARREL

Young man, going home to his father with his suitcases and his kids, said, "Dad, I don't know what happened. Angie and I had a little quarrel. And the next thing I knew, Wow!—she'd gained control of my construction business and she's given me custody of the kids!"

QUESTION

Suppose there were no questions, what would the answer be?
— Gertrude Stein

Bromidic though it may sound, some questions *don't* have answers, which is a terribly difficult lesson to learn.
— Katherine Graham

RATING

(When she earned B's in her Georgetown U. courses, except for an A in religion) As long as you've got A's with God, honey, those B's don't matter.

– Pearl Bailey

When Barbara Walters asked Bette Midler to rate herself on the 1-to-10 scale, Midler said, "Oh, I think I'm about a 55."

(At an Academy Awards ceremony, explaining filmdom's G, PG and R "rating" system to the audience) "If a man and a woman go into the woods with a picnic basket and a blanket, spread out the blanket and have a picnic, that's a G. If they go into the woods with a picnic basket and crawl under the blanket, that's a PG. And if they go into the woods without a basket or a blanket and have a picnic anyway, that's an R."

– Jane Fonda

READING

(On salacious literature) No girl ever got ruined by a book.

– Jimmy Walker

I just finished reading the *Iliad*. That's like baking bread. I read it to prove I can.

– Patricia Harris

I've never allowed myself to get lazy. Even sitting in the sun, I've got to be reading something that I can store in the back of my head....

– Kate Jackson

REAL ESTATE

New successful real estate saleswoman: "I'm gonna hang a 'sold' sign on my chest, meaning I'm sold on real estate as a career."

REBELLION

Well, I'd rather be myself than any one else. I've always had an absolute rebellion against worrying what other people think.
— Shirley MacLaine

Often I had thought of Vashti as the first woman rebel in history. Once when her husband, King Ahasuerus, had been showing off to his people his fine linens, his pillars of marble, his beds of gold and silver, and all his riches, he had commanded that his beautiful Queen Vashti also be put on view. But she had declined to be exhibited as a possession or chattel. Because of her disobedience, which might set a very bad example to other wives, she had been cast aside and Ahasuerus had chosen a new bride, the meek and gentle Esther,

I wanted each woman to be a rebellious Vashti, not an Esther; was she to be merely a washboard with only one song, one song? Surely, she should be allowed to develop all her potentialities. Feminists were trying to free her from the new economic ideology but were doing nothing to free her from her biological subservience to man, which was the true cause of her enslavement.
— Margaret Sanger

RECIPE

Family recipe: An advertising career woman decided to make a roast like her mother did. "Cut the ends off ... that's important," said the mother. "My mother always did that and I cook like she did." So the career cook carefully cut the ends off the roast and assured her friends, "This is our special family recipe!"

One day the ad executive visited her grandmother and asked why she always cut the ends off her roast. "Because," said Granny with annoyance, "that's the only way it would fit in that doggone pan of mine."

REFLECTING

If the power of reflecting on the past, and darting the keen eye of contemplation into futurity, be the grand privilege of man, it must be granted that some people enjoy this prerogative in a very limited degree.

         — *Mary Wollstonecraft*

REFUGEE

Letter to President Eisenhower from Queen Juliana of Holland: "How could refugees ever trust free society if it shows interest only for trained muscles or brains, but lacks respect for the higher values of life; if it looks at refugees only as labor potential, and refuses those who cannot work; if it separates them from their families?"

REGRET

Regret is an appalling waste of energy; you can't build on it, it's only good for wallowing in.

         — *Katherine Mansfield*

REJECTION

Once in a while I have allowed a man to reject me when I wished to initiate the rejection but believed it would severely injure the man's ego for me to do so.

         — *Margaret Mead*

(Talking to SRO audiences) But don't feel guilty about rejecting me. I'm used to rejection. Both my parents were musicians, so naturally when I was born, they were hoping for a piano. I spent the first six years of my life pushed up against the wall with a doily and a bowl of Hershey's kisses on my head.

         — *Marilyn Sokol*

RELAX

Because en route I've learned that the only way to enjoy life to the fullest is to slip up now and then—to occasionally let your defenses down as long as you keep your rib cage up.

         — *Dinah Shore*

She (the cow) charged! Slowly at first, then faster and faster. My legs started pumping like pistons. She chased me straight at a tough-looking barbed wire fence, which I dived through, leaving a flapping piece of jeans. My heart pounded and my knees shook and I rolled around in the lucerne roaring with laughter. I was so deliciously relaxed I could have slept in the sun and the wind for hours. That august lady had taken my psyche by the scruff of its neck and shaken it into a horse laugh.

– Anne Bancroft

RELIGION

Religion is induced insanity.

– Madalyn Murray O'Hair

I have done nothing. The Sacred Heart of Jesus has done everything. I am merely a witness of the wonders of God.

– Mother Cabrini

The religious people feel you can ignore laws with impunity if it furthers the cause of Jesus Christ.

– Madalyn Murray O'Hair

(On her husband Larry Flynt, publisher of *Hustler,* being introduced to religion and desiring to clean up his magazine) I told him, "God may have walked into your life, but $20 million a year just walked out."

– Althea Flynt

... we would stop in at the church very often because I wanted them (her children) to know that church was something for every day in the week, it wasn't just for Sunday, just for a special day or special hour; that you could pray or that you could talk to God any time and He would be there, He would listen to you. He would give you advice or sympathy or whatever it was you felt you needed.

– Rose Kennedy

Emily R. Atkins in the *Reader's Digest*: "Hospitalized after an automobile accident, I was visited by a contingent of nuns from the small Catholic college I was attending. They had been praying for me, they said. One priest had mentioned me at morning mass, another at afternoon chapel, and the sisters themselves prayed for me all the time. 'Thank you very much,' I said, feeling a little guilty. 'But will it count? I mean, I'm not a Catholic...' 'Don't you worry, my dear,' said one of the older nuns, placing her hand gently on mine. 'We just say the prayers. Then God can do whatever He wants with you.'"

RELIGION—ORDINATION

Jesus warned his own followers to study carefully the signs of the times.

That directive crosses centuries. Jesus would, I'm sure, ordain women today.

– Sister Camille D'Arienzo

Christian creativity for the present age must not depend on male leaders. Woman's contribution—from women properly trained and authorized—is essential.

– The Rev. Mary Michael Simpson

The Rev. Paul Washington, rector of Church of the Advocate, Philadelphia at the ordination of the first eleven women as priests in the Episcopal Church: "If the Church Fathers still claimed that women's time had not yet come in the Church, they should take note that, even though her obstetrician tells a woman that she will give birth on August 15, if the baby is coming on July 29, it is the woman and the baby who are right, not the obstetrician."

Alla Bozarth-Campbell, one of the eleven women ordained as priests in the Episcopal Church, 1974: "A key question for me is: Can women be Christian? If Christianity is chiefly a patriarchal religion of usurpation, the answer is No. If it is chiefly a religion of love and wholeness then the answer is Yes. Each woman must judge whether or not she can stay in the Church effectively without being diminished or destroyed by it. This is a question I live daily."

It seems almost unbelievable that there was an earlier age, and one that lasted from at least 30,000 B.C. until about 2,000 B.C., and in some few places until as late as almost A.D. 500, when men were subordinate to their wives and mothers. Not in all aspects of life, even then, but most certainly in the confines of the great temples of worship that existed in the cities of the ancient world when the Supreme Being—astounding as it may seem at present—was worshipped as a woman. The Great Mother was worshipped, furthermore, in her own right—not as the wife or daughter of some superior male god or the muse of poets, as in the familiar myths of the Greeks and Romans...No—before that age that we now call the Age of the Patriarchs in the Bible and stretching back into the dim recesses of time, the Great Mother ruled supreme and the priests who led all people to Her were both male and female.

– Elizabeth Rodgers Dobell

RELIGION—SUNDAY SCHOOL

Returning from Sunday school, actor Lloyd Nolan's daughter Melinda handed her father an envelope. "What's this?" asked Nolan. "Nothing. Just an ad from heaven." replied Melinda

– Andrew B. Hecht

REMARRIAGE

Woman executive at time of her second marriage: "I'm now looking for a wedding gown that goes with gray hair."

Divorced Princess Margaret of England once dismissed the idea of remarrying as a "bore."

I had an uncle who said he'd remarried as soon as he'd run out of clean socks.

— Woman poet

A newspaper reporter interviewed an 86-year-old man on remarrying for the sixth time. "Why did you tie the knot again?" asked the reporter. "Well, I'll tell you," confided the octogenarian, "for the little bit women eat I certainly wouldn't be without one."

(After his wife's death, when asked if he were contemplating remarriage) I say there is always a number one you put on top of the flower bunch,...No life is worth living if it's not "a deux," perhaps not a permanent one or the same one, although now and then there are new renewals, but it has to be "a deux."

— Baron Phillipe de Rothschild

RESILIENCE

What really works in life is being able to bounce back. Resilience ... That's what does it. If you stop and think, nothing is as bad as it seems. The worst moments, I've always found that something funny is happening—I mean really *funny* funny! And for that I give my mother all the credit. Judy Garland could cry, but she was also one of the world's great laughers.

— Liza Minnelli

RESISTANCE

Resistance to tyranny is obedience to God.

— Susan B. Anthony

RESPECT

Queen Victoria of England admired the tremendous talent of the writer Charles Dickens. When he was summoned for an audience with England's diminutive Queen at Buckingham Palace, court protocol didn't allow him to sit down. But out of her deep respect, Queen Victoria stood throughout the interview—one and a half hours!

RESPONSIBILITY

A female vice-president at an FM radio station noted: "Responsibility is assumed rather than given."

(About her grandmother's treatment of her in childhood) There's no use "to blame." Once you're mature, you take the responsibility.
— Elizabeth Ashley

REST

I think it's healthy for a woman over fifty to stay in bed mornings—if she can afford to.
— Mamie Eisenhower

RISK

To make it big, you have to risk.
— Woman headhunter

Although she admits staying away from the cameras could hurt her movie career, film star Sarah Miles says, "I like having my feet firmly planted in midair."

RETIREMENT

I may die, but I'll never retire.
— Margaret Mead

(Retiring at 62) Who wants to be the richest veterinarian in the cemetery?
— Woman veterinarian

I have hit lots of home runs, and when the cheering stops, I certainly will miss it ... I did it all. I'll put my voice to bed and go quietly and with pride.
— Beverly Sills

When British comedienne Gracie Fields partly retired, she began to putter around her house: "My life is split between being a charlady and a starlady."

I wanted to stop before I was asked to stop. I left the screen because I didn't want what happened to Chaplin to happen to me. When he discarded the Little Tramp, the Little Tramp turned around and killed him. The little girl made me. I wasn't waiting for the little girl to kill me.

– Mary Pickford

A striptease dancer explained why she went back to stripping, "I worked in a law library for awhile but I missed performing. The pay is no better, but the work is a lot more fun," she said. "I missed the applause. No one ever cheered when I checked out a book."

Why did Isabella Walton Cannon go into politics at 73, becoming mayor of Raleigh, N.C.? Her explanation: "I'm an active person—I couldn't sit still. I retired at 65 from the business office of the North Carolina State University library, and I figured I'd live to be 90. That's a good chunk of time. I'm not the book-club type."

When Britain's Queen Mother Elizabeth celebrated her 79th birthday, she declined to retire. However, a royal spokeswoman pointed out, "Of course, she has made some concessions to age. For instance, she is a fair weather fisherwoman these days and when the wind cuts sharply from the east and the temperature of the river is near Arctic, the Queen Mother no longer wades in up to her waist fishing for salmon."

I retired one time. It was the worst time of my life. I had made a great deal of money writing movies. With all that money I stopped working. I traveled, lived a life of ease in Paris, Palm Beach, California—in town houses, country houses, on ocean liners. It was one big party, going on all the time. And it was boring, awfully boring. When you're not working you only meet other people who are not working and you are all bored together.

– Anita Loos

REVIEWS

Actress Shirley Booth, commenting to Olga Curtis on her reviews: "The critics have given me lots of flowers. A few weeds will keep my soil moist."

REVOLUTION

Revolutions are not made with songs.

– Melina Mercouri

People who like red start revolutions. People who wear blue settle them.
— Katherine Nash

Many people have likened the women's revolution to the black revolution. The two are alike in that both women and blacks have been oppressed and exploited. Both groups enjoy second-class status and are treated as inferiors by the first-class citizens—the whites, the males.
— Shana Alexander

REWARD

My rewards came when I followed my own inside path, doing what is comfortable. I know that when I hang on, something wonderful will always happen!
— Eartha Kitt

RICH

You're rich when you buy your gas at the same service station all the time so your glasses match.
— Erma Bombeck

RIGHT MAN

Personally I think if a woman hasn't met the right man by the time she is 24, she may be lucky.
— Deborah Kerr

The reason I haven't met that right guy is that I haven't been the right girl.
— Waitress on "Mork and Mindy"

RIGHTS

I digress, for I am old now too, but differently. It is my favorite disputation, the rights that are owing to women, who are the mothers of all, denied them by the man-world, the war-world, the world that will destroy all if its senseless whirling is not stopped. We have made a start on Lesbos, and the Muses are on our side, and all the goddesses. I pray, and my prayer will be answered, long after me.
— Sappho, in My Name Is Sappho

ROMANCE

(When asked her advice to someone contemplating a romantic relationship) Take a chance!

— Lauren Bacall

It doesn't have to be a white charger anymore, but I believe something good is just around the corner.... There's a void in my life now.

— Dinah Shore

(On rekindling romance with your own husband) I understand that all you do is meet him at the door wearing nothing but high-heeled shoes and a rose in your teeth, and he snatches you up, foaming with passion, and drags you off to the bedroom. (A bonus side effect is that this gets your children and their little friends to glance up from the television for a minute, which doesn't happen often.)

— Barbara Holland

ROYALTY

(About meeting Queen Elizabeth) I'd seen her face on so many stamps that I wanted to lick the back of her head.

— Glen Campbell

When England's Princess Anne gave birth to a son, a member of Parliament commented, "How charming—another one on the payroll."

The queens in history compare favorably with the kings.

— Elizabeth Cady Stanton

About serving as monarch, Queen Frederika of Greece said: "We must put ourselves at the disposal of the people...We are not to be served but to serve."

Though I must take first place officially, it is possible for me to take second place in my marriage.

— Queen Margrethe, of Denmark

There is a famous story (certainly apocryphal) that when Queen Liliuokalani visited Queen Victoria, she said, "Your Majesty, they say that I have English blood in my veins." "How do you account for that?" asked the English queen. "Well," replied the dark-skinned ruler, "There is a rumor that my grandfather ate your Captain Cook."

— David Earl Campbell

(About her marriage to King Hussein) I'll never have the same friendships I had before. The relationships will be different. I'll never again be able to speak freely of everything that's on my mind. But there are things between a king and queen that aren't like anything else, that are exclusively private. It's not a problem, but it's part of my new life.

— Queen Noor el Hussein

A British civil servant who often accompanied Queen Elizabeth, the Queen Mother, on her public appearances, said that on one occasion the Queen Mother spotted a little girl in the crowd with a camera, turned backward, poised to take Her Majesty's picture. Queen Elizabeth went over to the youngster, turned the camera around, then stepping back said, "Are you ready?" The Queen graciously waited till the small fry snapped several shots.

SALES

I have ESP. That's Extrasensory Sales Perception.

— Real Estate Saleswoman

Always show psychology—but never let your psychology show.

— Saleswoman

SAN FRANCISCO

This is the only spot in America which resists the domination of the old lady next door.

— Edna Ferber

(When visiting San Francisco) Everyone here is so smart, as they are in New York. But as you get closer to the center of the country, the people get dumber and dumber. For some reason, people living near the ocean are smarter.

— Eydie Gormé

SAYING

My two favorite sayings are "Pacienza—patience" and "Don't think, ask."

— Ella Grasso

SAYING "NO"

My husband usually gets what he wants, but that don't mean I don't put up a battle. Better than I used to, now I can say no.

— Loretta Lynn

SCHOOLROOM

Just remember the world is not a playground but a schoolroom. Life is not a holiday but an education. One eternal lesson for us all: to teach us how better we should love.

— Barbara Jordan

SCIENCE

One single sentence which she (Marie Curie) was to repeat often as a sort of motto, which depicted character, existence and vocation—a sentence which tells more than a whole book: "In science we must be interested in things, not in persons."

— Eve Curie

SCRIPT

I don't like following scripts.... It's more satisfying *not* knowing what the ending is going to be

— Shirley Temple Black

SECRETARY

What are the two jobs with the most stress? A government survey on occupational safety and health found they were laborer and secretary.

What we need now is a computer to figure out what things in a secretary's life don't add up.

— Secretary

As for secretaries, some of them are treated as chattels or secondary wives or harem girls. One congressman got so possessive about the secretary who served as his "office wife" that when she said she had to stay late to catch up on work, he decided to check up on her to see if she was "cheating" on him. He pretended to be going on a trip and doubled back, using a ladder to look over the transom to see what she was doing. She was sitting at her typewriter. She looked up casually, after hearing the scratching of the ladder, and said, "Oh, there you are. Do you want carbons on this report?"

— William "Fishbait" Miller

After handling everything from keeping track of her employer's dental appointments to planning his business calendar to rinsing out coffee mugs to dusting shelves to taking care of the most urgent business questions when he was away, not to mention the usual load of typing and dictation, she (Ann Butler, a Phi Beta Kappa with a master's degree in English) realized: "I was completely unprepared for the rigors of a job I had heretofore considered a cinch...I will never sneer at secretaries again. They are superhuman fonts of practical and useful knowledge...I am convinced that if one can survive being a secretary, one can survive anything."

– Louise Kapp Howe

SECRETARY OF AGRICULTURE

... We probably ought to have a woman as Secretary of Agriculture. We could call it the "Goddess of Agriculture," something like that. The old mythology didn't have a god of agriculture, it was just a goddess.

– Eugene McCarthy

SECURE

I can afford to fool around and do-diddle with makeups and such things, because I'm secure in myself.

– Dolly Parton

Evangelist Billy Graham and his wife Ruth maintain security precautions around their mountain home. After they were installed, Ruth told friends that her Guardian Angel was "highly insulted."

SELF

I didn't value myself much so I was drawn to men who didn't value me much.

– Elizabeth Ashley

When I was younger ... it was very confusing to hear one day that I had such beautiful blue eyes and the next day that my eyes were crossed and was I going to get them fixed. I have a face like that, you know what I mean? I look a lot of different ways, and I like that now. I enjoy it in myself. I used to feel really nuts, schizophrenic. One day I'd feel very regal and self-contained, like a queen, and the next day I'd be like a clumsy thirteen-year-old. But lately what I've been accepting is that I'm really *all* of those things.

– Barbra Streisand

SELF-ACCEPTANCE

If people do find me glamorous, maybe it's because I accept myself. It would be nice to think you mature emotionally with the years. I know I'm not afraid to be myself now. And I think if you have that self-acceptance, people don't notice if a hair is out of place.

— Dinah Shore

SELF-APPROVAL

But I've finally stopped running away from myself. Who else is there better to be?

— Goldie Hawn

If you like yourself, you'll have good company and wind up with a man as well.

— Harriet Frank, Jr.

SELF-CONFIDENCE

If people do not snigger when I go by in the street, I feel that my hat has no style.

— Fernande Picasso

(Speaking of herself in the third person) Mae West would *never* cry over a man. She would just yell "Next!"

— Mae West

SELF-HELP

Self-help … I wish there were better words, but that is my whole credo. You cannot sit around like a cupcake asking other people to come and eat you up and discover your great sweetness and charm. You've got to make yourself more cupcakable all the time so that you're a better cupcake to be gobbled up.

— Helen Gurley Brown

SELF-IMPROVEMENT

(On Rose Kennedy's constant self-improvement) She reads *The New York Times* and the Hyannis newspapers every morning, cuts out worthwhile thoughts and possible quotations and then pins them on her bathroom towels and on the front of her bathrobe, to memorize them.

— Barbara Gibson

SELF-INTEREST

Women must retain a hard core of self-interest ... without it you can't grow.

— Kathryn Crosby

SELF-SUFFICIENCY

I have always regarded myself as the pillar in my life.

— Meryl Streep

SELF-SUPPORTING

Francoise Giroud, France's first State Secretary for the Condition of Women: " 'Learn a trade' is the most important piece of advice I'd give to a young girl today...I can support the idea that you let a man beat you four times a day because you love him, but not because you can't afford to leave him."

SEMINAR

Columnist Letty Cottin Pogrebin advises professional women to think of their job as a business seminar with pay.

SENIOR CITIZEN

I am 75 years old and proud of it. I like three things about old age: 1. I can speak my mind. 2. I have outlived much of my opposition. 3. When you reach out to others you have access to new energy.

— Maggie Kuhn

SERVICE

Yes, I think the girls will do all right as pilots. After all, airplanes don't have fenders.

— Bob Hope

Phyllis Schlafly said if women were drafted into the armed forces under the ERA it probably wouldn't do any good. "Historically," she said, "there's no mention of coed battles."

After speaking of a feudal warrior lady:
    ... "Where, lives there such a woman now?"
    Quick answer'd Lilia, "There are thousands now
    Such women, but convention beats them down:
    It is but bringing up; no more than that:
    You men have done it: how I hate you all!"
                                    – *Lilia in Tennyson's* The Princess

SETTLING DOWN

Friends and family are still waiting for me to outgrow this phase (Foreign Service work), get married and settle down. Not that I'm against settling down—I'm just against settling.
                                                        – *Marie Campello*

SEX

Sex with love is about the most beautiful thing there is. But sex without love isn't so bad either.
                                                        – *Christie Hefner*

Men are after one thing, and one thing only—and for that I say, Hallelujah!
                                                        – *Marilyn Sokol*

Companionship is the most important thing in life. Sex just for the sake of sex is about equal with washing your face.
                                                        – *Sophia Loren*

Sex is an emotional experience for a woman; she can't pop in and out of bed and not have it affect her character.
                                                        – *Barbara Cartland*

Feminist-actress Marie-France Pisier: "Sex should be like a delicate perfume—a few gentle drops will do all that is necessary."

(Woman to friend) Richard's every waking thought is of sex. Unfortunately, as soon as he is through thinking about it, he goes to sleep!

Not having a full (sexual) relationship with a man is a waste of yourself ... like leaving a Ferrari out in the garage.
                                                        – *Helen Gurley Brown*

(During a panel discussion, when chided by William Safire for "derogating sex" as a subject for the Washington novel) Well, who wants to read about sex with Nixon, we all know he did it twice.

— Barbara Howar

(About sex) There is no such thing as a lousy lay, there is no such thing as a great lay; it depends on the who and the circumstances... Sometimes there's magic, sometimes there isn't.

— Elizabeth Ashley

Sex is now seen as primarily a form of communication. This means that, no matter what or how we choose to communicate sexually, we are already living in a very different society from the old one in which the foremost purpose of sex was not to communicate but to reproduce, and sexual repression was the hallmark of high morals.

— Gloria Steinem

However, I don't think experimenting with sex can be fulfilling. In a way it's like experimenting with church—going to one church after another in search of a better religion. You can never try it all, not all the churches or all the sex in the world, and until you commit yourself to one church or one man you'll always wonder whether something better isn't just around the corner, so you'll never be satisfied.

— Debby Boone

I think a woman who is happy in her love life, her love expression, has a fluidity about her that other women may not have ... I said before that I do everything possible to present me at my best form, and I'm only speaking from my own personal point of view, but this is definitely one of the qualities that is extremely necessary for a polished, well-rounded performance. I'm lucky, because I'm extremely happy in my sex life. It's full and fruitful, and I know what it has done and continues to do for me as a woman.

— Leontyne Price

SEX APPEAL

(Reported by Sydney Skolsky) Sex appeal is 50 percent what you've got and 50 percent what people think you've got.

— Sophia Loren

Sydney Skolsky once said that "sex symbol" Raquel Welch's still photographs don't stand still.

I am a woman, mother and wife. If that means I am a sex symbol, I am for it 100 percent.

— Sophia Loren

(When asked to comment about Bo Derek stealing her title of sex symbol) I wish I could talk to her and tell her what to expect. First of all, don't believe your own press releases and don't take yourself seriously. The moment you take yourself seriously as a sex symbol, I think you're really in trouble. It's fun, being a sex symbol. But it's silly.

— Suzanne Somers

SEX—INFIDELITY

When I was younger I might have equated trust with sex—I don't any longer.

— Elizabeth Ashley

If my old man went out on me, I wouldn't want to know it. Why would he want to tell me and hurt me?

— Loretta Lynn

I believe all men at one time or another'll have these one night stands. It don't mean he don't love you. But if you catch 'em, kill 'em!

— Loretta Lynn

SEX OBJECT—MALE

Men are seldom, if ever, considered as sex objects at all. Except among groups of comparatively recent formation, men have for the last hundred and fifty years gradually been required to suppress all the erotic aspects of their appearance. Beards and whiskers disappeared, hair was cut back to the skull and limbs were hidden in drab clothes which were neither loose and flowing enough to enhance nor tight enough to reveal the wearer's shape.

The fear of being treated as a sex object derives not so much from masculinity itself as from sexual insecurity. Sexual insecurity is the result at least partially of a highly competitive performance ethic. The man who sets out to attract might find himself seduced into a degrading role because without his masculine armor he cannot carry through the bluff of omnipotence.

— Germaine Greer

SEX RELATIONS

I believe that the direction in which the endeavor of woman to readjust herself to the new conditions of life is leading today is not towards a greater sexual laxity or promiscuity or an increased self-indulgence, but toward a higher appreciation of the sacredness of all sex relations, and a clearer perception of the sex relation between man and woman as the basis of human society, on whose integrity, beauty, and healthfulness depend the health and beauty of human life as a whole. Above all, that it will lead to a closer, more permanent, more emotionally and intellectually complete relation between the individual man and woman.

— Olive Schreiner

SEXINESS

Writer Blair Sobol: "Sexiness is not some contrived trick-or-treat. It's always there, and you can't ignore it. For that reason, some folks may find sexiness an annoyance, like a single buzzing fly that gets in the way of the business at hand."

SEXISM

American Catholic bishops are currently under siege by reformers who want to have the words of the mass trimmed to say that Christ died, not "for all men," but "for all." The word "men," it seems, is thought to be "sexist" by the reformers, and prima facie proof of improper thinking. So the bishops are in a fix: changing the words of the liturgy would amount to admitting that what their critics charge is true—that they have "hated women all along." Not changing them, on the other hand, would mean that they are unrepentantly sexist.

— Dick Dabney

SEXUAL HARASSMENT

A woman lawyer points out many people do not take sexual harassment on the job seriously. When the Chicago Bar Association announced an upcoming seminar on sexual harassment, a male lawyer phoned her and asked: "Will it be a 'how-to' session?"

SEXUALLY AGGRESSIVE

Women with high IQs are frequently more sexually aggressive and less sexually inhibited than women of average intelligence.

— Coronet

SEXY

(Quoted in Hy Gardner's column) it gives any girl a lift to have any man, even a censor, say you're sexy.

— Gwen Verdon

SHOPPING

Women on shopping trips should exercise shelf-control.

My wife is like a baby—she always wants to go buy-buy.

— Evan Esar

SHOW BUSINESS

Sarah Vaughn, on entering show business: "I wanted to get up in the world without having to get up in the morning."

Milton Berle: I've been in show business for 72 years. Joan Rivers: Do you plan to make this a career?

Under no circumstances do I want my children in show business, for the same reasons my father (Henry Fonda) didn't want me to get into it. It's not a happy business, it's too competitive and it's not intellectually stimulating. You have to fight just to stay human. I'm amazed I've lasted.

— Jane Fonda

SHY

I like sensitivity, gentle men, shy people ... people that seem to care about other people.

— Dolly Parton

SIGN

Raises not roses

Every mother is a working mother.

Sign on a woman executive's desk: "I don't do coffee."

(A homemaker's embroidered sampler) A Clean House Is The Sign Of A Wasted Life.

Women don't get heart attacks ... they give them.

One newly-promoted woman keeps this adage in her desk drawer. "A true measure of a woman executive is how she treats co-workers and company suppliers who can do her absolutely no good."

A reporter once noted a cushion in the home of Alice Roosevelt Longworth with a piece of embroidery that said something like: "If you can't say something nice about someone, come sit down by me."

SIGHTSEEING

I'd rather look than be looked at.

– Kim Novak

SIN

Sin makes its own hell, and goodness its own heaven.

– Mary Baker Eddy

SING

To be able to sing, the whole personality must be developed. So is it with everything in life if we would reach any sort of beginning of perfection. We must look widely around us; no one-sided development.

– Jenny Lind

SINGER

I haven't done so badly for a gal who never had a singing lesson.

– Kate Smith

I started singing because where I grew up there wasn't a whole hell of a lot to do.

– Rosemary Clooney

I'm 44. I have teeth that were made by a mechanic. I wear glasses. And my legs—ee, lad, I'm glad I earn money with my throat.

– Gracie Fields

(About a pendant she wears which says "Never Assume.") I had that made up fer my manager. He's always assumin' things. You cain't assume things when yer doin' business.

– Loretta Lynn

Glenda Jackson's mother commented on the star's portrayal of a mad woman: "When you started to sing, I started to cry and kept crying and didn't see much after that. You're not a very good singer, dear."

(About a singer's not overeating) It requires effort—and hence tension—to lift a diaphragm that is full of fat! And the carrying power of a voice depends upon correct resonance rather than on adipose tissue. Try to eat for strength, not for bulk!

– Kathryn Grayson

SINGER—MESSAGE

When asked why she directs her messages toward women, country singer Loretta Lynn says that "... men just put the quarters in the jukebox—women buy the records."

An entertainer ... can put on the same performance no matter how he really feels inside. I sing exactly what's in my heart. If I'm depressed, my singing is sad and the audience knows how I feel.

– Joan Baez

SINGER—OPERA

To be an opera singer, you have to be an actress.

– Maria Callas

SINGING

I'm used to singing in church where they don't stop me till the Lord comes.

– Mahalia Jackson

Most of the time I'm not singing to the people out there ... I'm singing to myself, really I am. But I'd like the people to come along if they do it quietly.

– Lena Horne

Pop music star Joni James: "I like fantastic things and I like simple things, but I don't like anything in between ... Every time I do a number, I live it ... The heartbreak of it or the fun. I translate it so it means something to me and then I go to it."

(Reacting to the comment she was easy to write a song for) I suppose it's because I belt them out so loud and clear ... The only place where my pipes don't always work is in the nightclubs. There's always someone at the back complaining he can't hear—while you hear every word he's complaining.

— Ethel Merman

SINGING—BLUES

Anybody that sings the blues is in a deep pit calling for help, and I'm simply not in that position.

— Mahalia Jackson

SINGING—IMITATOR

I'm easy to imitate, those actions and the voice and all that stuff ... But those dames, they'll never really get on to me. They don't know what I'm thinking when I'm out there singing. No one does.

— Lena Horne

SINGING—SPIRITUALS

You have probably heard spirituals all your life. They were written in a type of shorthand like underground hymns. Many people think that they are about the afterlife. But they are actually about the times of this life in hope of a future change in the hard ways.

— Odetta

SINGLE

According to Charles W. Mueller, University of Iowa and Blair G. Campbell, University of Wisconsin: "If you're a highly successful single woman, chances are that you're less likely to marry than other single women."

Honey, I'm single because I was born that way. I never married because I'da had to give up my favorite hobby—men. I didn't want kids because they'd change me; besides I had such a good relationship with my mother, I didn't see how it could be improved upon.

— Mae West

Being single is a distraction. I mean one of the things about marriage that is good for both men and women is that it frees you from all that energy that you use to put into dating. You can put it into work. You don't have to worry about who is going to take you to the dinner party tomorrow. It takes time to be single, it seems to me.

— Nora Ephron

SINGLE BARS

Single bars are great if you want to stay single.

— Divorcee

SINGLE WOMAN

It is time that women who live alone help their hosts realize it is not the end of the world if they do not have a man supplied for them.

— Tish Baldridge

I feel that modern literature has slighted the single woman, the toughminded woman. There are books about weepers and wailers. I wanted to write a book about women who have a strong grasp on life.

— Harriet Frank, Jr.

SIZE

Once, a lady about size 96 asked me why I didn't design for fat ladies. I answered: "Madam, I am not in the upholstery business."

— Oscar de la Renta

SKYSCRAPER

Look at those Manhattan skyscrapers. They're like Tennessee mountains with lights on them.

— Dolly Parton

SLEEP

There's no such thing in any business as sleeping your way to the top.

— Lauren Hutton

I'm older now ... I've gotten to sleep with almost everyone I wanted.

— Elizabeth Ashley

I've been taken to dinner by some pretty classy escorts, but I let them know up front that I don't intend to sleep with them. Otherwise it seems unfair, letting them spend a lot of money on dinner and things.

– Sarah Miles

SLOGAN

Vivian Kellems, one of the country's leading feminists and a prolific speechmaker, had developed a slogan, "Let's put housekeeping back in the White House. And we'll put a woman president there, too." During one speech at Colby Junior College when she introduced this idea, a man dropped dead of a heart attack. She explained the unfortunate incident as the "whole idea's such a shock to men."

SMART

The heftier the hips, the smarter the student, according to a somewhat scientific study of DePauw University coeds.

– Family Weekly

SMILE

Your smile is a giant form of communication.

– Adrien Arpel

SMOKING

People have suggested I give up smoking, to which I reply, "Whatever for?"

– Bette Davis

Listen, I'm not going to deny myself one of life's little pleasures when I'm on the last lap. Who wants an extra decade in the nursing home?

– "Luvie" (Mrs. Drew) Pearson

Diana Ross in an interview with writer Elin Schoen: "I used to smoke, but I stopped because I didn't want to be dependent on anything.... I can't let a little cigarette run my body. "I just can't be that weak, I've got to be stronger."

SNEEZE

There are conditions under which the most majestic person is obliged to sneeze.

– George Eliot

SOCIAL SECURITY

Adlai Stevenson (as quoted by Earl Wilson), explaining what social security means to the sexes: "For a man—employment. For a woman engagement."

SOCIETY

(On going to the Carters' semidry parties) When you were born in bourbon and branch-water country, you have difficulty adjusting to those fine wines.

– Barbara Jordan

(In speaking of the high-living class of society which revolved around the Prince of Wales during Victoria's reign) We acknowledged that pictures should be painted, books written, the law administered. We even acknowledged that there was a certain class whose job might be to do these things. But we did not see why their achievement entitled them to recognition from us, whom they might disturb, overstimulate, or even bore. On rare occasions, if a book made a sufficient stir, we might read it, or better still, get somebody to tell us about it, and save us the trouble.

– Countess of Warwick

SON

(Rose Kennedy, speaking at a reception for her son Ted's Senate campaign) She told a story about how, when she became pregnant with her ninth child, everyone told her, "Why do you want to become pregnant again? ... it will ruin your figure, tie you down." She told the audience, "If I hadn't had the ninth, I would now have no sons." It was a poignant moment. I noticed lots of people with tears in their eyes.

– Barbara Gibson

SONG

When I don't particularly like a song, it's sure to sell.

– Rosemary Clooney

(Remarks on tour that later appeared on the *Joplin in Concert* album)
I'll do a song, man, that I'll tell you, you could apply it to, well, just
about anything you want to, but it could almost be even called the
truth. It's talking about everybody's life, and what passes by you, and
what you miss and what you grab. 'Cause it ain't gonna be there when
you wake up, man.

– Janis Joplin

SONG WRITER

The song "Amazing Grace" has always been magic for me. I heard this
story from Alex Hailey. He told me that the author of 'Amazing Grace'
was a sea-captain who was also a slaver. The captain's religion finally
caught up with him and he got out of slavery and further into his
religion. He became a preacher and wrote the song. His name was John
Newton.

Well, Hailey told me the story but didn't give me the captain's
name.... So the next time I was in Washington I called the Library of
Congress and asked if they had any information on the author of
"Amazing Grace."

I remember I was in a hurry and I had to call the airport. I
managed to get over there only to be handed a whole package on
Newton's life. I couldn't believe it.

– Odetta

SPEAKING

One of my most successful after-65 accomplishments was getting rid of
the fear of appearing in public. Sounds crazy? Well, it was never a
problem hiding behind a part I was playing on the stage, but facing a
group or audience cold, as Ruth Gordon, made my knees wobble. But I
licked it. I began with the talk shows—the Carson, Cavett, Griffin,
Donahue, etc., circuit—and took every booking I could get. And now at
last I've managed to take my own talk show on the road. I've developed a
lecture tour where I talk to as many as 1,500 persons on various subjects
and answer questions from the audience. This was my big giant step
after 65.

– Ruth Gordon

SPEECH

(Speaking at a hospital ground-breaking ceremony) My job is to charm. I stay out of politics.

— Miz Lillian Carter

Rosalynn Carter says she prays for courage before each speech. "I say, I can do it, Jesus, but you've got to help me."

Next to speaking in public oneself ... there is nothing which produces such feelings of nervousness and apprehension as to hear one's husband make a speech.

— Lady Randolph Churchill

At a testimonial dinner in her honor, Shirley Temple Black, former child star and Chief of Protocol under President Ford, said that she was just "... female, Black and unemployed."

There is a strong tendency among successful women in New York to accent their speech.... The day they acquire executive rank, they acquire an accent that would baffle Henry Higgins.... Accented speech is all right as long as it's intelligible and really your own.

— Jo Foxworth

Some of my Newport friends were in the front row and Marguerite (my sister) was in the second row on the aisle (so she could leave if my performance embarrassed her too much). Jim and Bess Farley were there, as were Mrs. Ogden Reid, and Countess de Kotzebue, Norman Thomas, and Lawrence Langner. Marguerite later said that when I came out on the stage, all she could do was stare at her feet—she was afraid to look at me. But as I started to talk and the people didn't laugh at me or get up and leave, she began to relax a little. Toward the end of my lecture, she said, she was listening to what I was saying about Russia instead of reminding herself constantly that it was her sister, Perle, who was doing the talking. I considered that one of the finest compliments possible.

— Perle Mesta

SPORT

Writer Glenna Collett: "More sports for matrons, fewer card parties and teas, and the beauty parlors will not be so full of the middle-aged trying to find synthetic youth!"

I've been called a boaster and a braggart.

But I don't think I'm that. I don't figure it's anything else than an extra large amount of confidence in myself....

I don't think its boasting to come right out and admit that I have officially or unofficially broken or equalled almost all of the Olympic records for women. That I won the National Women's A.A.U. track and field meet in Chicago in 1932 singlehanded. That I was twice given All-American honors as forward on The Golden Cyclones girls' basketball team. That I hold the women's record for the baseball throw. That I won the Texas Amateur Women's Golf Championship. That I hit the longest ball of any woman golfer. That the sports I have taken part in include running, jumping, hurdling, shot putting, discus throwing, javelin throwing, baseball, tennis, golf, hockey, boxing, wrestling, riding, billiards, pool, skating, football, fencing, basketball, swimming, shooting, weight lifting and diving.... So, to go around tittering bashfully when the subject comes up would be just a lot of false modesty and affectation, the way I see it.

— Babe Didrikson Zaharias

SPORTS—ACTING

There are a number of similarities between sports and acting. Both require tremendous concentration; both present obstacles that have to be surmounted; both teach you to set goals and then work hard to attain them, and both encourage you to truly appreciate others who are doing the same thing. When you get right down to it, playing sports is acting, and athletes are artists.

— Cathy Lee Crosby

SPORT—BASEBALL

Because of politeness, Ethel Barrymore, an avid baseball fan, usually pulled for the visiting team in most ballgames.

I know why more women don't coach. They have to go home and cook supper.

— Woman Coach in the Pony League.

Columnist Allison Sanders said that at an Astro-Dodger game in the Houston Astro-Dome a couple of tads fell into conversation. The girl, about 8 or 9, was dressed for the occasion in an Astros T-shirt and Astros cap. Her companion, noting the attire, posed a question.

"Do you know how to play baseball?"

"Sure," she told him. "I'm on a Little League team and I play outfield and shortstop and sometimes pitch."

Her seatmate then asked if there were any other girls on the team, and she told him no.

"How do the boys treat you?" he asked.

She reflected a moment, and then said·

"Like a lady pirate."

SPORTS—BASKETBALL

Description of a woman basketball coach: She radiates astuteness, caring, someone who reflects toughness over a mound of Jell-O.

SPORTS—BOWLER

I'm more momma than bowler.

— *Champion Woman Bowler*

SPORTS—CAR RACING

Woman race driver making a toast for male race drivers: "May the best man win ... which isn't likely."

(On opening car races) I definitely love (car) racing ... I love saying "Gentlemen: Start your motors!"

— *Zsa Zsa Gabor*

Drag racer Shirley "Cha Cha" Muldowney: "I knew I could be a success, but getting the guys to respect me took time. And winning. Flat dominating the whole field did it—blowing their doors right off!"

When male race drivers laugh at the idea of her being strong enough for big-time auto racing, Janet Guthrie says: "I drive the car ... I don't carry it."

(When asked why she raced cars) I don't suppose anyone has ever answered that question fully ... It's a challenge, like the mountain climber's cliche: "Because it's there." I know of no other activity that calls upon you to extend yourself 100 percent on all levels—physical, emotional, intellectual, spiritual.

— *Janet Guthrie*

(Practicing at Indianapolis before qualifying runs, she did 191 m.p.h. but tagged the wall and damaged her racing car. When asked if she was scared in a race) No, if you felt fear you'd be a danger to yourself and to other drivers. You're concentrating—on what you're doing, what the other drivers are doing, what's happening to the track.

– Janet Guthrie

SPORTS—FOOTBALL

I love football. There are so many handsome players.

– Mamie Van Doren

Why don't they give each of those boys a ball instead of their all running around chasing one?

– Minnie Pearl

SPORTS—GOLF

All his subjects be very glad, I thank God, to be busy with the golf, for they take it for pastime; my heart is very glad for it.

– Catherine of Aragon

Woman golf player: "I don't have any handicaps. I'm all handicap."

Boy, don't you men wish you could hit a ball like that!

– Babe Didrikson Zaharias

Replying to English reporters' queries as to how she won the Women's British Amateur in 1947, Babe Didrikson Zaharias stated: "Just loosen your girdle and let her fly."

(On playing the pro golf circuit) ... Here we are, the world is going up in flames, and all we can think of is three-putting a green. But that's it. Every bit of emotion and brains we've got is concentrated on the game. Wouldn't be any good otherwise.

– Betty Rawls

When I am reincarnated I'm coming back to earth as a golf ball—the men may knock them about and swear at them but they are faithful to them, and they will chase them farther than any vamp that ever lifted a lipstick.

– Elsie Janis

SPORTS—HORSE RACING

Thoroughbreds are just like women ... They must be petted and cared for the same way.

– Elizabeth Arden

Jockey Mary Bacon explaining her success: "Women have a better temperament for this work. Getting along with a horse is like winning over a child. You bullshit your way along."

"What's the difference between a 100-pound man and a 100-pound woman? Let's face it. No jock—or woman—is going to be stronger than a horse. You don't use muscles on a horse; you use brains."

– Mary Bacon

SPORTS—ICE SKATING

Taking off your warmups is like jumping in a frozen lake naked.

– Sheila Young

I think I'll always be connected with skating ... it's a change from housework.

– Peggy Fleming

(On his sister, speed skater Beth Heiden) She is a sparrow with a tiger hidden inside her.

– Eric Heiden

(On her brother, speed skater Eric Heiden) A thoroughbred horse on the outside with a stubborn mule inside.

– Beth Heiden

"It was exciting to be on the cover of Time magazine; it doesn't happen every day," she (Beth Heiden, winner of a Bronze Medal in Speed Skating at the Winter Olympics, 1980) said with her last smile. Now she really had to hold on. "But if you like that, and you like being on television, and you want attention for your sport." said the hugest man in the crowd, but with the gentlest voice, "What made it all go sour?" "It got in the way of our family," she said, and now she really started to go. "And that really got me mad." She went off trying to hide her tears in her cup.

– Tom Callahan

SPORTS—KARATE

When six of his women students graduated from his karate course, their instructor gave them framed mottoes: "Don't Maul Us—We'll Maul You."

SPORTS—RUNNING

S. F. Sunday Examiner & Chronicle writer John Crumpacker writes about Evelyn Ashford, a runner who won the World Cup competition: "The circumstances of Ashford becoming a sprinter are quite interesting.

"The Roseville (high school) football coach had noticed Ashford running in a P.E. class. Noting her speed and style, he invited her to run against his players.

" 'I beat all of them,' said Ashford, who ran 10.3 of 100 yards while a senior at Roseville. 'They didn't have a woman track team at the school, so I ran on the men's track team. There was no objection. Everybody thought it was fun. I never had any negative feedback from my running. They thought it was a joke.'"

SPORTS—TENNIS

At Wimbledon, the ladies are simply candles on the cake.
— *John Newcombe*

I wish you'd consider me a tennis player, not a Negro tennis player.
— *Althea Gibson*

Although she never won Wimbledon or any other major tournament, Gladys Heldman was inducted into the International Tennis Hall of Fame as the organizer of the women's pro circuit and founder of *World Tennis* magazine.

I've been playing tennis since before the Democrats started to play it!
— *Erma Bombeck*

Money aside, I still can't quite conceive of what being "No. 1" is all about. It's a category that few people in the world are ever able to attain, and it's scary. I guess I can prove I'm the best (even the computer says so), but it's a strange place to be. It's frightening to think that I am capable of playing tennis better than the other two billion women in the world. But, deep down, I know I can.

— Martina Navratilova

(On winning the Colgate Series that decided the "World Tennis" No. 1 world ranking for 1979) Deep down I'm all swirling around ... I had problems sleeping because I couldn't stop thinking about how I played. I was feeling the ball so well. I was moving so well. God, it was almost a perfect match. In a perfect match you don't make any errors and you get all your first serves in, but that's impossible. Last night was as close to perfection as I can play. I think. I want to still get better, but I don't know if I can.

— Martina Navratilova

SPORTS—TENNIS—FUTURE

(About getting good money and publicity in the Slims tournament) If we don't get satisfied, things will get even better. That's why I keep traveling like a madwoman, talking, making appearances, promoting. It's all good for me, but it also pulls the girls and the game along with me. I think ... we're grabbing the kids. Those twelve, thirteen and fourteen year olds. When they get ready to turn pro they won't worry if it's a "normal" life. No men are going to assign them their roles; they won't go through that phony amateur bit like I did ... these kids are really going to be liberated.

— Billie Jean King

SPORTS—TV

(On the addiction of her husband to televised sports) We don't plan a divorce, but if we did get one, the only way he would know it is if they announced it on "Wide World of Sports."

— Joyce Brothers

SPORTS—WRITERS

(Much of the work the former Olympic track star and three-time gold medal winner does on her books is scribbled on scraps of paper and stuffed in her purse while traveling.) You'd be surprised how you keep jotting things down and before long, you got enough. Put them together and you got a book.

— Wilma Rudolph

STAGE FRIGHT

I'm frozen with fear before (talk) shows. I'm very shy. I hate to talk about myself. I may look calm on the outside, but underneath it's hell.
— Sophia Loren

Waiting for the curtain to rise on opening night of her act at Las Vegas, Suzanne Somers barred visitors with the comment: "Suzanne will be busy vomiting."

STARDOM

Among other things ... stardom means you're always in a rush.
— Gwen Verdon

Young girl suffering from starlet fever.
— New York Daily News

(On being a poor child in the hills) I felt I never belonged I always wanted more ... to be a star.
— Dolly Parton

When a special program was presented on Gloria Swanson at Beacon Theatre in New York, a program note read: "Long before Hollywood made stars, there were stars who made Hollywood."

The starlet, whose rather frank interviews were bringing her good press coverage, said: "Telling the truth ... part of it ... can turn an actress into a star."

STARVING

Some people believe in Christianity or Judaism or Marxism. I believe in Not Starving.
— Actress

STATES

Woman pro golfer: "Texas is all achievement; South Carolina is all tradition."

STATURE

(Speaking of a tall girl) ... She can't relate to anybody while she's stooping. Whole conversations whiz past her, below ear level.

– Aimee Lee Ball

A five-foot-ten incher once dated a man two inches shorter—"and two inches was noticeable," she says. "Fractions made a difference. He was forever trying to arrange it so that if I was sitting on the floor, he was sitting on the rug."

– Aimee Lee Ball

(On short women) After all, we are jewel-like—tiny, with multifaceted personalities. We are quality versus quantity. We combine just the right attributes in one economic package (Japanese ideal). We are a small bundle bursting with goodies (Italian ideal). And for a sexy touch, everything is easily within reach.

– Aimee Lee Ball

(Dorothy, five-foot-two, never knew she was short until she went to college) "I had a new boy friend at another school and I thought he was gorgeous... For weeks I kept talking about how beautiful he was, but when my friends finally met him, they were stunned. 'Yes, he's very beautiful,' they said, 'but he's the size of a peanut.' I hadn't noticed—he cleared *me*."

– Aimee Lee Ball

Charlotte Observer columnist Dot Jackson: "The worst affront to short people ... must surely be the language. It was conceived by tall chauvinist pigs to put us down. Think of the derogatory terms that speak us ill: Low. Base. Puny. Runt. Sawed-off. Pixieish. Banty rooster. 'He is acting so little about this thing.' 'Don't you think she tried to make us look small?'

"Let us strike from print and speech mean references like 'short-sighted,' 'small-minded,' 'fallen short.'

"In fact, we ought to campaign to purge all references to size. From talk, newspapers, the Bible, the dictionary.

"We need to work at positive anti-Sizist PR. We need to point up that less is better. Short people are energy-efficient.

"Some of us don't use much energy at all. We eat less burger. We wear shorter pants."

I don't know exactly when it became okay or even fashionable for women to be tall, but I suspect it started to happen in the late 60's and I suspect it had something to do with the birth of the feminist movement. Remember the song "Five foot two, eyes of blue, But oh, what those five foot could do"? Remember "A doll I can carry the girl that I marry must be"? And "You are woman, I am man. You are smaller, So I can be taller than"? Remember how men talked of bringing the boss home to meet "the little woman"? Those songs and expressions now seem to be anachronisms. In fact, speaking of a woman as diminutive seems to be a pejorative way of speaking

– Aimee Lee Ball

STATUS

(When Grace Kelly married Prince Rainier of Monaco) Everyone likes to see a little American girl who has practically everything in the world—get the rest of it.

– Johnny Carson

STEWARDESS

A stewardess jokes that every Catholic girl's first ambition is to be a nun, and next, to be a stewardess.

STOCKHOLDERS

When a mining company took over a small Utah town for a refuse dump and declined to pay expenses for uprooted residents, an 81-year-old woman successfully twisted the Company's arm. At a stockholders' meeting she said. "We (residents) ARE stockholders—stockholders in human life."

STRESS

In the normal human being it is impossible to live every day under emotional stress; there have to be, on this seesaw, periods of even balance.

– Faith Baldwin

Company president Barbara Fields: "I think there are times we all feel the load is too immense. But you're nourished by your work, and you know that the times of strain will pass."

STYLE

Style is style is style is you.

– Gertrude Stein

SUCCESS

When people say how well I'm doing, I always look behind me.
– Joan Rivers

There is no deodorant like success.

– Elizabeth Taylor

I ain't done bad for an old lady.

– Grandma Moses

No matter what happens to me I still feel like a little girl from Detroit.
– Diana Ross

Success is counted sweetest by those who ne'er succeed.
– Emily Dickinson

In *Damn Yankees* ... whatever Lola wants Lola gets with a flip of the hip. The rest of us usually have to work hard to achieve any success.
– Gwen Verdon

(Speaking to a group of Saleswomen) Whatever you women do, you must do it twice as well as men to be thought good. Luckily, you'll not find this difficult.

– Sales Manager

The *Chattanooga* (Tenn.) *News-Free Press:* "A successful man is one who makes more money than his wife can spend. A successful woman is one who can find such a man."

I cannot tell you how tired I am of being one of "the few—the ten, the twenty, the thousand ... every successful woman is familiar with that particular isolation...."

– Marlo Thomas

I can't do much with my hands; so I will make a battering-ram of my head and make a way through this rough-and-tumble world.
– Louisa May Alcott

If you want to succeed, be willing to assume responsibilities and to work to the highest level of your capabilities. While it's hard to be objective about what that level is for you, it's not hard to assume responsibilities. Sometimes the demands of a profession, like working overtime, impinge on your personal life. The woman who considers such demands not a sacrifice, but a reordering of priorities, will be a success.

– Brigadier General Margaret A. Brewer

He has achieved success who has lived well, laughed often and loved much; who has enjoyed the trust of pure women, the respect of intelligent men and the love of little children; who has filled his niche and accomplished his task; who has left the world better than he found it, whether by an improved poppy, a perfect poem or a rescued soul; who has never lacked appreciation of earth's beauty or failed to express it; who has always looked for the best in others and given the best he had; whose life was an inspiration; whose memory a benediction.

– Bessie Anderson Stanley

SUCCESS—BUSINESS

When making $135 a week at a talent agency, Sue Mengers realized she could do a better job than some talent agents "making a hundred grand. So I went out on my own." From then on, she recalls, she never touched a typewriter or took public transportation.

Executive Pamela Nelson: "To what do I owe my success? Excellent results. At Sears, each national merchandise manager is measured in terms of sales and profits. That's the way it should be. The bottom line is a very big equalizer."

Songwriter Carol Connors: "The most important thing I've learned from men about being successful is: Make a decision. It's essential to make decisions fast, quick, snap."

SUGAR MOMMY

Some career women, going out with younger men, play Sugar Mommy.

SUPERSTITION

Every day of my life I wear something red because it brings me luck.

– Sophia Loren

SURPRISE

> The Riddle that we guess
> We speedily despise—
> Not anything is stale so long
> As Yesterday's Surprise.

— Emily Dickinson

SWEARING

Julie Andrews (as reported by Leonard Lyons): "I never use a naughty word unless the role calls for it. But never say that I don't *think* it."

TALENT

Talent is an ability to do something instinctively.

— Cicely Tyson

A Southern grandmother once said, "Talent ain't nothin' but wantin' to bad enough."

I think if you have a talent, then you must absolutely give it to people as long as you can.

— Ingrid Bergman

If a person doesn't fulfill his talent ... the talent God gave him, he might as well lay down and die the way I look at it.

— Althea Gibson

As father Richard said at the turn of the century, "There is only one aristocracy and that's talent! Our breed is a helluva lot nobler than anything you'll find in that damn Blue Book!"

— Joan Bennett

(On being interviewed for a job on the *New York World Telegram*) The editor said, "What makes a provincial punk like you think she can write for the big-city Telegram?" I was very cheeky and pulled myself up and said, "I wasn't aware that geography was a measure of talent." I was hired.

— Gail Sheehy

I think talent is very sexy. It could be anything, like a gardener's skill, if he's developed that specific talent, it really expresses who he is. When

someone is doing what he does best, it's really sexy. Like Carol Burnett, when she does what she does, it's so sexy because she's so good.
— Sally Field

TALK

We women do talk too much, but even then we don't tell half we know.
— Nancy Astor, M.P.

Rolfe Neill, publisher of *The Charlotte Observer*: "I'd rather talk with an interesting woman than a beautiful woman. It's even nicer to talk with an interesting, beautiful woman."

The way a man speaks lays bare the texture of his mind, the goodness of his heart, the inner pain or the sweet serenity that are his companions in solitude.

— Harriet Van Horne

Without anyone to talk to, a person is not quite real. Sounds are very important—we are like bats tapping at each other with sounds, making sure there is someone there, groping along.
— A character from The Goddess and Other Women
by Joyce Carol Oates

When feminist Vivian Kellems, who opposed high taxes and bureaucrats, would find herself talking to someone who didn't agree with her, she would say: "I can see you don't agree with a word I've said, but didn't I put it well, though?"

In a TV special, Goldie Hawn and Liza Minnelli played two roommates divulging long-suppressed feelings about one another. Goldie suddenly says to Liza, "Don't say it because once you do, I'll never forget it."

Written in the back of an 1879 Methodist Episcopal Church hymnal: "To whom it may concern, this is to certify that Cora M. Moody on the 18th of Dec. 1989 A.D. did not speak for 15 min., 20 seconds. She made a very good beginning.—M."

TAME

Three things have been difficult to tame—the ocean, fools and women. We may soon be able to tame the ocean; fools and women will take a little longer....
— Spiro Agnew

TASTE

Taste is an innate talent, one that has nothing whatsoever to do with money ... I try to make a woman look as sexy as possible and yet look like a lady.

— *Sophia Gimbel*

TAXPAYER

Even if the issue (ERA) is unpopular, I still owe it. I'm a taxpayer and when it comes to that, we are all equal.

— *Carol Burnett*

Golden rule for business women: Do unto others and use it as a tax deduction.

TEACHER

Rose (Kennedy) is the finest teacher we ever had. She made our house a university that surpassed any formal classroom in the exciting quest for knowledge.

She was also the quiet at the center of the storm, the anchor of the family, the safe harbor where little ones could tow their capsized boats and set their sails again, confident her hand was on the rudder.

She could spot a hole in a sock from a hundred yards away. She could catch an error in our grammar, or sense a wandering eye at the grace before our meals.

For half a century in ways like these, she has been gently stretching each child and grandchild toward her goal of excellence. And always, she mixed her tonic of education and self-improvement with a dose of love so overflowing that her potion was irresistible.

— *Edward Kennedy*

TEEN-AGER

The only reason a teen-age girl eats heartily is so she can grow up fast and go on a diet.

— *Fletcher Knebel*

The best way to keep children home is to make the home atmosphere pleasant—and let the air out of the tires.

— *Dorothy Parker*

Writer Peter Evans once spoke of a teen-age actress as facing the classic dilemma of childhood stars bridging the gap between pigtails and cocktails.

TELEPHONE

I'm afraid of using telephones except when I'm talking to somebody I know.

– Eartha Kitt

A woman executive recalls answering the telephone after 5 p.m. in her office. "When the caller heard my voice," she said, "he lamented to someone with him, 'It's no use. There's no one there. A girl answered.' and the caller hung up."

Whenever the phone rings I have, of course, the wonderful thought that something remarkable and astonishing is going to happen. Need you in California; plane tickets arriving special delivery ... Investigation proves you only surviving heir of ...

– A character in Queen of the May
by Shirley Jackson

Margaret Chase Smith often sent her staff home at 5:30 p.m., only to stay on longer herself to finish up the day's remaining letters. When calls came in on these nights alone, she had no problem covering up her Skowhegan, Maine, accent and asking, "Is there any message for the senator?"

TEMPERAMENT

I have only two temperamental outbursts a year—each lasts six months.

– Tallulah Bankhead

TERRARIUM

Postage stamp garden
I wet it and
send it with love.

– Betsy Bostian

THANKS

… when we learn to give thanks, we are learning to concentrate not on the bad things, but on the good things in our lives.

– Amy Vanderbilt

THANKSGIVING

Charlotte Observer columnist Ina Hughs: "I'm going over the river and through the woods to grandmother's house for a self-basting turkey and homemade corn pudding. And love. Lots of love.

"Don't season my weekend with scenes of hollow-eyed children wrapped in black rags, old men vomiting on each other inside blue refugee tents—people without names who become numbers on the 6 o'clock news.

"Don't make me have to wrap up my leftovers in newspapers with pictures of mothers holding dead children. Don't interrupt my list of blessings with scenes from the valley of the shadow of death.

"After all, it's Thanksgiving

"Let me eat in peace.

"Don't rain on my parade.

"I'm counting blessings.

"Let me sleep. 'Remember the starving Chinese' we are told. And we clean our plate.

"But what if the only way to spell relief for all these nameless, frightened, haunting, hurting people is if people like you and me get a good case of heartburn this Thanksgiving?"

As we gather together to count the Lord's blessings today, the 375th anniversary of the first Thanksgiving Day, we thank Thee, God of our fathers, for Camp David and campfires and campers (when someone else cooks) and Camelot, for Indian summer and independence and intimations of immortality, for colleges and colleagues and collages and choirs.

For 10,000-runner marathons and 10-yard gains, for a $2 trillion GNP and 10 billion brain cells, for the Dow Jones when it goes up and unemployment statistics when they go down, for 20 percent off and fringe benefits added on, and for 36-26-36 and 1776, we give Thee grateful thanks this Thanksgiving week, O Lord.

O God, our help in ages past, our hope for years to come, we are grateful, too, for peacemakers and pacemakers and pizzamakers, for salt that adds savor and SALT that gives hope, for paramedics and parachutes and parables and parades; for elections, affection and Thy divine protection....

For catalogues and cathedrals and catamarans and catcher's mitts, make us thankful, God. But most of all, Lord of all, to Thee we raise our words of grateful praise for the American dream and the amazing grace and the ancient assurance that "Neither death, nor life, nor angels, nor principalities, nor powers, nor things present, nor things to come, nor height, nor depth, nor any other creature shall be able to separate us from the love of God."

— Joan Beck

THEATER

I remember when I was three, my grandfather would drive me around Constitution Square—our principal public place—and he would say, "Salute your subjects, my queen." I would bow and wave, making an exhibition of myself, and I guess that it was my first step toward the theater.

— Melina Mercouri

What would I do were platforms, microphones ... and screens denied me? I'd go to the races ... Cooking? Writing? These require powers of concentration and industry I don't possess. The theater has spoiled me for the more demanding arts.

— Tallulah Bankhead

I played it (Peter Pan) about one thousand, five hundred times. As you might expect all the matinees were attended by many children who thought that I was really a boy. I remember one incident that happened nearly forty years ago, as I pushed my way through the crowds after a matinee at the Empire Theater to my electric automobile at the curb, I caught the eye of a small boy. The profound disappointment on his face seemed to tell me: "You're not Peter Pan, or even a boy; you're an actress, and a lady." From that time on, during the run of the play, I never again left the theater after a matinee, lest too many little boys became disillusioned.

— Maude Adams

We decided that it would be best for Dorothy (Gish) to take the contract. She was then a Griffith player but by the terms of the new contract to be made with Paramount and Mr. Griffith she would star in seven films that would earn her a total of a million dollars. Mother didn't go with Dorothy to the conference at which the contract was to be discussed, thinking it would be good for her to handle it on her own. Dorothy attended the conference, listened politely, and then just as politely said, "no." When she came home and told Mother, she asked, "Why, Dorothy, did you do that?" Dorothy said, "Why, Mother, all that money at my age. It might ruin my character."

– Lillian and Dorothy Gish

THIN

(After she'd been complimented on how thin she'd become, she quipped) It was easy! They put me in a crib with high sides and they chopped off my leg; how was I gonna get to the refrigerator?

– Totie Fields

THINKING

For as a (woman) thinketh in (her) heart, so *is* (she).

– Proverbs 23:7

Rising at 5 a.m., Gloria Vanderbilt says she enjoys "dreaming, and thinking and planning," before she sees her sons off to school.

THOREAU

Everything Thoreau says hits something deep within me. From the time I was sixteen years old I kept some of his material with me most of the time. Many times I slept with it under my pillow in case I woke up in the night, just to read and read. In those early days of having all my babies there was nothing intellectual in my life, just babies, doctors, bottles and diapers. Thoreau was like blood in my veins. When I first became aware that I had that job to do, I asked my husband if I could build a Walden. We had very little money at the time, but my desire was so great that he found enough so that I could build just a tiny little shack. That's where I went every summer and took my children.

– Ruth Carter Stapleton

THOUGHT

A (woman's) life is the direct result of (her) thoughts.

– Buddha

THRIFT AWRY

It really was nice
Buying things at half price
The day after Christmas last year;
I labeled and twined them
(And wish I could find them
Now that this Christmas is here!).

– Gloria Rosenthal

TIME

A woman confessed, "My attitude toward time is defensive—I'm always out to get it before it gets *me*."

Bring the past into this eternal present only to guide your actions, or when, in some dark moment, you need to be cheered by happy memories. Bring the thought of the future into your mind only when it spurs you to action now.

– Clare Boothe Luce

TIME—PAST

Don't live in the past. No matter how good everything was in the past, the future is still a dream—with who knows what great possibilities.

– Virginia Graham

TOKENISM

Women have not even reached the level of tokenism that blacks are reaching.

– Shirley Chisholm

TOMBOY

Tomboy: A girl who has yet to discover that her strength is her weakness—and vice versa.

(About C. Z. Guest) Who could have imagined that lurking inside this cool vanilla lady was a madcap, laughing tomboy?

– Truman Capote

TOMBSTONE

No hits, no runs, no heirs.

— A spinster's epitaph

You know what I'm going to have on my tombstone? "She did it the hard way."

— Bette Davis

At last I know where he is at night!

— Middlesex, England widow

Written by a widow on her adulterous husband's tombstone: "Gone. But not forgiven."

> Sixteen years a maiden
> One 12 months a wife
> One half hour a mother
> And then I lost my life.

— English tombstone inscription

(On a tombstone Harry Benton ordered for his wife, Effie (1894-1931).)
> Say not good night;
> But in some brighter clime,
> Bid us good morning!

TOUCH

One touch of a woman's hand can be paradise, if the touch is not for too much.

— Will Durant

TOUR

(When Irene Meyers, Supervisor of Women's Activities, led a large group of General Electric's factory and office women employees on a tour to Europe) Each girl chose a basic color—navy, black, brown or green—and built her entire wardrobe around it. Each girl purchased an orlon suit that could be washed out and hung up to dry overnight, a nylon slip, three nylon blouses, and five identical pairs of nylon hose—so that if one stocking became snagged, its mate could be worn with any outfit.

Months before their departure date, Miss Meyers arranged orientation lectures ... One girl, on learning that in France it was the custom to drink only wine with meals, went into training, and soon was able to consume a quart a day without visible effects.

– Frederick G. Brownell

TRAINING

When training to play the film role of an Olympics track star, beauteous Mariel Hemingway commented about her muscles: "You can see them get larger, they feel stronger. You become real conscious of them but not in a vain way."

TRAITOR

"And in certain parts of Albania, a woman enjoys a unique privilege," went on my hostess. "If she is tired of being a woman, she can renounce her sex. She declares herself a 'Holy virgin'—even if she is married or a widow—and can claim all the privileges of a man. She does no more housework, but carries a gun and goes around with the men. She joins their hunting expeditions and is accepted by them without reserve. But she must observe the rules of the game. If, after she has publicly made this change, she has any love affair with a man, she is shot."

"Ah, then there is punishment for erring women," I said.

"She is not shot as an erring woman. She is shot as a traitor ... a traitor to the male sex."

– Lillian T. Mowrer

TRANSLATION

Translator Steven Seymour: "Translations are like women. When they are pretty, chances are they won't be faithful."

TRAVEL

Once you've been to a place, it never seems far away.

– Woman Travel Agent

Travel takes you outside of yourself and makes you look inside.

– Loretta Swit

TROUBLE

Women and slaves give equal trouble.

— *Confucius*

TRUTH

I always tell the truth. I cannot be bothered to lie—you need such a good memory.

— *Sophia Loren*

I always mean what I say when I say it, but tomorrow I may change my mind.

— *Joanne Woodward*

If you want to write the truth, you must write about yourself.... I am the only real truth I know.

— *Jean Rhys*

TV

(On her TV re-runs) I've been a baby sitter for three generations.

— *Lucille Ball*

I found the most divine sleeping pill—television.

— *Eva Gabor*

One woman's definition of TV: "Candy for the mind."

(On concluding her TV variety show) I just want to exhale for a year.

— *Carol Burnett*

Television beams into the home a message of unreality: "It's Fun, It's New, You need it."

— *Shirley Chisholm*

(Advising 50 school children interviewers not to go overboard in television watching) "You must be doers and not watchers."

— *Margaret Thatcher*

After returning from school, seven-year-old Marian settled down to watch TV. When a friend came to the door and asked her to come out and play, Marian replied, "I'm so sorry, but I'm closed."

(Cartoon—Woman explaining a broken TV screen) What happened was, Jean Harlow was on an old movie and my husband lunged forward to flick his Bic for her.

– Bic advertisement

Actress Celeste Holm, as quoted by Leonard Lyons: "Television has all the intimacy of a night club, the vast market of the movies, the audience response of the theater—and all the insecurity of summer stock."

TWINKLE

Helen Keller remarked after meeting Mark Twain, "I can feel the twinkle of his eye in his handshake."

TYPEWRITER

I remember one day we had a bunch of people here for a beach party, and the house was filled with people. I began to feel scattered, upset, not myself. I could have gone and sat in the bathroom for a while by myself. I could have gone for a walk on the beach. Instead, I went to my office and just sat in front of my typewriter, and it was okay. I got control. I calmed down. I'm only myself in front of my typewriter.

– Joan Didion

The girl Lillian (Sholes) had ... learned the keyboard (of the newly invented typewriter) ... On a certain day ... Miss Sholes was asked by her father to show ... the inventors that she could run the machine ... And so she wrote:

"Dear Friend: This is a writing machine by which words can be written easily and read by all." ...

Lillian thus became the spiritual mother of the thousands of young women who have, are now, and will ever pursue the profession of typist. Seated at one of her father's early models, prophetic of the millions of women who have since earned their livelihood in this way.

– Arthur Toye Foulke

ULCERS

Celeste Holm, as quoted by Walter Winchell: "The tragedy of ulcers is that you can have them and still not be a success."

UNDERGRADUATE

When Pearl Bailey, at 59, enrolled in classes at Washington, D.C.'s Georgetown University, she decided to skip classes in drama because "I took it 40 years of my life."

UNDRESS

Hollywood's undressing madness has gone as far as it can go. I've started putting clothes on and the only thing I plan to reveal in the future is talent.

— Terry Moore

A letter in an advice column once pointed out that husbands and wives who undressed in front of each other stayed happily married and that the greater number of married partners who undressed in closets split up. The columnist commented, "Where there's light there's heat."

UNMARRIED

She laughs, she cries, she feels angry, she feels guilty, she makes breakfast, she makes love, she makes do, she is strong, she is weak, she is brave, she is scared, she is ... an unmarried woman.

— Ad for the film "An Unmarried Woman"

VACATION

Sunday! My glorious day off.

– Rosalind Russell

A woman travel agent says, "A lot of men should stop treating a vacation as sort of a homework assignment."

When writer Robert Crandall learned that The Women's Club in Norway, an affiliate of the General Federation of Women's Clubs, was campaigning to achieve vacation for all housewives, he commented that it "strikes me personally as a dangerously subversive idea."

VEIL

In Arabia before the advent of Islam it was customary to bury female infants alive. Mohammed improved on the barbaric method and discovered a way by which all females could be buried alive and yet live on—namely, the veil.

– Annie Van Sommer and Samuel M. Zwemer

VICE

Chewing gum is my vice and knitting my avocation.

– Joan Crawford

(Her biggest vice) Always blaming myself for anything that happens. Guilt. Terrific guilt.

– Bette Davis

VIRGIN

I knew Doris Day before she was a virgin.

– Oscar Levant

You watch. In five years, it is going to be very smart to be a virgin.

– Barbara Cartland

Sometimes when I look at all my children, I say to myself, "Lillian, you should have stayed a virgin."

– Miz Lillian Carter

VIRTUE

Woman's virtue is man's greatest invention.

– Cornelia Otis Skinner

VIRTUOUS

Who can find a virtuous woman? for her price is far above rubies....
    Strength and honour are her clothing; and she shall rejoice in time to come.
    She openeth her mouth with wisdom; and in her tongue is the law of kindness....
    Her children arise up, and call her blessed; her husband also, and he praiseth her.... A woman that feareth the Lord, she shall be praised.
Proverbs 31:10, 25, 26, 28, 30

VOICE

A critic once called an actress' singing voice "more willing than thrilling."

(By the time she was graduated) I discovered that all you really need to be a glorious singer is a gorgeous voice. All the rest can be fed into you, but all the rest won't do it if you don't have a glorious voice....

– Anna Russell

You can't reach for the stars at once. The human voice is slow in the making and demands years of painstaking effort and study. There are no shortcuts. Auditions may be excellent in focusing attention on your voice, but they can also be harmful. Too much sudden adulation misleads you into thinking the way is easy.

– Lotte Lehmann

VOICE—TIMBRE

Timbre again, belongs according to my idea to the *expression of the soul*. My timbre must obey my feelings. Therefore a correct declamation and careful phrasing in all its fine and endless shadings together with a right development of the *inner being* must absolutely help me over the technique to the real subject (emotion) which the vowels stand for. If I sing of joy, sorrow, hope, love, my Saviour, folk-songs, moonlight, sunshine, etc., I feel naturally quite differently, and my voice takes on my soul's timbre without that I need in the least care with what tone color I sing.

— Jenny Lind

VOLUNTEER

A note for "help" posted on the Women's National Democratic Club bulletin board (in Washington, D.C.) was not soliciting volunteers for a presidential task force. It was soliciting volunteers to help address the President's Christmas cards.

Newspaper writer Pat Borden, a volunteer "friend" at Alexander Children's Center) " 'You know what a volunteer is for?' Bobby asked.... 'No, what?' I asked. I'd been Bobby's volunteer for several months.... 'They help you get that happy feeling,' he told me, 'so the frown lines will go away.'"

I manage to keep on the go, what with writing a column for our newspaper, serving on PTA and Girl Scout committees, and conducting meetings for 28 Brownies. One evening my husband was kept busy answering phone calls which were for me. When one woman asked, "Will she be home later" he replied, "I expect so. She usually stops in between meetings."

— Mrs. Kenneth Neville

(About their mother Lillian) Mother did take an active part in the Sunday school work, though. She didn't teach a class, but she served on a number of committees. Once she called on a woman who had just moved to town, to ask her to serve on a fund-raising committee. "I'd be glad to if I had the time," the woman said. "But I have three young sons and they keep me on the run. I'm sure if you have a boy of your own, you'll understand how much trouble three can be." "Of course," said Mother. "That's quite all right. And I do understand." "Have you any children, Mrs. Gilbreth?" "Oh, yes." "Any boys?" "Yes, indeed." "May I ask how many?" "Certainly, I have six boys." "Six boys?" gulped the woman. "Imagine a family of six!" "Oh, there are more in the family than that. I have six girls, too." "I surrender," whispered the newcomer. "When is the next meeting of the committee? I'll be there, Mrs. Gilbreth. I'll be there."

— Frank B. Gilbreth, Jr. & Ernestine Gilbreth Carey

VOLUNTEER—DISASTER

(Speaking of a situation which occured in Kentucky during an Ohio River flood) One of the Red Cross volunteers had worked hard at the school gym, where they had set up a mass shelter for those families who had been flooded out of their homes. This volunteer had noticed a little old man and a shriveled little woman sitting on their cots way back in the corner. Neither said a word to one another or to anyone else. They looked so pitiful and befuddled that she decided to take them to her home that night, so they wouldn't have to spend the night in that noisy, cold gym. When she asked them to go with her, they both resisted. She kept insisting, and they both held back, but she wouldn't take "no" for an answer, and dragged them off to more comfortable quarters. When she got them to her home, she gave them a hot cup of tea and a piece of cake. She got out a pair of her husband's pajamas for the old man and one of her nightgowns for the little old lady, and took them up to the guest room. As she was saying good night and was about to shut the door, she asked if there was anything else she could do to make them comfortable. The man said, "Yes, ma'am, if you don't mind, please. Would you introduce me to this-here woman?"

— Jane Clay Sutherland

VOTE

The first U.S. Congresswoman Jeanette Rankin said that at the polls people are given a "choice of evils, not ideas."

(Declaring she has voted only in one presidential election) I don't vote generally ... It doesn't matter what they (politicians) say anyway. They do what they have to do to stay in and be popular and keep the votes.

— Joan Baez

After casting the *only* dissenting vote in the U.S. House of Representatives on the United States Declaration of War against Japan, Congresswoman Jeanette Rankin said, "I voted against it because it was war."

I do not think women go sheep-like to the polls voting only as the head of the house directs. Most of us, I suppose, *do* mark the same ballot as our spouses but that is more a testament to domestic felicity than to coercion. In our house, my husband and I have often supported opposing parties and we are rather proud that we can do so without rancor. (We have always felt it was more important to happiness that we agree on the small things like the color of the bedroom wallpaper or whom to invite to dinner than on issues which only conscience can determine.)

– Phyllis McGinley

VOTE—WORKING FOR

I have lived to realize the great dream of my life—the enfranchisement of women. We are no longer petitioners, we are not wards of the nation but free and equal citizens.

– Carrie Chapman Catt

When I read President (Theodore) Roosevelt's long (birthday) tribute to her, Miss (Susan) Anthony rose to comment on it.

"One word (about women's suffrage) from President Roosevelt in his message to Congress," she said, a little wearily, "would be worth a thousand eulogies of Susan B. Anthony. When will men learn that what we ask is not praise, but justice?"

– Anna Howard Shaw

There was nothing Mrs. (Amelia) Bloomer could do, but before returning to Council Bluffs, she sat down in her hotel and wrote a letter to the Des Moines Reporter in which she attacked and ridiculed the reasons Senator Gaylord had given in his speech for not enfranchising women.

"A female ought not to be compelled by law to work out a poll-tax on the public highway," had argued the Senator, "Nor to learn the art of butchery on the battle field." He claimed that if women received the vote, then it was only right that they should become liable to perform the same civic duties as men.

Mrs. Bloomer thought such reasoning absurd. Why couldn't a woman hire a substitute to do these things, just as the Senator himself did? "I venture the assertion, without knowing, that he did not earn his rights to the ballot by the bullet or by shovelling dirt on the highway. If only those who do these things were allowed to vote, the number of voters would be small indeed."

– Charles Neilson Gattey

WALKING

I have often thought that God may have taken away President Roosevelt's power of locomotion to save him from a second-rate career.

— Sister Kenny

WALL STREET

I am in earnest; therefore they (the people on Wall Street) picture me heartless. I go my own way, take no partners, risk nobody else's fortune, therefore I am Madame Ishmael, set against every man.

— Hetty Green

The girl who put the sparkle into what has been called the "dismal science" of finance dislikes people to think that her occupation is freakish for a woman. A Wall Street financier who tried to squelch her by being patronizing was brought up short by Miss (Sylvia) Porter's caustic comment on his attitude. She ended her remarks with, "You see, sir, I believe that the brain has no sex."

— Jack Sher

(About a country-wide recession) I saw this situation coming ... and I predicted it. I saw that the rich were approaching the brink and that a panic was inevitable. Some of the solidest men in the Street came to me and wanted to unload all sorts of things, from palatial residences to automobiles. When the crash came I had money, and I was one of the very few who really had it. The others had their securities and their values. I had the cash and they had to come to me.

— Hetty Green

If one is rich and one's a woman ... one can be quite misunderstood. I'm afraid that on Wall Street they think all I'm after is prizes and ego trips; that how the stock does, doesn't matter to me. Half of them think I don't work at all and just go to parties; the other half think I'm obsessed with Watergate. I get a lot of flak at the Post, too, when I talk about profitability. They get up pretty tight at the mention of M-O-N-E-Y; they think I'm some heartless bitch. I have to do an endless song and dance about how excellence and profitability go hand in hand—which isn't an act. I really think they do. It costs plenty to put two people on a story for sixteen months, and profit-making is my priority. If it weren't, I shouldn't be here.

— Katherine Graham

WANT

I know what women want—and that's to be flung across a man's saddle or into the long grass by a loving husband.

— Barbara Cartland

Orchestra conductor Antonia Brico: "You die inside when you don't do what you want to do more than anything in the world."

I want someone who knows what he's about ... a success in his own line of work. Someone who—hopefully—has a brain!

— Lauren Bacall

WAR

Former Congresswoman Jeanette Rankin on the Vietnam War: "The world must finally understand that we cannot settle disputes by eliminating human beings."

This war is the ultimate conflict, the final collision, of two conceptions of life: on one side, liberty, individualism, Christian civilization; on the other, oppression, aggression, torture, and the law of the jungle.

— Eve Curie

WASHING MACHINE

Raconteur Joel Sasser in the *Reader's Digest:* "Washing machines in an upstate New York apartment complex are labeled with human names for easy identification by the repairman. In Chelsea Chatter, a local newsletter, the repair clerk reported: "One work order gave me pause. It said that Mary, a machine on Canterbury, gets hot but won't tumble. She still takes money, though."

WASHINGTON

Washington is a town of famous men and the women they married when they were young.

— Mrs. Oliver Wendell Holmes

Your private life and your public life are identical in Washington.

— Barbara Walters

WASHINGTON MONUMENT

Alice Roosevelt Longworth became so well known in Washington, D.C. for her wit and longevity that she was referred to as the other Washington Monument.

WATERGATE

One reason for the Watergate scandal, I think, was that Nixon and his associates didn't have any women to tell them they were daft.

— David Cornwell (aka John le Carré)

WAY

Novelist Pamela Hansford Johnson's school motto: "If you don't find a way, make one."

WEAKER SEX

Men should think you're a poor little thing who can't cross the road or carry a parcel.

— Barbara Cartland

WEAKNESSES

We love everybody who justifies our weaknesses.

— Virginia Graham

WEALTH

I've been poor and I've been rich, and believe me—rich is better.
— Sophie Tucker

WEATHER

Among the most famous traitors in history, one might mention the weather.
— Ilka Chase

WEDDING

Hollywood is becoming more formal. At a wedding the other day, the bride wore a veil so long it almost covered her pants.

Chick Hosch, in the *Atlanta Constitution:* "The reason why so many mothers cry at weddings is that their daughters are marrying a man just like dad."

(Cartoon) Newly married bride and groom in wedding clothes, about to enter an automobile. Bride: "You get in first, I'll be getting out at mother's."
— Chon Day

Young people nowadays want to add personal touches to their wedding vows; they want to repeat words to each other in the ceremony that mean the most to them. Last week I was at a wedding where the couple did just that. They read each other their Honda guarantees.
— Kaye Ballard

An aunt stopped to ask her six-year-old niece Kathy and her two little friends what game they were playing, "Oh, Aunt Jane, we've had a wedding. I was the bride," said Kathy. And Barbie played the flower girl. Pam was the minister." Who was the groom?" Aunt Jane asked, "Oh, it was a small wedding, so we didn't have a groom." said Kathy complacently.

WEDDING—ELOPEMENT

Writer Cameron Shipp in an article gave this description of the announcement of the elopement of French movie actress Leslie Caron to George Hormel: "Geordie Hormel, a twenty-three-year-old one-man band who plays as many as thirteen instruments when he makes recordings, sent the following telegram to his father, Jay Catherwood Hormel, chairman of the board of George A. Hormel & Co., of Austin, Minnesota, famed for ham and Spam: 'You have just become the father of a 110-pound French girl.'

Mr. Hormel considered this announcement in the best of taste and offered only one mild protest. Newspaper accounts had described Geordie as heir to a seven-million-dollar meat fortune.

'Are they trying to low-rate me?' he asked his son."

WEDDING—SHORT NOTICE

"What do you say, El?" asked Lou (Gehrig). "Let's be married today."
"How can we?"

"I'll get the mayor to marry us," he said, eagerly. "You call up your mother and your aunt. Tell 'em to get over here right away. I'll get Fred Linder to help hold me up. He's a big, strong guy. And we'll be married at noon."

It was ten o'clock. The carpenter, the plumber and the carpetlayer were busily hammering and clattering.

The mayor, Walter Otto, answered our call. My aunt entered, breathless. Mr. Linder hurried to the scene. At noon we were married.
— El (Mrs. Lou) Gehrig

WEEPING

I will never weep again. The heart can only break once.
— Pearl Buck

WEIGHT

Extra cash
Bought fudge
Extra bulge
Won't budge.

— Sonia Masello

When I'm asked how much I weigh, I always quickly answer, "One hundred and too-much."
— Dental assistant

(About her weight) There's been more tension in my zipper than there has in the Middle East!

— *Kaye Ballard*

When Sister Elaine consulted the doctor because she was underweight he prescribed nun fattening foods.

(Joking about her 4-ft., 11-in., 190-lb. figure) Obese, hefty, overweight, rotund. I never knew there were so many ways to say fatty.

— *Totie Fields*

> Since chocolate's plain old cocoa beans
> And whipped cream's mostly air
> My scale and I, we wonder how
> Those pounds land here and there!

— *Sonia Masello*

Esther Manz, founder and president of TOPS ("Take Off Pounds Sensibly") had two dieting tips: "Follow your doctor's advice and if you're built like a robin, don't try to become a hummingbird."

I've never had a problem with weight because I *think thin*. Every night before I go to sleep I decide it doesn't matter what I ate that day, I'm thinking thin and I'll wake up thin.

— *Hermione Gingold*

WEIGHT—SLOGAN

TOPS ("Take Off Pounds Sensibly"), non-profit slimming association, has the slogan: "See You Lighter."

WELFARE STATE

Unless we are very careful, this welfare state will turn into a farewell state.

— *Nancy Astor, M.P.*

WHISTLE

If a good-looking man went by I'd *think* a whistle, but I wouldn't really whistle ... You can whistle with your eyes.

— *Angie Dickinson*

(Said to Humphrey Bogart in the movie "To Have and Have Not.") If you want me—just whistle.

— Lauren Bacall

(As a lad Benjamin Franklin once paid too much at a store for a whistle he fancied. Later in life he often saw others whom he felt "paid too much for a whistle.") When I see a beautiful, sweet-tempered girl married to an ill-natured brute of a husband, what a pity, say I, that she should pay so much for a whistle!

— Benjamin Franklin

WHITE HOUSE

To the question, would you like to live in the White House, Martha (Mrs. Robert A.) Taft answered: "Who wouldn't!"

Upon moving into the White House, Mamie Eisenhower hung up a little sign that read: "This Is Our Home."

Lyndon Johnson once moved a young female guest from her seat next to him at a White House dinner so that Mrs. (Alice Roosevelt) Longworth could take her place. When a White House aide chided that the president "didn't know what he was missing," Johnson replied, "Ah, but I know what I'm getting."

— Myra MacPherson

While Dwight D. Eisenhower was President, his popular First Lady, Mamie, went shopping in a Washington store and bought a blouse. 'Send it to the White House, please,' she said.

Totally unaware of her famous customer, the clerk said in a bored way: 'What's the address, please!'

'1600 Pennsylvania Ave.,' said Mrs. Eisenhower, giving the most famous address in America.

"What apartment?" asked the clerk.

WHITE HOUSE—RECEIVING LINE

(When asked if she were bored standing in reception lines at the White House) Bored? Why no, I love it. These women from all over the country are so interesting, and you know, they can scarcely name a place that I haven't visited or campaigned in with Ike. We never run out of things to say.

— Mamie Eisenhower

After all the guests were gathered in the Blue Room, it was explained that when the President, the First Lady and the Visiting Head of State entered, the guests would pass by the receiving line and were to "give their names to the page" so that he could announce 'em to the President. In the din and excitement, Mrs. Beré understood him to say, "give your name and age." So, when the moment came, she came forth with "Barbar Beré, age 38."

— Malcolm S. Forbes

WHITE HOUSE—WAKING UP IN

One time a television quizmaster said to Maine's Margaret Chase Smith, the then only woman in the U.S. Senate: "I know you don't want to be President, Senator Smith, but suppose you woke up some morning and found yourself in the White House. What would you do?" Mrs. Smith, who was known in Washington circles as ladylike, answered quickly: "Well, I'd go straight to Mrs. Truman and apologize, and then I'd go home."

WILDFLOWER

Charlotte Observer columnist Harriet Doar "Hunting an identity in a wildflower guide, I get interested—Southerner that I am—in the family connections. The mountain ash, with its spill of scarlet seed clusters, is a member of the rose family, and so is the serviceberry, the cranberry-colored, blueberry-sized fruit so easy to miss, so habit-forming to eat from the bush. They taste a little like apples, another rose cousin; our hostess makes them into preserves—delicious!

"After all these years of reading about it, I finally have 'poke sallet,' the wild greens gathered fresh, par-boiled and then cooked like spinach, and decide it's an acquired taste. But then so is caviar."

WOMAN

One is not born, but rather becomes, a woman.

— Simone de Beauvoir

I still like women best in the bedroom and the kitchen.

— Bobby Riggs

New York Gov. Hugh Carey: "You never ask a woman why."

Woman was made from man's ribs which, as any butcher will tell you, isn't the best cut.

— Robert Orben

The woman is the ridge pole of the tent.

— Arab saying

Being a woman has only bothered me in climbing trees.

— Frances Perkins

There is no worse evil than a bad woman; and nothing has ever been produced better than a good one.

— Euripides

A woman who is strong is not masculine; she is a *strong woman*.

— Lynda Huey

My idea of a real woman is someone who can make a young man feel mature, an old man youthful and a middle-aged man feel completely sure of himself. Unfortunately, I have never met her.

— Cary Grant

Ever since woman's consciousness has looked beyond the material, man's consciousness has feared her vaguely; he has gone to her for inspiration, he has relied on her for all that is best and most ideal in his life, yet by sheer material force he has limited her.

— Nancy Astor, M.P.

WOMAN—HOME EXECUTIVE

Modern woman must be, by all modern standards, an executive who makes and keeps a schedule; who manages wisely the ever-shrinking dollars in her trust; who, authoritatively, settles disputes with a wisdom greater than Solomon the king. She must be a cook, chauffeur, seamstress, gardener, sportswoman, solicitor, a member of the Red Cross, Cancer, Mental Health, Tuberculosis, Heart, and Et Cetera Associations. She is expected to march when the mothers march, to camp out with the Cubs, to bake with Brownies, to attend music recitals, PTA programs, and never miss a day of being informed on world affairs. She must know how to make a cheap home permanent look like a twenty-dollar one, to make witch's hats, pirate's swords, angel wings, a triangular flower arrangement or a Hogarth Curve. She must be continually learning new ways to solve new problems as she discovers such basic truths as that changing a baby's diapers is much, much easier than changing a teen-ager's mind. She must strive never to lose her self-control, figure, temper, teeth, good standing with her in-laws, direction booklets that come with electrical appliances, or the once-a-week cleaning woman in her life.

— Mary Lou Lacy

WOMANLY

For women to remain womanly does not necessarily mean that they need be silly, ignorant, touchy, artful, spiteful, jealous, envious, and generally ninny-minded. The pity is that "womanly" should ever have trailed such adjectives in its wake. There are few things more gracious and lovely than a woman who is womanly in the better sense—serene, capable, intelligent, mellow, generous, wise, charming. She is perhaps the most desirable type of all, and also, of course, the rarest.

— V. Sackville-West

WOMAN'S PLACE

Is woman's place in the home? It certainly is, but the difficulty lies in deciding whose home she wants to be in.

— Elsie Janis

Most men believe that a woman's place is in the home. They expect to find her there immediately after she gets off work.

— Sparks

Jehan Sadat, wife of Egyptian President Anwar Sadat, told 1,000 prominent Arab women: "Because of biological defects, a woman's place is in the home."

WOMEN

Oh, yes, I like women better than men ... Who doesn't?

— Gore Vidal

I divide women into two categories. The female and the broad. Me? I'm a broad.

— Bette Davis

(On why he likes to write about women) ... the life of the slave is always more interesting than that of the master.

— Gore Vidal

Erma Bombeck once described a woman as being too old for a paper route, too young for Social Security, too clumsy to steal and too tired for an affair.

New York Times columnist John Leonard: "Personally, I prefer New York women because they all come from somewhere else."

You know, even as a kid I always went for the wrong women. I think that's my problem.

   When my mother took me to see "Snow White," everyone fell in love with Snow White; I immediately fell for the Wicked Queen.

— Woody Allen in "Annie Hall"

Gibbon, writing about the breed of Germans that lived almost 2,000 years ago: "... treated their women with esteem and confidence, consulted them on every occasion of importance, and fondly believed that in their breasts resided a sanctity and wisdom more than human."

The Western man has, without knowing it, westernized the harem mind of the East. I don't believe he knows it yet, so we must break it to him gently. We must go on being his guide, his mother, and his better half. But we must prove to him that we are a necessary half, not only in private, but in political life. The best way that we can do that is to show him that our ambitions are not personal. Let men see that we desire a better, safer, and cleaner world for our children and their children and that we believe that it is only by doing our bit, by facing unclean things with cleanliness, by facing wrongs with right, by going fearlessly into all things that may be disagreeable, that we will, somehow, make this a little better world. I don't know what we are going to do this—I don't say that women will change the world, but I do say that they can if they want to.

— Nancy Astor, M.P.

WOMEN—AMERICAN

They are the prettiest, youngest-looking, most energetic (only superlatives will do here), most educated in some ways, most ignorant in others, most hopeful, most practical, the dreamiest and most wildly romantic, the most independent and the most enslaved (for isn't it a kind of slavery never to have an hour of your own?) and, summing up, the most entirely "engaged" and "committed" young women of any time, any country. They have almost as many children as their grandmothers, who didn't have to help support them; as a rule they do as much housework and baby-tending as their mothers, but without servants; and yet they go out into the world of business every morning with their husbands to help make a living—that is the main thing. But this creature with her four big jobs thinks of herself as freed from the treadmill of the purely domestic life and as being more useful than ever! No shop, no office, no trade, industry, profession, art, science or craft, including politics, but is humming with her dynamic presence. I am convinced that if, on a single given morning, every employed woman in the country should decide to stay at home that day, this whole system would fall into economic and moral chaos. Men wouldn't be able to find anything, for instance, because the women have got everything filed and tucked away and are carrying the keys.

– Katherine Anne Porter

WOMEN—CATEGORIES

There are those that are humble in the shade and those that are arrogant in the sun. There are those that wish to climb on others and those that prefer to stand alone. There is also an intermediate kind, those that respond gratefully to a stake against the wind. Let us, by all means, divide our women into types. This system is quite fair. The only unfair system is to call all women "woman."

– V. Sackville-West

I think people have only to face reality to see how foolish it is to divide women into categories. Some men seem to idealize the image of the porcelain beauty from afar. How terribly boring for them if women like this really existed! To act noble, regal and remote all the time, with no other qualities of vitality, sparkle and sexual passion, would be most unsatisfying for a man.

– Deborah Kerr

WOMEN—NEW PATTERNS

Now that women have broken through the mystique, they can attack the problems that remain, from the discrimination in paychecks and income tax to child-care centers and misguided remnants of male resistance. All they need to do is simply to become themselves, and affirm, help each other; ask for, create, the new patterns all women need—in voices loud enough to be heard. For no woman can truly make this breakthrough, tolling the bell alone.

– Betty Friedan

WOMEN—SPECIAL SUBJECT

Look up WOMEN in the card catalogue of the library and you find a pack of entries as long as your arm. There are almost as many entries under NEGRO, and YOUTH. JEWS and CATHOLICS are represented respectably, too.

Most of the books in the library are by individuals who happen to be middle-aged male, white, Anglo-Saxon Protestants, but there are few or no books about the middle-aged, men, white people, Anglo-Saxons, or even Protestants.

Middle-aged, male, white, Anglo-Saxon Protestants are all treated as individuals.

Because it is assumed that all individuals are middle-aged male WASPS, people who don't look like them are classified by the way they differ. They become not people, but subjects, and all too often, problems—problems for, and to be solved by middle-aged male WASPS.

As long as women remain a special subject—and I hope some day they won't be—you are going to hear more and more talk about them because it's getting harder and harder to generalize about them—and that always produces clouds of words, too.

– Caroline Bird

WOMEN VS. MEN

In work situations I find men more interested in acquiring and possessing territory than women. I assume the difference is because women look at property differently—as something they have to clean.
– Patricia Schroeder

The war between the sexes has been going on for several thousand years, and men's propaganda about it is just as silly as war propaganda. Men say women are less courageous; it's notorious that they are *more* courageous. That they are less realistic; it's notorious that they are *more* realistic. Women are more concerned with the question of war and peace than men are.

– Erich Fromm

A woman merchandising manager says, "For a man to be called ruthless, he needs to have been involved in Watergate. For a woman to be called ruthless, all she has to do is put someone on hold."

A magazine writer, interviewing a group of successful businesswomen, asked one: "Are the requirements for men and women the same?" "No," the woman answered. "The women don't have to wear suits."

Women have perpetual envy of our vices; among which is warmaking; they are less vicious than we, not from choice, but because we restrict them; they are the slaves of order and fashion; their virtue is of more consequence to us than our own, so far as concerns this world.

— Samuel Johnson

What's the difference in women's and men's activities? A newspaper article pointed out that one man had been the paper's sports editor for almost 50 years. His wife, said the article, had made an afghan during every baseball season for nearly 50 years.

WOMEN VS. MEN—BIOLOGY

Biologically, a woman is younger and lives longer; it's the men who give up.

— Gloria Swanson

Of forty-eight chromosomes only one is different; on this difference we base a complete separation of male and female, pretending that all forty-eight are different.

— Germaine Greer

WOMEN VS. MEN—CHARACTER

Generally, women are better than men—they have more character....

— Lauren Bacall

I prefer men for some things, obviously, but women have a greater sense of honor and are more willing to take a chance with their lives....

They are more open and decent in their relationship with a man. Men run all the time. I don't know how they live with themselves, they are so preoccupied with being studs.

— Lauren Bacall

WOMEN VS. MEN—FEELINGS

Women are supposed to be very calm generally: But women feel just as men feel; they need exercise for their faculties, and a field for their efforts as much as their brothers do; they suffer from too rigid a constraint, too absolute a stagnation, precisely as men would suffer; and it is narrow-minded in their privileged fellow-creatures to say they ought to confine themselves to making puddings and knitting stockings, to playing the piano or embroidering bags. It is thoughtless to

condemn them, or laugh at them, if they seek to do more than custom
has pronounced necessary for their sex.

> *– Charlotte Brontë, 1847,*
> Jane Eyre

WOMEN VS. MEN—HELPFULNESS

I have noticed over the years that there seems to be a great difference
between the way a woman writer lives with a man and the way a man
writer lives with a woman. So often you hear a male novelist say (this is
extreme, but somewhat representative, anyway), "Oh, my wife has been
terrific: when I start a novel I just tell her to take the kids and get lost.
She brings me my lunch on trays and does all my typing and she's just
great." On the other hand, in cases of successful cohabitation with a
woman writer and a man, it seems the very best thing she can say is,
"He's really nice about it." Or to take it one step up, "He's been very
supportive."

> *– Alice Adams*

WOMEN VS. MEN—TOUGHNESS

Company president Barbara Fields: "A woman has to be much stronger
and tougher than a man to survive in this (retail) business. I don't mean
tough in manner, but tough inside. That's really the core of it. To make
it as a woman in this business, you have to have inner toughness."

Women are built for endurance and wired for empathy. We are the
overland trucks of the species. Our antennae pick up all the stations ...
Men are the test planes. They make excitement and danger and
breakthroughs, and they burn out early. Women just keep on truckin'.

> *– Gail Sheehy*

Stephanie M. Bennett, Dean, Westhampton College, University of
Richmond pointed out in a speech: "Not too long ago it was common, in
work situations, to differentiate between a businessman and a businesswoman by observing that he was aggressive, she was pushy; he was
careful about details, she was picky; he was decisive, she was preju-
diced; he was a leader, she was a tyrant. In short, by displaying the
characteristics associated with competence, the businesswoman trans-
gresses invisible barriers and becomes victim of sex-role stereotyping.
She is then caught in a "double bind": if she displays typically feminine
behaviors she is rejected as incompetent, if she does not display
typically feminine behaviors she is rejected as inappropriate."

WOMEN'S CONTRIBUTION

Nobody can influence me, nobody at all. And a woman still less. In a man's life, women count only if they're beautiful and graceful and know how to stay feminine. You've never produced a Michelangelo or a Bach. You've never even produced a great cook. And don't talk of opportunities. Are you joking? Have you lacked the opportunity to give history a great cook? You have produced nothing great, nothing.
— Mohammed Reza Pahlavi

WOMEN'S LIB

You've come a long way, baby.
— Virginia Slims ad

God made man. Then He stepped back, looked and said: "I can do better than that."
— Erma Bombeck

Do women really want to give up their superiority?

One man said: "A libber is a term used to suggest what otherwise is a pushy, aggressive broad."

Women's liberation is to find you're an individual.
— Cathy Handley

When God made man she was only joking.
— Ad for Quality T-Shirt

I thought there's more to me than just being an attractive armpiece or having children.
— Beverly Sassoon

When Harvard men say they have graduated from Radcliffe, then we've made it.
— Jacqueline Onassis

We have to be reminded of the past to see how much fighting we need to do in the future.
— Bella Abzug

When a man streaked across the stage attired only in a black scarf around his head as she was speaking, Gloria Steinem dryly commented, "For men, liberation is streaking. For women, it's not *having* to streak."

(On the National Women's Political Caucus): It was so easy for me to embrace the issue when I realized this thing called fame can be utilized so constructively.

— *Jean Stapleton*

I believe in women's lib. But I would wish there wasn't that faint edge of hostility toward men. I like men. We have a common cause. I don't want my near and dear left out in the cold.

— *Harriet Frank, Jr.*

Regarding Women's Lib, author Barbara Cartland said: "Equal pay is one thing—I'm all for it. But you can't have equal sex. One partner's got to dominate, and what women's lib seems to forget is that men have to be aroused. Literally. Women can't just lie back and think of England.... If a woman's going to leap into the bedroom, waving a sex manual and demanding 15 orgasms every five minutes, men are going to lose their pride and confidence."

WOMEN'S LIB—CRYSTAL BALL

Wilma Scott Heide, President of the National Organization for Women: "If women are 'natural' secretaries (and typing is not a secondary sex characteristic of all females), why not Secretary of Labor, of Defense, of Health, Education and Welfare, Transportation, Commerce, Housing and Urban Development, Interior and Agriculture?

"If the best communication is indeed 'telewoman,' why not a woman for Postmaster or Postperson General?

"If women 'intuitively' sense and value the good of the whole—family or community and the justice of this, then are not women the 'naturals' for Attorney Generals and Supreme Court Justices? While the recent U.S. Supreme Court decision vis á vis abortion may represent *something* of our 'emancipation proclamation,' can we continue to depend on the sufferance and largesse of men only for this and related overdue decisions?

"If black defendants have a right to determine if jurors and/or judges are racists (and I support this approach) must not women of all races demand nonsexist judges and juries and police of both sexes?"

WOMEN'S LIB—MEN

I told you good things would start happening to men if we helped women get liberated.

My friend Mike was sitting at the counter, having an introspective mid-morning cup of coffee, when a good-looking woman walked up, murmured "Congratulations!" and handed him a card. Then she disappeared while he was reading it.

The card said: "You have been rated Most Watchable by an Official Man-Rater. Please phone her at XXX to arrange for award ceremony and Official Prize." Mildly flabbergasted, Mike went back to his office and dialed the number. She pretended to be serious and asked a number of questions, ending with "Are you married?"

"I don't get the prize if I'm married?" Mike asked.

"Oh, you are definitely a winner," she responded. "but the awards do vary." So they had dinner that night and, in fact, they are still dating.

"What was the prize?" I asked. "I've been pledged to secrecy," Mike said.

– Jim Sanderson

WOMEN'S LIB—QUIRK

I don't understand exactly why it happens but women who are really quite strong and independent and who really do live their own lives, will in very odd ways do what they are told by men. They are very ready to be obedient. I once had a teacher—she was my role model—and I was at her house one day when her husband came home and said, "I need a handkerchief." She got up and scurried around and could only find Kleenex, which she offered him. But she kept saying, "I'm so sorry I didn't have a handkerchief. I'm so sorry."

– Mary Gordon

WOMEN'S MOVEMENT

It is and was a woman's assumption of full personhood in our society.

– Betty Friedan

First woman to be elected to Congress, Jeanette Rankin speaking about the women's movement: "And when the men make fun of you, that's when you know you're getting on well."

WOMEN'S RIGHTS

(About Women's Rights) I like both sides of them ... a man is only as old as the woman he feels.

– Groucho Marx

Typical woman, she just can't make up her ... mind ... I think women have rights. They ought to have the right to be a good cook and good housekeeper, look after the baby.

— Billy Carter

WOMEN'S SOCIETIES

Nobel prizewinner for medicine Rosalyn Yalow: "I think that the goals of women's societies should be to self-destruct. The most talented women should not be in women's groups but in men's groups. That's where the power is."

WONDERFUL

Too much of a good thing is wonderful.

— Mae West

WORK

There's only one way to work—like hell.

— Bette Davis

(The) least disappointing relationship you can have is work.

— Bette Davis

Sign on a woman editor's desk: "Pandemonium doesn't reign here ... it pours."

... telling me not to work is like telling a 747 not to fly.

— Shirley MacLaine

To love what you do and feel that it matters—how could anything be more fun?

— Katherine Graham

Work is the most important thing in life and ultimately the most satisfying.

— Britt Eckland

Work is the best therapy for anything—it's good for your health and good for your soul.

— Claudette Colbert

One's life should be concentrated on work, everything else should be fringe. Work is the rewarding and lasting thing.

— Lauren Bacall

Child to telephone salesman: "No, the lady of the house is at her office running her business ... but the house husband's here."

I've found that being a woman is a tremendous asset in business. I believe the greatest attribute a woman has is—being a woman.
— Pearl Nipon

... women who work in offices ... get blamed when things go wrong, and when they go right, the boss gets all the praise.
— Louise Kapp Howe

My work is a reflection of me. It makes me self-reliant and it is a good feeling to know you don't have to depend on anyone other than yourself to survive.
— Cloris Leachman

All of my children are hard workers, and that is important, because no matter how rich you or your parents are, work gives you a reason to get up in the morning.
— Ingrid Bergman

Rachel Mussolini, the widow of Italian Dictator Benito Mussolini, on running a restaurant: "With all the troubles in my life, if I couldn't make a plate of tortellini or bring somebody a glass of wine, I'd have jumped out the window long ago."

I am only alive when I work. I have been working since I was six, when I was a child actress, and that was a long time ago. I thought then and still find that all work is a challenge, the overcoming of obstacles. I still have a sense of victory in getting to be expert.
— Anita Loos

Sometimes, on the other hand, the trouble is that girls do not exert themselves to see the possibilities in their work. Many a job is an inanimate thing until a bright girl gets hold of it. She can give it life and vigor, make it put out new branches, strengthen its roots and bear fruit. No job in the world is a static thing. It is what somebody makes it.
— Hazel Rawson Cades

WORK—CAREER

Work is all joy to me, it really is—every moment of it. I like earning money, I like it when companies seek me out and sign me up to design no matter what—sheets, yard goods, glassware, scarves, wallpaper, table linen, valentines. I like being every year in greater demand. I like having to face every week my all-but-impossible deadlines. The fame you earn has a different taste from the fame that is forced upon you.

– Gloria Vanderbilt

WORK ETHIC

(Editor Marse Grant about his mother, Elsie, a feisty 81.) I'm not sure Mama will like these, her husband once joked when he was given new permanent-press pajamas. She will probably go out and exchange them for some she has to iron.

"My mother invented the work ethic ... She was the driving force. The emphasis in our home was on action, work."

WORK—QUITTING

My family no longer has to ask, "Where are the *clean* towels?" or ask for an appointment to have a button sewn on.

– Homemaker

WORK—RETURNING

(From a case history about a woman returning to work) The children were old enough to do without a full-time mother. And people were always asking me what I *do*. I joked that I sit in the tub and eat bon-bons—or I answered, "I make mischief." It didn't seem enough to say I was a community activist, a fundraiser for the school fair or a neighborhood environmentalist.

– Letty Cottin Pogrebin

WORKAHOLIC

I'm a workaholic ... every minute of life has been a joy—with working.

– Arlene Francis

WORKER

(When she went to Paris as a journalist) Obviously I was not rich. If I had been, there would have been quickly gathered around me a group to offer entertainment as well as treasures to buy; but it was clear I had little money, so that was out of the question. There are other things by

which the French label you, a woman particularly—charm, beauty,
chic, l'esprit, seriousness, capacity to work, intelligence, bônté. Those
with whom I had dealings for any length of time hit perfectly on my
chief asset. I was a worker. "A femme travailleuse," they said to one
another, and if they passed me to an acquaintance that was the
recommendation. No people believe more than the French in the value
and dignity in hard work. I was treated with respect because of my
working quality.

– Ida M. Tarbell

WORKING

Everything works better when you're working.

– Lauren Bacall

The most shocked women in the world are those who get married
because they got tired of working.

– Sam Levenson

I've been working since I was very young—out on the courts practicing,
practicing. It's a big investment of time. I'm one of the lucky ones—I got
a return on my investment ... Money is good, money makes things
happen—it's how you direct it, what you do with the money that's
important. When money starts owning you, you're in trouble.

– Billie Jean King

WORKING ROOM

Now I've been able to concentrate on my search for a house, and finding
it has told me something about what's really important for me. It's
clearly designed to be lived in relatively alone, it's magnificently
designed for working, and most important, after making a living, more
or less, as a writer for more than 20 years, I finally feel entitled to give
my work its own room. No longer do I have to be sent upstairs to the
bedroom to write as if I was being punished.

– Jill Robinson

WORKING WOMAN

Often the first question leveled at Washington wives at cocktail parties
is "What do you do?" Columnist Art Buchwald's friend Lucy gave him

her solution on what to answer: "It (the solution) came by accident one night when a man sitting next to me asked, 'What do you do?' I told him 'I'm a paper clip inspector for the State Department.'

"He said, 'You're kidding me.'

"I said, 'I am not. They have to be twisted just right or the State Department papers won't stick together, and some of them could get lost.' What do you do? He just blushed and said, 'Nothing.'"

WORLD

Helen Chapman, president, General Federation of Women's Clubs: "Let us help mold the world, and not be molded by it!"

The American people cannot carry the whole world on its back and survive.

— Vivian Kellems

I have no use for women who want the world to be run by women. I could not think of anything more ghastly.

— Mme. Vijaya Lakshmi Pandit

(On her move from Minnesota to Washington) Everybody was a stranger. It was a lot bigger stage in Washington. Now the stage is even bigger. It's the world.

— Joan Mondale

The world is a welter and has always been one: but though all the cranks and the theorists cannot master the old floundering monster, or force it for long into any of their neat plans of readjustment, here and there a saint or a genius suddenly sends a little ray through the fog, and helps humanity to stumble on, and perhaps up.

— Edith Wharton

WORRY

Worry Borrows: It's a disease of the future. It borrows the unknown trouble of tomorrow. The worrier loses the beautiful spirit of hope because worry paints such a gloomy, shocking, dreadful picture of the future. She becomes deeply troubled about something that happened 30 years ago that can't possibly be changed.

- Joyce Landorf

WRINKLES

She has so many wrinkles, her facial cream is Prune Whip!
*   — Patricia Daniels*

I don't like to complain about our Creator's handiwork, but if God had to give a woman wrinkles, He might at least have put them on the soles of her feet.
*   — Elizabeth Taylor*

WRITER

I shall live bad if I do not write and I shall write bad if I do not live.
*   — Francoise Sagan*

The writer must be willing, above everything else, to take chances, to risk making a fool of himself—or even to risk revealing the fact that he *is* a fool.
*   — Jessamyn West*

New Yorker columnist, Janet Flanner, explained that one of her secrets of writing well was that she kept going over a sentence/ "I nag it, gnaw it, pat and flatter it."

I like to see my books in the stores and libraries ... What's wrong with leavin' behind a little of yourself on paper? Like I always say, it's better to be looked over than overlooked!
*   — Mae West*

Murder springs nine times out of ten out of the character and circumstances of the murdered person. Because the victim was the kind of person he or she was, therefore he or she was murdered.
*   — Agatha Christie*

As an aspiring writer growing up in Queens, novelist Mary Gordon, Catholic, greatly admired another Catholic writer, Mary McCarthy, for her ability and glamour. Gordon said that until then she'd thought that "only Protestants were glamorous and smart."

I would like to discover why I wrote the books I have written. Why those particular books and not others. It's astonishing to look at what one has done in the light of the wild ambitions one had at twenty. One planned, one expected to give the world an important message. Yes, now I want to find out precisely why I have written what I have written.
*   — Simone de Beauvoir*

WRITER—COLLABORATING

Writer Nanette Kutner and Mamie Eisenhower once discussed collaborating on a book about General Eisenhower. Kutner recalled: "When in my presence she told General Eisenhower of the plan, he seemed delighted. Leaning over her bedside he said, 'You can learn to type. I'll get you a little typewriter.'

"At mention of a typewriter Mamie dismissed the book idea with an airy gesture. She said cheerfully, 'You know I don't like to work.'"

WRITER—WOMEN DINNER GUESTS

I perceived that on this tide (of women writer dinner guests) Mr. (Max) Beerbohm was beginning to bob like a cork. It seemed a pity that he had come. He had no doubt been encouraged to form other dreams of the evening's personnel by the invitation cards which had bidden us dine in the Charles II suite of the Carlton Hotel. I had thought myself that, in view of the notorious fact that King Charles's dinner companions were far other than women writers, this was not too suitable for a literary dinner. When we rose to go to the table, still more of the dangerous breed pressed in on us. The average woman writer, I was suddenly conscious, runs to height and force and mass. More and more did Mr. Beerbohm seem minute, perilously fragile, enormously precious. Finally we sat down in our appointed places, which was at the very end of the immensely long table. But though we were now out of the crowd Mr. Beerbohm was not relieved. Up the long vista travelled the clear blue eye, and remained protuded in horror; for no one, save the All-seeing Eye of Providence, can ever have seen so many women writers at once.

Were we literary women, I inquired of him, like the violets that had been strewn on the tablecloth with prodigality but no very successful decorative effect?—rived from our right place in secluded dells to pursue an aesthetic aim that we never could quite realize? In the faintest of moans he assented. So hypnotic an effect is exerted by the delicate, fixed perfection of his personality, and so single-minded is he in his concentration on the thing which seems to him most beautiful—and that is the society which died with the 'nineties—that I had by now entirely passed over to his state of mind.

— Rebecca West

WRITING

Journalist Janet Flanner thought of writing as "the persuasion of words."

Newspaper columnist Dot Jackson: "Writing is just something that if you have to do it, you will do anything else but."

The best friend a would-be writer can have is a talkative mother. Verbal facility is acquired very early in life, long before a child goes to school.
                                                                    – Sloan Wilson

Film critic/writer Pauline Kael about her stint as a film producer: "Writing sensitizes you ... producing de-sensitizes you."

To me, writing is a natural extension of acting, just as painting is an extension of sketching. It's a more demanding, involved kind of expression, but I think all actresses and actors are secret novelists. For women, especially, writing offers a means of ending the stereotyped roles most of us get stuck with.
                                                                      – Jane Fonda

(On Anne Morrow Lindbergh) When I picked up a volume of *Gift from the Sea*—and there seems to be one in every room in the house—I find that hers is humility of the kind a candle shows when shining alone in the dark ... And between the rich gentle home life and cultured education, this woman writer of all others has produced an utter *simplicity,* a purity of style and plainness of speech, a value of content that is outstanding. It had to come from that Higher Source.
                                                          – Adela Rogers St. Johns

WRITING—AUTOBIOGRAPHY

The nicest thing about an autobiography is that you can leave out certain things.
                                                                 – Ethel Barrymore

Hiring someone to write your autobiography is like paying someone to take a bath for you.
                                                                      – Mae West

(About a book, *Wildflowers,* she's writing) It's almost autobiographical. It's sort of exaggerated, with a little bit of truth, a little bit of humor, and a little bit of dirty stuff to make it sell!
                                                                    – Dolly Parton

When I saw what was written after Joan Crawford dropped dead, I thought I'd better get my side of the story in first.
                                                                     – Bette Davis

(About writing her autobiography) I'm in awe of really fine writing. I love the language. They must think I have some damn nerve!
— Lauren Bacall

(On her 81st birthday, she gave what she called "natural birth" to her memoirs) I've been 80 for a whole year—long enough to announce that it's the manuscript that's finished and not me. It was a natural delivery, the kind I hoped for. Nobody can claim that it was premature.
— Gloria Swanson

WRITING—CLASSES

You can take too many writing classes, and after the first one it's like trying to recapture love. An impossible task.
— Doris Betts

WRITING—COOKBOOK

In *Miss Beecher's Domestic Recipe Book,* the first edition of which was published by Harper and Brothers in 1842, Catherine Beecher wrote:

"You find yourself encompassed by such trials as these.... You go to the experienced housekeepers or cookery books and you are met by such sorts of directions as these: 'take a pinch of this or a little of that and considerable of another and cook them until they are about right.'...

She then gave some of her philosophy and objectives for her cookbook:

"... (her purpose) to present a good supply of the rich and elegant dishes demanded at such entertainments, and yet to set forth so large and tempting a variety of what is safe, healthful, and good, in connection with such warnings and suggestions as it is hoped may avail to promote a more healthful fashion in regard both to entertainments and daily table supplies....

"... in the work of *Domestic Economy,* together with this, to which it is a supplement, the writer has attempted to secure a cheap and popular form, for American housekeepers....

"Lastly, the writer has aimed to avoid the defects complained of by most housekeepers in regard to works of this description issued in this country, or sent from England, such as that, in some cases the recipes are so rich as to be both expensive and unhealthful; in others, that they are so vaguely expressed as to be very imperfect guides; in others that the processes are so elaborate and fussing as to make double the work that is needful; and in others, that the topics are so limited that some departments are entirely omitted and all are incomplete."

WRITING—FICTION

For me the goal of all fiction is simply this: to make more understandable, more bearable if you will, the muddle of human life.
— Shirley Ann Grau

Fiction at its best is a mirror of that constantly changing reality. Each serious writer with each successive book is describing another facet of his world of reality.
— Shirley Ann Grau

Mr. Susskind asked Miss (Dorothy) Parker (who is currently *Esquire* magazine's book reviewer) what she thought of the fiction that came her way. Miss Parker said she found it appalling. She was especially distressed by the sex scenes. "They're all the same!" She wondered why most of the books got published in the first place.
— Janet Winn

I assume, then, that you want to write fiction. And that is the first requisite. Wanting to hard enough. Not next year some time when little Sally has gone to school, not even next week when you're through with the dentist or that important conference, but today, and tomorrow, and the day after, until the working habit is established and you're lost without it. If you want to hard enough you'll find time. Life is malleable and the hammer is desire.
— Anya Seton

WRITING—FREE-LANCE

As a profession, free-lance writing is notoriously insecure. That's the first argument in its favor. For many reasons, a few of them rational, the thought of knowing exactly what next year's accomplishments, routine, income, and vacation will be—or even what time I have to get up tomorrow morning—has always depressed me. Perhaps because I spent my formative years not going to school (except when we happened to stay three months in one place), getting attached to the routine of no routine, and absorbing my father's philosophy ("I can stand anything today as long as I don't know what tomorrow might bring"), I am wonderfully well-prepared for the precariousness of writing. Or, to look at it another way, I am unprepared for anything else.
— Gloria Steinem

WRITING—MARRIAGE

I think marriage and writing books are very difficult to combine. If things don't go well between you, then there's a tendency for the partner to blame it on the book, and quite right. The person a writer marries is forced to take a certain role in relation to the writer, and may not like that role. It happens with all creative people, actors, musicians ... but writers are particularly difficult, because they have to be so solitary.

— Jill Robinson

WRITING—NOTEBOOK

(On keeping a notebook of ideas) I tried to keep one, but I never could remember where I put the damn thing.

— Dorothy Parker

WRITING—NOVEL

(About writing the Washington novel) The problem is sex and power are no longer sexy.

— Barbara Howar

My book *(Gone With the Wind)* belongs to anyone who has the price ... but nothing of me belongs to the public.

— Margaret Mitchell

(A wife, mother and grandmother who wrote her first novel after raising her family) I'm a one-thing-at-a-time person, and car pools and writing didn't mix.

— Belva Plain

Writing at a little desk in the family parlor, ready to shove her pages under the blotting pad should guests intrude, she (Jane Austen) invented the modern novel—that is the novel that keeps to the likely behavior of ordinary people in ordinary circumstances, forgoing the seductive implausibilities of high romance.

— Bookviews

WRITING—PLANNING

The best time for planning a book is while you're doing the dishes.

— Agatha Christie

WRITING—PLAYWRITING

It is a discouraging thought to consider the possibility of American
playwriting becoming as parasitical as popular song writing, which has
the unenviable reputation of picking the brains of old masters.

– Maude Adams

WRITING—PSEUDONYM

We (the Brontë sisters) agreed to arrange a small selection of our
poems, and, if possible, get them printed. Averse to personal publicity,
we veiled our own names under those of Currer, Ellis, and Acton Bell;
the ambiguous choice being dictated by a sort of conscientious scruple
at assuming Christian names positvely masculine, while we did not like
to declare ourselves women, because—without at that time suspecting
that our mode of writing and thinking was not what is called "feminine"—we had a vague impression that authoresses are liable to be
looked on with prejudice; we had noticed how critics sometimes use for
their chastisement the weapon of personality, and for their reward, a
flattery which is not true praise.

– Charlotte Brontë

WRITING—RESEARCH

Every worker invents his own techniques for warding off fatigue during
the research period. Experienced librarians recognize the problem. The
Folger Shakespeare Library in Washington opens at nine a.m. By nine-
five the scholars are glued to their tables and their books. At eleven-
thirty a buzzer sounds. Readers go outside and cross the square to a
cafeteria in the Supreme Court building, where they sit at a long table,
eat frugally so as not to grow sleepy, and talk to each other briefly about
their problems. Then they return to their books until half-past three,
when the buzzer sounds again; the scholars troop downstairs for tea and
a smoke—twenty minutes out—after which they read until the library
closes at five. Hardy souls then cross the street to the Library of
Congress which stays open till ten at night.

– Catherine Drinker Bowen

WRITING—SECOND CAREER

(About her writing career) It's very nice to discover halfway through your life something you really want to do, instead of sitting home playing mother or worrying about your figure.

– Lilli Palmer

WRITING—SHORT STORIES

I could not write my old stories again, or any more like them: and not because I do not see the same detail as before, but because somehow or other the pattern is different. The old details now make another pattern; and this perception of a new pattern is what I call a creative attitude toward life.

– Katherine Mansfield

America has always been a country in a hurry. The pioneer had too much work to do in exploring and developing new frontiers to afford the time for either writing long works or reading them. The frontier is gone, yet Americans are still impatient and restless, still mobile, as proved by the traffic on any interstate highway. Short stories are ideal for such a culture....

– Martha Foley

YARD SALE

Caution—this vehicle stops for yard sales.

— Bumper sticker on woman's car

YOUNG

Being young—who wants to go through that again?

— Dinah Shore

(Quoting her mother) To insist on staying young is to grow old with pessimism, like a wine which little by little turns to vinegar.

— Princess Grace of Monaco

YOURSELF

A friend who was pastor of a local church said to me, "Tell me all about yourself." I proceeded to tell him about my Christian service, my experience as a wife and mother. I delighted in doing so for an entire hour. When I concluded, he responded by saying, "Now tell me about you."

— Ruth Carter Stapleton

YOUTH

Role models of success, for many of our young people, are those who have "beat the system."

— Shirley Chisholm

Not for everything that the world could give would I consent to live over
my life unchanged, or to bring back, unchanged, my youth....
                                                             – Ellen Glasgow

British singer Lulu: "I look at all the wanderers, young people who are
trying to escape and those who are in fact runaways. And I wonder
about their parents. I wonder about love, respect, understanding. Would
any of us run if we had those?"

If half the kids in the country could follow their creative impulse, it
would be a different world. But it takes money to go into ballet or
whatever or to really study something. So they suffer.
                                                               – Linda Blair

The thing that impresses me most about the youngsters is that they are
totally uninterested in the group of people who try to tell you something
simply because they want to make money. They are ready for good
whole-grain breads, they do their own baking, do organic gardening to
grow their own food, and I think there is great hope for them.
                                                              – Adelle Davis

YOUTH—ETERNAL

The secret of eternal youth is arrested development.
                                              – Alice Roosevelt Longworth

PERMISSIONS AND ACKNOWLEDGMENTS

The editor wishes to thank the following for their kind permission to use extracts from their publications.

Advertising Age. From article. January 30, 1978; From "Nine Commandments for Women in Business" by Jo Foxworth. Reprinted with permission from the June 5, 1978 issue of *Advertising Age.* Copyright 1978 by Crain Communications, Inc.: From article. February 1979. From "Syndication: Stars' social security," by Bob Williams. Reprinted with permission from the February 18, 1980 issue of *Advertising Age.* Copyright 1980 by Crain Communications, Inc.

B. Altman & Company. From B. Altman & Co. Advertisement.

Ambiance. From "Pearl Nipon" interview with Barbra K. Sadtler in "Off the Cuff" column. January 1979.

America. From "The Church and the Fiction Writer" by Flannery O'Connor. March 30, 1957. By permission of America Press Inc.

American Express. Advertisement. Reprinted with the permission of American Express Company.

American Way. From "Age 65 and Kicking Even Higher," by Milton Rockmore. July 1978. Reprinted by permission of *American Way,* the inflight magazine of American Airlines. Copyright 1979 by American Airlines.

Arlington House Publishers. From *The Power of the Positive Woman* by Phyllis Schlafly. Copyright 1977. By permission of Arlington House Publishers.

Associated Press. From " 'Single' Novel Looks at the Strong Woman." AP Newsfeatures in *The Charlotte News.* January 19, 1978; From "She's Earned a Badge and Is Hanging Onto It." AP Newsfeatures in *The Charlotte News.* February 7, 1978; From "King Says Skip College..." by Will Grimsley. AP Newsfeatures in *The Charlotte News.* March 23, 1978; From "Super Sisters." AP Newsfeatures. Re-printed in *The Charlotte News.* May 18, 1978; From "Ex-Hooker Helps Others Off Streets." AP Newsfeatures. Reprinted in *The Charlotte Observer.* May 29, 1978; From "Strong-Willed Mothers Reared 'Mama's Boys' to be Presidents," by Dave Goldberg. AP Newsfeatures in the *Atlanta Journal-Constitution.* August 13, 1978; From "Billy Carter Says He's His Family's Alcoholic." AP Newsfeatures in *The Charlotte Observer.* November 5, 1979; From "U.S. Born Queen Misses 'Burgers, Casual Lifestyle," by Ann Blackman. AP Newsfeatures in *The Miami Herald.* June 22, 1980.

Atheneum Publishers. From *Myself Among Others* by Ruth Gordon. Copyright 1971.

Julian Bach Literary Agency, Inc. From "How To Be A More Perfect Person," by Elin Schoen in *Redbook* magazine, September 1978.

A.S. Barnes & Co, Inc. From *Gloria Swanson* by Richard Hudson and Raymond Lee. Copyright 1970.

Bic Pen Corporation. From Bic Advertisement.

Book Digest. From "Conversation with an Author: Erica Jong," interview conducted by Martin L. Gross. January 1976; From "Conversation with an Author: Gail Sheehy," interview conducted by Martin L. Gross. June 1977.

Books for Libraries Press, Inc. From *Ending in Earnest* by Rebecca West. Copyright 1931. Reprinted by Books for Libraries Press. Distributed by Arno Press Inc.

Bookviews. From "Jill Robinson," by John F. Baker. Reprinted from *Bookviews,* August 1978. Published by the R.R. Bowker Company, a Xerox company. Copyright 1978 Xerox Corporation: From "The Name Below the Title," by M. George Haddad. Reprinted from *Bookviews,* published by the R.R.

Bowker Company, a Xerox company. Copyright 1978 Xerox Corporation.

The Boston Globe. From "Sissela Bok: The Truth About Lying," by Georgia Litwack. February 17, 1980.

Brandt & Brandt Literary Agents, Inc. From *National Velvet* by Enid Bagnold. William Morrow & Co., Inc., Publisher. Copyright 1949.

Cambridge University Press. From *The Letters of Emily Dickinson,* edited by Thomas H. Johnson and Theodora Ward. Cambridge, 1958. Vol. II.

Candan Productions. Quotes by John Cantu and Patricia Daniels.

The Charlotte News. From article by Emery Wister, February 27, 1978; From "Bette Davis 69 and still feisty," by Emery Wister, March 31, 1978; From article by Dr. Herbert Spaugh, April 24, 1978; From "If You Want A Happy Marriage...," by Dr. Herbert Spaugh, May 29, 1978; From "Atheist Leader To Open Charlotte Office," by Larry King, June 15, 1978; From "Lillian Gish— History With a Heartbeat," by Bob Wisehart, January 11, 1979; From "Carol's TV Series Failed," by Emery Wister, January 27, 1979; From "Now Wilma Runs the Speaking Circuit," by Ruth Moose, February 21, 1980.

The Charlotte Observer. From Kays Gary's column; From "In the Full Moon?" by Mary Kratt, September 23, 1977; From column by Ina Hughs, November 25, 1977; From Rolfe Neill's column, November 27, 1977; From "The Key Is Responsibility," by Elizabeth Rhodes, December 24, 1977; From article by Dannye Romine, January 1, 1978; From "Jane: She's Life's Best Banana Peel," by Ina Hughs, February 17, 1978; From "Praise Julia, Pass the Haute Cuisine," by Helen Moore, March 26, 1978; From "Creative Writing Class," by Dannye Romine. April 9, 1978; From "Playing Hardball In The Fields Of the Lord," by Lew Powell, May 7, 1978; From "If I Were Hiring a Mom," by Ina Hughs, May 12, 1978; From "I've Come Back to (giggle) Write," by Dot Jackson, May 15, 1978; From "We Don't Know Our Place," by Elizabeth Rhodes, May 25, 1978; From "Just Daahling!" by Elizabeth Rhodes, May 27, 1978; From "A Kid Named Bobby Let Me Be His Friend," by Pat Borden, June 25, 1978; From "A Spunky Mary Pickford Is Feeling Terrific at 85,"

November 8, 1978. By permission of Chas. Buddy Rogers; From "For All This We're Thankful, Lord," by Joan Beck, November 23, 1978. Copyrighted 1978, *Chicago Tribune.* Used with permission, all rights reserved; From "How Much Should What a Person Is Shade What He Did?" by Dannye Romine. December 10, 1978; From "Fannie Farmer, She Created a Stir in 1896," by Helen Moore. January 11, 1979; From "If You Lose Your Job," by Sylvia Porter. February 19, 1979; From "The Subject Was Themes," by Dannye Romine. September 16, 1979; From "Little Do I Know (And Now I'll Share It)," by Dot Jackson. November 5, 1979; From "How Do We Spell Relief for The Suffering People?" by Ina Hughs. November 23, 1979; From "The Comer News Was A Cheer-Up Bundle For A Dreary Day," by Dot Jackson. February 6, 1980; From "Midsummer In the Mountains," by Harriet Doar. July 2, 1980.

The Charlotte Weekly Uptown. From "Talking with Odetta Much Like Chat with Friend," by Bob Dawson. April 29, 1980; From "Writer Let Ann-Margret Down," by Emery Wister. April 29, 1980.

The Chicago Tribune. From "The Bard of Gothic Romance," by James O. Jackson. Reprinted in *The Charlotte Observer,* November 14, 1976; From "Barbara Cartland: Mother of the Melting Ice Maidens," by Jon Anderson. Reprinted in *The Charlotte Observer.* April 16, 1979. Copyrighted 1979, *Chicago Tribune.* All rights reserved; From "Former Flying Nun Reaps Just Rewards," by Gene Siskel. Reprinted in *The Charlotte Observer,* April 20, 1980. Copyrighted, *Chicago Tribune.* All rights reserved.

Chosen Books Publishing Co., Ltd. From *To Live Again* by Catherine Marshall. Copyright 1957 by Catherine Marshall. Published by Chosen Books Publishing Co., Ltd., Lincoln, VA 22078. Used by permission.

Christianity Today. From "A Face Aflame," an interview with Annie Dillard, conducted by *Campus Life* editor Phillip Yancey. May 5, 1978.

The Christopher Publishing House. From *Mr. Typewriter* by Arthur Toye Foulke. Copyright 1961. By permission of The Christopher Publishing House.

Columbus Dispatch. From "Pat Harris Knows

P's and Q's," by Margaret McManus. August 26, 1979. Reprinted from *The Columbus, Ohio, Dispatch.*

The Commonweal. From "Sacred and Profane Success," by Anne Fremantle. July 27, 1945.

Coward, McCann & Geoghegan, Inc. From *The Rest of the Story* by Sheilah Graham. Copyright 1964. By permission of Coward, McCann & Geoghegan, Inc. From *The Bloomer Girls* by Charles Neilson Gattey. Copyright 1967. By permission of Coward, McCann & Geoghegan, Inc.

Delacorte Press. *Milton Berle: An Autobiography* with Haskel Frankel. Copyright 1974.

J. M. Dent and Sons Ltd. From *Florence Nightingale at Harley Street: Her Reports to the Governors of Her Nursing Home 1853-4.* Copyright 1970.

The Dial Press. From *The Real Isadora* by Victor Seroff. The Dial Press. Copyright 1971.

Dodd, Mead & Company. From *Our Hearts Were Young and Gay* by Cornelia Otis Skinner and Emily Kimbrough. Copyright 1942.

Doubleday & Company, Inc. From *Madame Curie* by Eve Curie. Copyright 1937 by Doubleday & Company, Inc. Reprinted by permission of the publisher; From *Always In Vogue* by Edna Wollman Chase and Ilka Chase. Copyright 1954 by Edna Woolman Chase and Ilka Chase. Reprinted by permission of Doubleday & Company, Inc.; From *Some Are Born Great* by Adela Rogers St. Johns. Copyright 1974 by Adela Rogers St. Johns. Reprinted by permission of Doubleday & Company, Inc.; From the *Introduction to Clare Sheridan* by Anita Leslie. Copyright 1976, 1977 by Anita Leslie. Reprinted by permission of Doubleday & Company, Inc.

Dun's Review. From "Watch the Moneymen!" by A.H. December 1969.

E. P. Dutton & Co., Inc. From *Child Of The Dark: The Diary of Carolina Maria de Jesus,* translated by David St. Clair. Copyright 1962 by E. P. Dutton & Co., Inc.; From *Ten Years of Exile* by Madame de Staël, translated by Doris Buk. With introduction by Peter Gay. Saturday Review Press, 1972. Reprinted by permission of E.P. Dutton: From "48-38-48, 199 Pounds—and Proud of Every Ounce & Inch," excerpted from *Great Big Beautiful Doll* by Stella

Jolles Reichman. Copyright 1978 by E. P. Dutton & Co., Inc.

Ebony. From " 'Finally, I've Begun to Live Again,' an intimate, revealing interview with Mrs. Martin Luther King, Jr.," by Charles L. Sanders. November 1970; From "Lady Didn't Always Sing the Blues," by Charles L. Sanders. January 1973. Reprinted by permission of *Ebony* magazine, copyright 1973 by Johnson Publishing Company, Inc.

Esquire. From "Helen Gurley Brown only Wants to Help," by Nora Ephron. First appeared in *Esquire* magazine February 1970. Permission granted by International Creative Management; From "Women," by Nora Ephron. First appeared in *Esquire* magazine February 1970. Permission granted by International Creative Management; From "John Rennon's Excrusive Gloupie," by Charles McCarry from *Esquire* magazine. December 1970. Copyright 1970 by Esquire Publishing, Inc. Used by courtesy of the magazine; From "The Feminine Mistake," by Helen Lawrenson. January 1971. Copyright 1970 Esquire Publishing Inc. Used by courtesy of the magazine; From "What Turns Women On?" by Germaine Greer. July 1973; quote by Vivian Vance in "The Great Celebrity Ball Breaker," by Eric Lax. April 1976; From "Country's Angels," by Roy Blount, Jr. First appeared in *Esquire* magazine March 1977.

FemIron. From FemIron Advertisement.

The First Church of Christ, Scientist Publishing Co. From *Science and Health with Key to the Scriptures* by Mary Baker Eddy. Published by the Trustees under the will of Mary Baker Eddy, Boston, U.S.A.

Forbes. From article by Malcolm Forbes; From "You'd Never Know." "Luvie" Pearson as quoted by Malcolm Forbes, January 22, 1979; From "Fact and Comment," by Malcolm S. Forbes. November 26, 1979.

Foreign Affairs. From "Israel in search of lasting peace," by Golda Meir. Quoted by permission from *Foreign Affairs,* April 1973. Copyright 1973 by Council on Foreign Relations, Inc.

Fortune. From "I am a famous woman in this industry," by Elizabeth Arden. October 1938.

Glamour. From article on "Professors" as quoted by Janice Harayda. August 1977.

The Globe. From article by Bob Borino. July 1,

1979. Copyright 1979; From "Mrs. Billy Carter," by Phyllis Batelle. August 1979. Copyright 1979; From "Jane Fonda," by Louise Farr. Copyright 1980. All copyrighted by LHJ Publishing, Inc. All reprinted with permission of *Ladies' Home Journal,*

Lady's Circle Magazine. From "The Over-Packaging Disease," by Sonia Masello. April 1975.

The Literary Guild Magazine. From "Interview ... Belva Plain," by Ruth Fecych. June 1980.

Little, Brown & Co. From *Yankee From Olympus: Justice Holmes and His Family* by Catherine Drinker Bowen. Copyright 1944 by Catherine Drinker Bowen. By permission of Little, Brown & Co. in association with The Atlantic Monthly Press; From *Biography: The Craft and the Calling* by Catherine Drinker Bowen. Copyright 1968, 1969 by Catherine Drinker Bowen. By permission of Little, Brown & Co. in association with The Atlantic Monthly Press.

Macmillan Publishing Company. From *The Life of Clara Barton* by Percy H. Epler. Copyright 1915 by Macmillan Publishing Co., Inc., renewed 1943 by Percy H. Epler.

Mad Magazine. Permission *Mad Magazine* Copyright 1978 by E. C. Publications Inc. March 1978.

Mademoiselle. From "The Intelligent Woman's Guide to Sex," by Judith Coburn. March 1978. Copyright 1978 by the Condé Nast Publications Inc.; From "No More Ms. Nice Girl," by Amy Gross. June 1978.

Matrix Magazine. From "Talk," by Margot Sherman. Summer 1974.

McCall's. From *Queen of the May* by Shirley Jackson. First published in *McCall's* magazine. Copyright 1955 by Shirley Jackson. Reprinted by permission of Brandt & Brandt Literary Agents, Inc.; From "An Interview with Erich Fromm," by Richard Heffner. October 1965; From "Katharine Hepburn," by Roy Newquist. July 1967; From "Take The Lilies and The Lace," by Judy Collins. April 1970; From "The Feminine Eye," by Shana Alexander. June 1970; From "A Visiting Feminine Eye," by Shirley Chisholm. August 1970; From "What Have Women Really Won?" by Betty Friedan. November 1972; From "How Jacqueline Onassis Is Shaping Her Children," by Stephen Birmingham. January 1973;

From "We Don't Have to Be That Independent," by Betty Friedan. January 1973; From "The Joyous Arrival of Sophia's Second Son," by Helen Markel. April 1973; From "McCall's World." April 1973; From "Lady Bird Johnson," by Liz Carpenter. July 1973; From "The Bright Light of His Days," by Jacqueline Kennedy Onassis. November 1973; From "Rose Kennedy Talks About Her Life, Her Faith and Her Children." December 1973; From "Barbra: The Superstar Who wants to be a Woman," by Elizabeth Kaye. April 1975; From "The Kissingers Talk About Their Marriage," by Trude B. Feldman. February 1976; From "Betty Ford Talks About Her Mother," by Lynn Minton. May 1976; From "Mary Richards: 1970-1977 (Mary Tyler Moore)," by Gloria Emerson. May 1976. Reprinted with permission of Wallace & Sheil Agency, Inc., as agent for the author; From "My Life Is a Little ... Complicated," by Gwen Davis, about Elizabeth Taylor. June 1976; From "The Disenchantment of Elizabeth & Margaret," by Natalie Gittelson. July 1976; From "Jimmy Carter's Remarkable Women," by Kandy Stroud. July 1976; From "The Gossipers," by Natalie Gittelson. November 1976; From "How Faith Can Heal," by Jessamyn West. April 1977; From "My Wife, Roz," by Frederick Brisson as told to Helen Markel. April 1977; From "The Americanization of Stalin's Daughter," by Harrison E. Salisbury. April 1977; From "My Father, Charlie Chaplin," by Natalie Gittelson, March 1978; From "Suzanne Somers Is Very Happy, Sort of," by Barbara Grizzuti Harrison. March 1978; From "Of Two Minds," by Dorothy and Mary Rodgers. April 1978; From "Why Goldie Hawn Is Smiling Again," by Gwen Davis. June 1978; From "Marlo Thomas and Phil Donahue," by Mary Ann O'Roark. August 1978; From "Secretaries: Are Bosses Getting Their Message?" by Louise Kapp Howe. September 1978. By permission of the author; "Doris Day's Surprising New Life," by Gerald Astor. September 10, 1978. Copyright 1978 by Gerald Astor. Reprinted by permission of The Sterling Lord Agency, Inc.; From "Rich, Famous—and Vulnerable," by Penelope McMillan. September 1978; From "Linda Lavin Can Take Care of Herself," by Carolyn See. October 1978; From "Bargain Hunting," by Gloria Rosenthal. December 1978; From "A Christmas Without Bing," by Sheila Weller. December 1978; From "How to Look Your Best All Your Life," by Dinah Shore. July 1979.

McGraw-Hill Book Company. From *Perle: My Story* by Perle Mesta with Robert Cohn. Copyright 1960; From *My Father Marconi* by Degna Marconi. Copyright 1962.

McIntosh & Otis, Inc. From "That's All There Is...," by Barbara Holland. *Woman's Day.* November 1976.

Modern Maturity. From "Helen Hayes Drops Her Guard," by Joan Saunders Wixen. April-May 1978. Reprinted with permission from *Modern Maturity* and Joan Saunders Wixen. Copyright 1978 by the American Association of Retired Persons. Article copyrighted by Joan Saunders Wixen; From article. February 3, 1978. Reprinted with permission from Modern Maturity. Copyright 1978 by the American Association of Retired Persons.

Modern People. From "Eye Openers." Quote by Suzanne Somers' son Bruce. August 27, 1978.

William Morrow & Company, Inc. From *Journalist's Wife* by Lillian T. Mowrer. Copyright 1937.

Ms. From "Billie Jean King Evens the Score," by Bud Collins. July 1971; From "Phyllis Schlafly: 'The Sweetheart of the Silent Majority,'" by Lisa Cronin Wohl. March 1974; From "Ella Grasso of Connecticut: Running and Winning," by Joseph B. Treaster. October 1974; From "Katherine Graham: The power that didn't corrupt," by Jane Howard. October 1974; From "Why I Never Married," by Oriana Fallaci. December 1974; From "Bernadette Now," by J. Fitzgerald. January 1975; From "Sarah Caldwell: The Flamboyant of the Opera," by Jane Scovell Appleton. May 1975; From "And Now From Hollywood: The Sweetening of Sue Mengers," by Louise Farr. June 1975; From "An Interview with Doris Day," by Molly Haskell. January 1976; From "Glenda Jackson: A Triumph of Talent," by Valerie Wade. February 1976; From "Lillian Carter Talks About Racism, The Kennedys, and 'Jimmy's Reign,'" in conversation with Nanette Rainone and Mary King and husband Peter Bourne. October 1976; From "Is There Sex After Sex Roles?" by Gloria Steinem. November 1976; From "A Day in the Life of Joan Didion," by Susan Braudy. February

1977; From "Barbra Streisand: People Who Love Power," by Marjorie Rosen. May 1977; From "Pornography—Not Sex but the Obscene Use of Power," by Gloria Steinem. August 1977; From "Article on Marian McPortland," by Annie Gottlieb. March 1978, Copyright Ms. Foundation for Education and Communications Inc.; From "Can Women Really Have It All?" by Letty Cottin Pogrebin. March 1978; From "Can Marilyn Sokol Find Guilt Without Sex?" by Sheila Weller. August 1978; From "Alma Thomas, A One-Woman Art Movement," by Judith Wilson. February 1979.

National Education Journal. From "A Greeting to Teachers," by Helen Keller. February 1956.

National Geographic. From "The Society's Special Medal Awarded to Amelia Earhart." September 1932.

The New Republic. From "The Irish Remember," by Lady Augusta Gregory. Reprinted by permission of *The New Republic,* Copyright 1923 *The New Republic,* Inc.; From "Capote, Mailer and Miss Parker," by Janet Winn. Reprinted by permission of *The New Republic,* Copyright 1959 The New Republic, Inc.

Newsletter, Wheaton College, Norton, Mass. July 1979 Series II, Issue 4. by Lesley R. Stahl, CBS News.

New Woman. From "C.Z. Guest Is Into More Than Looking Great," by Truman Capote. *New Woman* magazine. Copyright 1977; From "Conversation With Barbara Jordan," by Marilyn Gardner. Copyright 1978.

New Yorker. From "Profiles," by Penelope Gilliatt. December 25, 1978.

New York Magazine. From "After Moro: An interview with Oriana Fallaci," by Phillip Nobile. May 22, 1978.

New York News. From "Men, Women Need Interpreters to End War Between Sexes," by Beverly Stephen. Reprinted in *The Charlotte Observer,* January 20, 1980. Copyright 1980 *New York News,* Inc. Reprinted by permission.

North American Newspaper Alliance 1979. From "Jacqueline Bisset Tells Why—Marriage Is Not For Me," by Charles Parmiter. Printed in *National Enquirer,* January 1, 1980.

Northwestern Alumni News. From "Durable Miss Mary," by Helen M. Tillman. November 1977.

W. W. Norton and Company, Inc. From *Margaret Sanger* by Margaret Sanger. Copyright 1938. Permission granted by Dr. Grant Sanger; From *A Glorious Third* by W. W. Norton. Copyright 1979.

Opera News. From "Price on Price," by Stephen E. Rubin. March 6, 1976.

Oxford University Press. From *First and Last Notebooks* by Simone Weil, translated by Richard Rees. Copyright 1970.

Parade. From "My Favorite Jokes," by Joey Russell. August 7, 1977 & April 8, 1979; From "My Favorite Jokes," by Kaye Ballard. January 1, 1978; From "Women FBI Agents—Cool and Tough As Wildcats," by Pam Proctor. February 26, 1978; From "My Favorite Jokes," by Joey Villa. February 26, 1978; From "Women of the Baton—The New Music Masters," by Herbert Kupferberg. May 14, 1978; From "Durants on History From the Ages, With Love," by Pam Proctor. August 6, 1978, (One quote by Ariel Durant amplified in a letter.); From "Why Congressmen Want Out," by Marguerite Michaels. November 5, 1978; From "Conversation Piece: Jojo Starbuck and Jesse Owens," by Jojo Starbuck and Jesse Owens. February 10, 1980.

The Paulist Press. From "Womanpriest," by Alla Bozarth-Campbell. Copyright 1978 by The Paulist Press.

People. From "Blue Jeans By A Vanderbilt?...." by Harriet Shapiro. June 25, 1979.

People Weekly. Quote by Phyllis Schlafly. April 28, 1975.

The Philadelphia Inquirer. From "From Doggie Bags to Divorced Guests," by Jill Gerston. March 23, 1980.

The Pittsburgh Press. From "Loretta, Sissy Share Spotlight," by Jerry Sharpe. March 16, 1980.

Prentice-Hall, Inc. From *The Movies, Mr. Griffith and Me* by Lillian Gish with Ann Pinchot. Copyright 1969; From *The Jersey Lily* by Pierre Sichel. Copyright 1958 by Pierre Sichel; From *Jennie: The Life of Lady Randolph Churchill, Volume I* by Ralph Martin. Copyright 1969 by Ralph G. Martin; From *Fishbait: The Memoirs of the Congressional Doorkeeper* by William "Fishbait" Miller as told to Frances Spatz Leighton. Copyright 1977 by William Moseley Miller and Frances Spatz Leighton. All published by Prentice-Hall, Inc., Englewood Cliffs, New Jersey 07632.

G. P. Putnam's Sons. From *Young Lady Randolph:* the life and times of Jennie Jerome by Rene Kraus. Copyright 1943; From *Garbo: A Biography* by Fritiof Billquist, translated by Maurice Michael. Copyright 1960: From *Miss Tallulah Bankhead* by Lee Israel. Copyright 1972. From *All Said and Done* by Simone de Beauvoir translated by Patrick O'Brian. Copyright 1974; From *My Name Is Sappho* by Martha Rofheart. Copyright 1974; From *Intermission* by Anne Baxter. Copyright 1976. All by permission of G. P. Putnam's Sons.

Quest/80 Magazine. From "The Novelist Who Came in From the Cold," by Tom Buckley. Reprinted in Review, March 1980.

Randolph-Macon's Woman's College Alumnae Bulletin. From "Alumnae Banquet Address," by Jane Sutherland. Summer 1967.

Random House, Inc. From "Biographical Notice," by Charlotte Brontë in *Wuthering Heights* by Emily Brontë. Copyright 1943.

Reader's Digest. From "Barbara Jordan—New Voice in Washington," by Irwin Ross, *Reader's Digest*, February 1977; From "Go Go Girl," by Kenneth Neville. Reprinted with permission from the January 1978 *Reader's Digest;* From "Life in These United States," by Meg Quijano. Reprinted with permission from the January 1978 *Reader's Digest;* From "A minister's wife..." by Janet Cardell. Reprinted with permission from the May 1978 *Reader's Digest;* From column by Joel Sasser. Reprinted with permission from the September 1978 *Reader's Digest* and Joel Sasser; From "Life in These United States." by Emily R. Atkins. Reprinted with permission from the September 1978 *Reader's Digest*.

Redbook. From "The Growing Strength of Coretta King," by Alice Walker. September 1971; From "Jane Fonda: A Long Way From Yesterday," by Martha W. Lear. June 1976; From "Jesus Would Ordain a Woman Today," by Jean Todd Freeman. June 1977. By permission of Russell & Volkening, Inc., as agents to the author; From "This Is Your Life (And It Could Be Yours Too)," by Aimee Lee Ball. November 1977; From "God and Woman, the Hidden History," by Elizabeth Rodgers Dobell. March 1978. Permission granted by the author; From "Short People & Tall Ones..." by Aimee Lee Ball. May 1978; From "Between the Lines," by Sey Chassler. May 1978; From "The Case For

Virginity," by Debby Boone as told to Nancy Anderson. June 1978; From "Barbara Walters' New York," by Joyce Winslow. October 1978; From "People On The Cover" by Aimee Lee Ball. November 1978; From "Liza Minnelli: Which Way Is Up?" by Elizabeth Kaye. January 1979. Permission granted by Russell & Volkening.

Redken Laboratories, Inc. From Redken Advertisement in *Cosmopolitan*. August 1973.

Fleming H. Revell Co. From *Our Moslem Sisters* by Annie Van Sommer and Samuel M. Zwemer. Copyright 1907.

St. Martin's Press, Inc. From *Joyce Grenfell Requests the Pleasure* by Joyce Grenfell. Copyright 1976. By permission of St. Martin's Press, Inc.; From *What Is a Husband* by Richard and Helen Exley. Copyright 1979.

San Francisco Examiner. From "The Giant Killer Who Outran Myth," by John Crumpacker. February 17, 1980.

The Saturday Evening Post. From "The Feel of the Audience," by Fanny Brice. Reprinted from *The Saturday Evening Post,* Copyright 1925 The Curtis Publishing Company; From "Hit on the Head With a Wand," by Barbara Haggie. Reprinted from *The Saturday Evening Post,* Copyright 1945 The Curtis Publishing Company; From "Bad Little Bad Girl," by Toni Howard. Reprinted from *The Saturday Evening Post,* Copyright 1958 The Curtis Publishing Company; From "Mercurial Mercouri," by Robert Emmett Ginna. Reprinted from *The Saturday Evening Post,* Copyright 1963 The Curtis Publishing Company; From "The Face Looks Vaguely Familiar" by Mary Alice Sharpe from *The Saturday Evening Post,* Copyright 1977; The Curtis Publishing Company; Excerpt that appeared May 6, 1978, "Dare To Be You," from *The Experience of Inner Healing* by Ruth Carter Stapleton. Copyright 1977 by Word Books, Inc.

Scrooge & Marley, Ltd. From "What's Happening," column by Gene Shalit. February 1978.

Sepia. From "Diana Ross: America's No. 1 Female Star," by Bill Lane. January 1979.

*Saturday Review.*From "A SR panel takes aim at 'The Second Sex': (pt. 4) Housewife," by Phyllis McGinley. February 21, 1953.

Scientific American, Inc. From Scientific American Advertisement.

Charles Scribner's Sons. From *Ethan Frome* by Edith Wharton. Copyright 1911, 1938 by Charles Scribner's Sons; Renewal Copyright 1939 by Frederic R. King and Leroy King; From *A Backward Glance* (An Autobiography) by Edith Wharton. Copyright 1933 Charles Scribner's Sons; From *Joan of Arc* by John Holland Smith. Copyright 1973.

Seventeen. From "Boy meets girl: Teen reporters come face to face with glamour and success," by Gary Waldman. January 1964; From "Oops," by Sue Hogshead. September 1973. Reprinted from *Seventeen* magazine. Copyright 1973 by Triangle Communications Inc. All rights reserved; From "Close Up," by Linda Blair. Reprinted from *Seventeen* magazine. Copyright 1977 by Triangle Communications Inc. All rights reserved.

Sheed Andrews & McMeel, Inc. From *My Prisoner* by Janey Jimenz, as told to Ted Berkman. Copyright 1977.

Simon & Schuster. From *You Don't Have to Be in Who's Who to Know What's What* by Sam Levenson. Copyright 1979

Excerpt reprinted courtesy of *Sports Illustrated* from the July 8, 1963 issue. Copyright 1963 Time Inc. "Sweet Explosion In The Air," by Paul Ress.

The Star. Quote by Dolly Parton. March 21, 1978; From article on Kathryn Crosby by Tom Martial. March 28, 1978; From "*MASH* Girl reveals her secret getaway plan," by Robin Leach. May 9, 1978; From "What Cindy (Williams) and others vow in New Year." January 2, 1979; From "Sally Field Opens Up Her Private World to Talk About Sex, Jealousy—and Burt," by Celeste Freman. July 10, 1979; From "The 80's Celebrity Resolutions." Quote by Lillian Carter. January 1, 1980; From "A Poised First Lady Tells How She's Filling Jimmy's Shoes and Loving It," by Norma Langley. March 18, 1980; From "Letters/Things Kids Say." June 3, 1980; quote by Dr. Joyce Brothers; quote by Jean Kennedy Smith.

Stein and Day. From *Laughing All the Way* by Barbara Howar. Copyright 1973 by Barbara Howar. Used by permission of The Sterling Lord Agency, Inc.

Suburban Features Inc. From his column "One Big Step for Man-Watching," by Jim Sanderson. Copyright 1980 Suburban Features Inc.

Taplinger Publishing Co Inc. From "Indira Gandhi speaks on democracy, socialism, and third world nonalignment." Edited by Henry M. Christman. Copyright 1975.

Tar Heel, The Magazine of North Carolina. From "Louise Thaden," by Nancy Oliver. July-August 1978.

Time. From "Mary's Museship," by Melvin Maddocks. October 18, 1976.

Town & Country. From "The Fine Art of Dressing," by Alice-Leone Moats. October 1978; From "The Great American Walk," by Jeanine Larmoth. October 1978; From "The New Elite, Women of Accomplishment," by Nan Tillson Birmingham. October 1978; From "Candice Bergen: The Essence of Cie," by Candice Bergen. August 1979.

University of Minnesota Press. From *Sister Kenny: The Woman Who Challenged the Doctors* by Victor Cohn. Copyright 1976.

Vanguard Press, Inc. Reprinted from *New Heaven, New Earth* by Joyce Carol Oates. Copyright 1974 by Joyce Carol Oates; From *The Goddess and Other Women* by Joyce Carol Oates. Both by permission of the publisher, Vanguard Press, Inc. Copyright 1974 by Joyce Carol Oates.

Victor Books. From *The Fragrance of Beauty* by Joyce Landorf.

Virginia Slims. Advertisement. Courtesy of Phillip Morris.

Vital Speeches of the Day. From "On Being Born Female," by Caroline Bird. November 15, 1968.

Vogue. From "Surprises in a Woman's Life." February 1979; From "In praise of bad memory; the fine art of forgetting—from an expert's point of view," by John Simon. April 1980.

The Wake Forest Magazine. From "In Praise of Walking," by Emily Herring Wilson.

The Wall Street Journal. From Review & Outlook—"Gardening," by Rosemarie Williamson. May 30, 1978; From editorial page, June 27, 1978 by Honey Greer; From "Vanderbilt Signature on Jeans Pockets Spells Success for Murjani Industries," by Anthony Spaeth. May 27, 1980. Reprinted by permission of *The Wall Street Journal,* Copyright Dow Jones & Company, Inc. 1980. All Rights Reserved.

The Washington Post. From "Discouraging Words," by Dick Dabney. November 20, 1979; From "Women's Caucus Girds for '80," by Elizabeth Bumiller. November 20, 1979; From "Women Still Promoted Up From the Ranks," by Martha M. Hamilton. November 20, 1979; From "The Heidens," by Thomas Boswell. *The Washington Post Magazine,* February 10, 1980; From "Fratianne," by Tony Kornheiser. *The Washington Post Magazine,* February 10, 1980; From "John Derek: Keeper of the Bo," by Henry Allen. Reprinted in *The Charlotte Observer,* February 17, 1980; From "Washington Society Queen Dies," by Myra MacPherson. Reprinted in *The Charlotte Observer,* February 21, 1980: From "The Barbara Walters Special: Babsy, Bette, and '8,' '9' and '10,'" by Tom Shales. April 1, 1980; From "Lady Henderson and the Art of Dining," by William Rice. April 3, 1980; From "Prime Ribs From The Prima Donna, The Zany Art and Voice of Anna Russell," by Sandy Rovner. April 16, 1980; From "The Princess in Exile," by Henry Mitchell. April 25, 1980; From "The Pill's Pioneer Wants a Better Contraceptive for Men," by Sandy Rovner. Reprinted in *The Charlotte Observer,* June 12, 1980. All copyright *The Washington Post.*

The Washington Star. From "Olympian Avalanche of Words," by Judy Flander. February 14, 1980; From "It's Not Easy Being Eric's Sister," by Tom Callahan. February 21, 1980; From "Lena Raises Roof—and Money," by Jurate Kazickas. May 13, 1980.

The Washington Writers Group. From "Winging It," by Coleman McCarthy. November 20, 1979.

Weekly World News. From "The Adventure of Being a Wife," by Ruth Stafford Peale. January 22, 1980; From "Woman collects a cool $1,000 for every episode of 'The Love Boat' that's aired." January 22, 1980; From "Hollywood's newest sex symbol doesn't think she's beautiful," by Roderick Barrand. February 19, 1980.

H. W. Wilson Co. From *Carrie Chapman Catt, A Biography* by Mary Gray Peck. Copyright 1944. By permission of the publisher.

Woman's Home Companion. From "The Gift of Woman," by Katherine Anne Porter. December 1956.

Women's Sports Publishing Co. Julie Staver as quoted by Billie Jean King. October 1977.

Women's Sports. From "The Play's The Thing!" by Greg Hoffman. March 1980.

Working Woman. From "Active, Successful, on their way up…" by Ann Foote Cahn: July 1978; From "Sexy vs. Sexist," by Blair Sabol: June 1978; From article by Toni Kosover. September 1978; From interview by Caroline Urbas. October 1978; From "Carol Burnett Talks Up ERA." December 1978. All reprinted with permission from *Working Woman.* Copyright 1978 by HAL Publications, Inc.

Worlds To Explore Handbook for Brownie and Junior Girl Scouts. Quote by Juliette Low.

World Tennis. From "Martina at Number One: Controlled Aggression," by Susan B. Adams. March 1980; From "Where Do You Go From No. 1?" by Martina Navratilova. March 1980. Both reprinted with permission from *World Tennis* magazine, CBS Publications, CBS Inc., 1515 Broadway, New York, NY 10036.

The Writer. From "From The Ground Up," by Edna O'Brien. October 1958; From "The Essence of Writing," by Shirley Ann Grau. May 1974.

Writer's Digest. From "Nice to See Nora Ephron Happy in Her Work," by Michael Laskey. April 1974; From "Porter on Prose," by Marguerite Hosbach. November 1977.

Special appreciation for quotes from the following individuals:

Alice Adams; Elizabeth Ashley; Tish Baldridge; Hambla Bauer (quote by Elizabeth Arden in *The Saturday Evening Post,* April 24, 1948); Joan Bennett; Erma Bombeck (quotes in *The Charlotte Observer,* 12/13/79. 12/21/78, 2/18/78, 2/3/78, 1/10/78, 10/20/77, 11/18/76. By permission of Aaron M. Priest, literary agent): Betsy Bostian (for her brief poems and quotes); Art Buchwald (from "Housewife's Guide to Answering When They Ask, And What Do You Do?" *The Charlotte News,* May 30, 1978); Pierre Cardin; Liz Carpenter; Miz Lillian Carter; Rosalynn Carter; Bonnie Cashin; Shirley Chisholm; Chon Day (cartoon quote); Philip Dessauer (quote in *The Charlotte Observer,* January 16, 1978); Betty Ford; Eileen Ford; Ella Grasso; Germaine Greer; Janet Guthrie; Helen Hayes (as quoted by Rose Heylbut in "My Life with Music—An Interview with Helen Hayes." From The *Etude,* August 1946, and other quotes); Edith Head; Christie Hefner (as quoted by Judy Klemesrud in "Christie Hefner: Playboy's Hare Apparent." In *Cosmopolitan,* February 1975); Lady Bird Johnson; Barbara Jordan; Nancy Kassebaum; Judge Cornelia G. Kennedy; Florence King; Irv Kupcinet (from his column in *The Chicago Sun-Times* reprinted in *The Charlotte News.* February 25, 1978); Angela Lansbury; Mary Wells Lawrence; Sonia Masello (from two poems and one saying); Louise Nevelson; Minnie Pearl; Letty Cottin Pogrebin; Sylvia Porter; Dr. Estelle Ramey; Harry Reasoner; Joan Rivers; Lynda Johnson Robb; Isabel Sanford; Phyllis Schlafly; Patricia Schroeder; Gail Sheehy; Jim Shumaker (quote from "Don't Draft Women—Please" by Jim Shumaker in *The Charlotte Observer,* February 17, 1980); The Rev. Canon Mary Michael Simpson, O.S.H.; Gloria Carter Spann; Judge Arthur J. Stanley, Jr. (permission to quote his mother, Bessie Anderson Stanley); Gloria Steinem; Jessamyn West; Earl Wilson.

It was not possible to contact all living contributors (or their agents) quoted in the following pages. However, this book's compiler/editor wishes to express deepest thanks to all the publishers, periodicals and other sources from which these excerpts have come.

She would also like to express her great appreciation to the following libraries and their devoted librarians: The New York Public Library, The Chicago Public Library, The Charlotte Public Library, The University of North Carolina Library at Charlotte and at Raleigh, and The Charlotte Observer Library.

American Heritage. From "Faces From the Past—VI," by Richard M. Ketchum. April 1962.

American Magazine. From "Calling All Women!" by Robert Crandall. May 1955; From "High, Low, Ace and Jane," by Jerome Beatty. January 1949; From "I Blow My Own Horn," by Mildred (Babe) Didrickson. June 1936; From "If I Were Seventeen," by Helen Gahagan Douglas. September 1947; From "Kelland Doesn't Know What He Is Talking About," by Emily Post. December 1928; From "Laugh Your Troubles Away," by Don Eddy. November 1954; From "Meet Hollywood's Most Exciting Family," by Al Stump. October 1955; From "People Who Want to Look Young and Beautiful," by Allison Gray. December 1922; From "See You Lighter," May 1954; From "She Solves the Problems of Working Wives," by Frederick G. Brownell. August 1954; From "What I've Learned About Men," by Rosalind Russell. August 1953; From "We All Can't Be Beautiful, But...," by Helena Rubenstein. June 1936; From "What it takes to be a big-time model." November 1955; From "Wing-Ding Mayor," January 1954.

The American Mercury. From "The War Against Birth Control," by Margaret Sanger. June 6, 1924.

Blue Ribbon Books, From *Emerson: The Wisest American,* by Phillips Russell, copyright 1929.

Book Digest. From *Americans,* "Rosalaynn Carter: The First Lady," by Desmond Wilcox. April 1978.

Bookviews, From "Classic Corner." February 1978.

Century. From "Talks with Katherine Mansfield," by A. R. Orage. November 1924.

The Charlotte News. From "Donna's Fighting Back Against MS," by Jack Hurst. January 6, 1979; From the "Green Section," in a story by Jay Sharbutt; From "Her Zingers Pack A Message," by Deborah Randolph. September 8, 1977.

The Charlotte Observer. From "Good Embroidered Slogans Will Keep You in Stitches," by Dot Jackson. October 3, 1979; From "Goren on Bridge." July 14, 1979. (Distributed by *The Chicago Tribune.*): From "The People Page," April 30, 1978; From "Schlafly & Friedan: 2 Worlds of ERA." May 9, 1978; From "She's Tinkering With Chicago's Machine," by Patricia O'Brien. November 1, 1979. (Distributed by Observer Washington Bureau.)

The Christian Science Monitor. From "Frontiers of Science," by Shirley Horne. August 10, 1978; From "Nadia Boulanger's worldwide legacy," by Harold Rogers. October 31, 1979.

The Christian Science Publishing Society. From *Science and Health with Key to the Scriptures* by Mary Baker Eddy.

Collier's. From "Adlai's Lady," by Helen Worden Erskine. October 11, 1952; From "All About Me: Marriage ... Moppets ... Maine ... and More Movies," by Bette Davis. December 9, 1955; From "Allison in Wonderland," by Bill Fay. March 4, 1950; From "Baseball Bride," by Mrs. Lou Gehrig. June 1, 1935; From "Broadway's busiest babe," by James Poling. February 14, 1953; From "Everything's Rosy for Clooney," by Evelyn Harvey. November 15, 1952; From "Fastest Woman in the World," by Helen Markel Hermann. January 12, 1952; From "Kim Novak; She Walks at Sunrise," August 17, 1956; From "Life in the Solomons," by Osa Johnson. September 26, 1942; From "Mitzi's a Merry Madcap," by Ezra Goodman. February 16, 1952; From "Mrs. Smith Really Goes to Town," by Lilian Rixey. July 29, 1950; From "The Actress Nobody Knows," by Eleanor Harris. October 7, 1950; From "The Magic of Lilly Daché," by Hämbla Bauer. February 26, 1949; From "The return of Lorelei Lee," by John Keating. January 7, 1950; From "The Woman All Women Want to Be—Deborah Kerr," by Robert W. Marks. December 7, 1956; From "The Woman Spends," by Betty Thornley Stuart. October 4, 1930; From "The Yankee Peeress," by John B. Kennedy. October 23, 1926; From "Wall Street Sex Appeal," by Jack Sher. June 7, 1947; From "Woman's Preferred Candidate," by Mary Austin. May 29, 1920.

W.B. Conkey Company, Chicago. From *Everyday Thoughts,* by Ella Wheeler Wilcox, copyright 1901.

Cosmopolitan. From "Linda Blair," by Peter Evans. October 1977; From "Margaret Mead: Portrait of an American Original," by Tom Burke. September 1977.

Creation House, Inc. From "Maria" by Maria Von Trapp.

Current Literature. From "The Future of

Woman As Olive Schreiner Sees It," May 1911.

Delineator. From "I envy American women," by Anita Joachim-Daniel. November 1936; From "Lonely Hearts Tell All," by Sheilah Graham. June 1935; From "Men you shouldn't marry," by Gladys Oaks. September 1926; From "Portrait of a Lady," by Ida M. Tarbell. October 1931.

Duke Power News. September 1978.

Editor & Publisher. From a news story. March 25, 1978.

The Etude. From " 'Aloha Oe' and Its Royal Composer," by David Earl McDaniel. September 1944; From "A Visit With Belgium's Musical Queen," by Walter Rummel. December 1932; From "Comeback—Words and Music," by Rose Heylbut. December 1948; From "How Music Helps the Salvation Army," by Evangeline Booth. July 1944; From "If you hope for a film career," by Jeanette MacDonald, secured by Rose Heylbut. November 1953; From "More Than Teaching," by Norma Ryland Graves. November 1955; From "Opportunity Needs Preparation," by Roberta Peters. April 1956; From "Singing in the movies," by Kathryn Grayson, as told to Gunnar Asklund. November 1952; from "The Amazing American Tour of Jenny Lind," by Charles F. Collisson. June 1946; From "The Secret of Public Reaction," by Rose Heylbut. February 1943; From "You Can Sing—If You Will!" by Ernestine Schumann-Heink. January 1934.

Family Circle. From "Marriages That Work: Norm and Frances Lear," by Bill Davidson. March 11, 1978; From "She Looks Better Now Than She Ever Did," by Muriel Davidson. September 1976.

Forum. From "Are Men Mice?" by Margaret Fishback. July 1938.

Glamour. Quote by Alexis Smith in "Big Time Glamour, Showstoppers."; From "Have You Enough Self-Discipline for the Marriage, Man, Career, Family You Want?" by David P. Campbell. June 1969.

Good Housekeeping. From "My Home in the African Blue," by Osa Johnson. January 1924; From "My Husband, George Wallace," by Cornelia Wallace. March 1976. Excerpt from *C'nelia,* by Cornelia Wallace. J. B. Lippincott Co., 1976; From "Practically Anybody Can Do It," by Dorothy Kilgallen. September 1954; From "The Debbie Reyn-

olds Scrapbook," by Joseph N. Bell. March 1978.

Harper & Brothers Publishers. From *Elizabeth Cady Stanton,* edited by Theodore Stanton and Harriot Stanton Blatch, copyright 1922. Vols. I & II; From *History of Alfred the Great,* by Jacob Abbot, copyright 1903; From *Miss Beecher's Domestic Recipe Book,* copyright 1842; From *Story of a Pioneer,* by Anna Howard Shaw, D.D.,M.D., copyright 1915.

Harper's Bazaar. From "1872 Was Not the Year of the Woman," by Eve Anthony. July 1972.

Holiday. From "Paris! City of Love," by Colette. April 1953.

Houghton Mifflin Co., The Riverside Press, Cambridge. From *The Princess,* by Alfred Lord Tennyson, Edited with notes by William J. Rolfe: copyright 1884, James R. Osgood & Co., copyright 1912, John C. Rolfe, George W. Rolfe and Charles J. Rolfe.

Alfred A. Knopf. From *Carry Nation,* by Herbert Asbury, copyright 1929.

Ladies' Home Journal. Quote by Gene Shalit in his monthly column.

Life. From "At 91, Jeannette Rankin Is the Feminists' New Heroine," by Elizabeth Frappollo. March 3, 1972; From "Gracie Fields: English Comedienne Mugs and Sings." December 21, 1942; From "Just Crazy ... We're Happy." December 1, 1952; From "100 Candles For a Gay Lady: Grandma Moses." September 19, 1960; From "Gospel Queen Mahalia." November 29, 1954; From "Shirley MacLaine: Free Spirit," by Eleanor Harris. September 15, 1959.

The Living Age. From "Preface to a lost battle," by Eve Curie. August 1940.

Look. From "Adelle Davis and the new nutrition religion," by John Poppy. December 15, 1970; From "All I Got's Sincerity," by George Eells. April 21, 1953; From "Althea Gibson ... Tragic Success Story," November 12, 1957; From "An Apple for Miss Brooks," November 4, 1952; From "Audrey ... The New Hepburn," by Jack Hamilton. October 21, 1952; From "Dinah Goes Glamorous," April 30, 1957; From "Dyan Cannon booms," by Stanley Gordon. July 14, 1970; From "Eleanor Roosevelt today," by Laura Bergquist. April 17, 1956; From "Fade-out: Now you see 'em, now you don't," by Louis Botto, editor. September 7, 1971; From

"Frederika of Greece: a modern monarch," by Michael Manning. October 20, 1953; From "Gloria Vanderbilt Starts a New Life," by Laura Bergquist. July 12, 1955; From "Gwen Verdon: Beauty and Baseball." July 12, 1955; From "Happy 40th, Dear Liz," by Thomas Thompson. February 25, 1972; From "I Hate Young Men," by Lauren Bacall. November 3, 1953; From "I'm Not Afraid Any More," by Ava Gardner. December 18, 1951; From item about Mrs. Lytle Hull. March 19, 1957; From "It's Hard to Be a Lady." September 4, 1956; From "Joan Crawford—unhappy success." October 29, 1946; From "Josephine Baker: World's Top Exotic." July 3, 1951; From "Ladies of the Links," by Vivian Gornick. May 18, 1971; From "Ladies of the Press," by Vivian Gornick. May 5, 1971; From "Leonore Fights Alone," by Al Rothenberg. October 20, 1970; From "Lucille Ball, The star that never sets...," by Laura Bergquist. September 7, 1971; From "Lulu." July 28, 1970; From "Mamie," by Ruth Montgomery. February 23, 1954; From "Martha Raye." March 22, 1955; From "My Life With George Burns," by Gracie Allen. December 16, 1952; From "Patti Page's New Life." February 18, 1958; From "Polly Bergen: She Can't Make Up Her Mind," April 29, 1958; From "Portrait of an Actress: Eartha Kitt." October 6, 1953; From "Raquel Welch, Mae West Talk About Men, Morals and 'Myra Breckinridge.'" by Jack Hamilton. March 24, 1970; From "She wouldn't give up." May 5, 1953; From "Song for Horne." May 8, 1951; From "Sophie Gimbel: Designing Woman," by Patricia Coffin. March 24, 1953; From "Susan Grows Up." March 18, 1958; From "Tallulah's 5 Lives." February 24, 1953; From "The Babe and I," by George Zaharias. December 11, 1956; From "The living faith of Mrs. Peter Marshall." March 6, 1956; From "The Mystery of Margaret Mitchell," by Medora Field Perkerson. November 15, 1955; From "The remarkable Zita Potts: she fights poverty," by David Maxey. June 16, 1970; From "The strange case of Suzy Parker," by Laura Bergquist. August 19, 1958; From "The Wonderful Wizardry of Roz," by Laura Bergquist. May 28, 1957; From "They hardly ever make passes at Glenda Jackson," by Henry Ehrlich. December 29, 1970; From "TVs No. 1 Female Clown." March 22, 1955; From "Yvette Mimieux," by Henry Ehrlich. November 17, 1970.

The Macmillan Company, New York. From *Women and the French Tradition,* by Florence Leftwich Ravenel, copyright 1918.

McCall's. From "How We Entertain in Southern California," November 1976.

McGraw-Hill Book Co. *If Life Is a Bowl of Cherries—What Am I Doing in the Pits* by Erma Bombeck.

The Mentor. From "A Life of Love and Tragedy," by Clement King. June 1926.

Musical Quarterly. From "Jenny Lind's Singing Method," by Jenny Lind. October 1917.

The New Republic. From "Aimee Rises from the Sea," by Morrow Mayo. December 25, 1929.

New Woman. From "Can You Control Your Life with Your Thoughts?" by Edward L. Rocks. July-August 1979.

The New Yorker. From "Profiles" by Penelope Gilliatt. December 25, 1978; From "The Talk of the Town." April 23, 1949.

The New York Times. From "Thoughts on Tennis Success and Goals," by Billie Jean King. August 6, 1978.

The New York Times Book Review. Review of Erma Bombeck's *If Life Is a Bowl of Cherries—What Am I Doing in the Pits* by Richard R. Lingeman. April 30, 1978.

Newsweek. From "Newsmakers." October 22, 1979.

North American Review. From "Portrait of Louisa May Alcott," by G. Bradford. March 1919.

Opera News. From "Dame Judith Speaks ... of Shakespeare, Verdi and the Theater," by Florence Stevenson. May 1973.

Outlook. From "Vaudeville at Angelus Temple," by Shelton Bissell. May 23, 1928; From "Personal Glimpses: Hetty Green's Philosophy," August 5, 1916.

People. From "From Lady Antonia's Golden Brow Springs Another Figure of History," by James Salter. April 28, 1975.

People Weekly. From "Startracks." March 10, 1975.

Pictorial Review. From "How I came to write about Etiquette," by Emily Post. October 1936; From "Our Future Beckons," by V. Sackville-West. November 1933; From "The Woman Who Wrote 'Gone With the Wind,'" by Faith Baldwin. March 1937.

G. P. Putnam's Sons. From *If I Know What I Mean* by Elsie Janis. copyright 1925.

Ramparts. From "Janis Joplin: Death Watch," by Richard Lupoff. July 1972.

Redbook. From "A *Redbook* Dialogue: Ingrid Bergman, Van Cliburn." January 1962.

Regina Leader Post. Item reprinted in *Ms.* magazine, June 1978.

The Reporter. From "A union without issue," by Madeleine Chapsal. September 29, 1960.

Rona Barrett's Hollywood. From "Show and Tell" by Rona Barrett. June 1978.

The Saturday Evening Post. From "High Priestess of Beauty," by Hambla Bauer. April 24, 1948.

The Star. From "Disco Sally, 80, shrugs off 53-year age gap of disco kid husband," by Leon Freilich. July 8, 1980.

TV & Movie Screen. From "Dolly Parton: Hollywood Hails Her As a New Marilyn Monroe." August 1980.

Stores. From "Today's Women Execs Evening the Score." March 1978.

Theatre Arts. From "Maude Adams' Blueprint for A Campus Drama Workshop," by Louise Dudley. August 1954.

Time. From "I've Never Won An Argument With Her," by Jimmy Carter. July 31, 1978; From "On the Record." May 1, 1978; From "On the Record." February 5, 1979.

Town & Country.

U.S. Department of State Bulletin. "Letter to President Eisenhower," by Queen Juliana of the Netherlands. May 4, 1953.

Vital Speeches of the Day. From "Charter of Economic Human Rights," by Sylvia F. Porter. September 1, 1957; From "Feminism: The Sine Qua Non for a Just Society," by Wilma Scott Heide. April 15, 1972; From "Revolution," by Wilma Scott Heide. May 1, 1973; From "The Re-entry Woman," by Stephanie M. Bennett. June 1, 1980; From "The 'Rule of Law': democracy vs. ochlocracy," by Madame Chiang Kai-Shek. July 1, 1943; From "What Do You Wish to Accomplish?" by Marjorie Bell Chambers; From "Women in Leadership and Decision Making," by Virginia Y. Trotter. April 1, 1975.

Vogue. From "Set Your Budget Free," by Bess Myerson. March 1973.

V.F.W. Magazine. From "Jest-a-minute." September 1965.

The Washington Star. From "Jackie Is Still the Dazzling Campaigner," by Jurate Kazickas. April 22, 1980.

Woman's Home Companion. From "Babes in the Holly-Woods." September 1946; From "Don't Kid the Women," by Barbara Wendell Kerr. October 1956; From "First Ladies in Waiting," by Patricia Lochridge. July 1947; From "I Remember Mamie," by Nanette Kutner. August 1953; From "I've Never Been in Love Before," interview with Debbie Reynolds. June 1955; From "Letter to an Unknown Man," by Phyllis McGinley. July 1952; From "Living With Your Job," by Hazel Rawson Cades. July 1930; From "Mademoiselle in Blue Jeans,:' by Cameron Shipp. December 1952; From "Our babies will be happy," by Lucille Ball, as told to Cameron Shipp. May 1953; From quote by Anita Loos. May 1956; From "Shirley Temple Expects," by Llewellyn Miller. February 1948; From "Sister Kenny Tells 'Why I Left America.'" March 1951; From "Sports for Women," by Glenna Collett. September 1924; From "Tallulah Goes to the Ball Game," by John Lardner. September 1951; From "Talking Through My Hats," by Lilly Daché. April 1946; From "The Right to Grow," by Lillian Smith. October 1946; From "The Story I've Never Told," by Joan Crawford. January 1955; From "What I Have Learned From My Clients," by Evangeline Adams. August 1930; From "What I Know of Love," by Deborah Kerr, as told to Barbara L. Goldsmith. July 1956.

World's Work. From "Alice in the Looking Glass," by Helena Huntington Smith. August 1930; From "Frances Perkins: Industrial Crusader," by Inis Weed Jones. April 1930; From "From the Home to the House," by Viscountess Nancy Astor, M.P. April 1923; From "Our Changing Stage," an interview with Ethel Barrymore by Keyes Porter. June 1928.

The Writer. From "Talent! The Most Dangerous Word," by Sloan Wilson. May 1980; From "Vocation and Vacation," by Phyllis A. Whitney. April 1952.

Also: Art Buchwald. From his column in *The Charlotte News*, December 14, 1977; Bette Davis. Quoted from "60 Minutes," July 27, 1980; Chicago Feedback, Educational Channel Television; The Merv Griffin Show; Maggie Kuhn. From a talk at Sharon Presbyterian Church; Charlotte, NC. September 13, 1979; Bill Kurtis, NBC-TV News; Lee Phillip Show, CBS-TV; The Dinah Shore Show, CBS-TV.

My deepest thanks to the people who helped make this book:

Researchers—Betsy Bostian, Carroll Backman, David Cannon, Shereen Cannon, Margaret Clayton, Sonia Masello, Jennifer Moyer and Barbara Richards;

Editorial Assistants—Jim Crawford, Sharon Horne and Scott Scher;

Typists/Xeroxers—Belinda Bruce, Mabel Day Daniel, Barbara Goodin, Beth Nutter, and Nancy Shinn.

And, most especially, appreciation for the fine editorial assistance of Stanley Spain.

Cathy Handley

INDEX